IN THE MARGINS OF THE MIDRASH
Sifre Ha'azinu Texts, Commentaries, and Reflections

SOUTH FLORIDA STUDIES IN THE HISTORY OF JUDAISM

Edited by
Jacob Neusner
William Scott Green, James F. Strange

Number 11
In the Margins of the Midrash
Sifre Ha'azinu Texts, Commentaries, and Reflections

by
Herbert W. Basser

IN THE MARGINS OF THE MIDRASH
Sifre Ha'azinu Texts, Commentaries, and Reflections

by

Herbert W. Basser

Scholars Press
Atlanta, Georgia

IN THE MARGINS OF THE MIDRASH
Sifre Ha'azinu Texts, Commentaries, and Reflections

©1990
University of South Florida

Publication of this book was made possible by a grant from the Tisch Family Foundation, New York City. The University of South Florida acknowledges with thanks this important support for its scholarly projects.

Library of Congress Cataloging in Publication Data

Basser, Herbert W.
    In the margins of the Midrash : Sifre Ha'azinu texts,
commentaries, and reflections / by Herbert W. Basser
    p. cm. -- (South Florida studies in the history of Judaism ;
no. 11)
    English and Hebrew.
    Includes original text of Sifre Ha'azinu with a commentary in
Hebrew as well as an English translation.
    Includes bibliographical references and index.
    ISBN 1-55540-536-3
    1. Sifrei. Ha'azinu--Commentaries. 2. Bible. O.T. Deuteronomy
XXXII--Commentaries. I. Sifrei. Ha'azinu. 1990. II. Sifrei.
Ha'azinu. English. Basser. 19990. III. Title. IV. Series: South
Florida studies in the history of Judaism ; 11.
BM517.S75837 1990
296.1'4--dc20   90-44268
                     CIP

Printed in the United States of America
on acid-free paper

In memory of my aunt, Bernice Wenus, who passed away
at the end of Passover 5750 and
in honor of my son Shmuel born four weeks afterwards.

"And the sun shall rise for the sun has set" (Qoh. 1:5). On the day Rav
Hamnuna died, Abin, his son, was born. (Qohelet Rabba 1:10).

Table of Contents

ACKNOWLEDGEMENTS ix

Part One
TOPICS IN THE STUDY OF MIDRASH SIFRE HA'AZINU

1. TRADITION AND MIDRASH 1
   Jewish exegesis 1

2. DESIGN AND STRUCTURE OF MIDRASHIM 14
   Generic exegetical forms 14
   The antiquity of midrash 20
   Form criticism 25
   Midrash Halakha 31

3. THE ANTIQUITY OF LEGAL MATERIALS 40
   Ancient legacy of the Rabbis 40
   The common conception of the exegetical enterprise 42
   Cross referencing 47

4. SIFRE'S PRIMACY 49
   The primacy of Sifre's version of the death of
      Rabbi Hanina ben T'radyon 49
   The date of Mekhilta published by Kahana in relation
      to that of Sifre 63

5. FORMAL COMPOSITION 67
   The Song of Moses in Sifre as a unit 67
   The antiquity of the structural understanding
      of the Song 67
   Biblical verses 70
   Midrash and Halakha 71
   The manner of composition and compilation 72
   Rabbinic theology and midrash 74
   Internal design 74
   The value of medieval commentary 77

Part Two
SIFRE HA'AZINU WITH COMMENTARY (English)

Sifre Ha'azinu 80
Song and Commentary 164

Part Three
SIFRE HA'AZINU WITH COMMENTARY (Hebrew)

Sifre Ha'azinu 182
Perush 204

INDEX 217

Acknowledgements

In the period between my earlier *Midrashic Interpretations of the Song of Moses*, New York and Berne: Peter Lang, 1984, and now, I have had occasion to reflect upon the text I had studied then. Since that time I have come to know some invigorating minds. These people have helped me to understand Rabbinic text and commentary in a more mature way. I refer to such people as the late Frank Talmage who welcomed me into his home for lively study. Menahem Kahana, likewise displayed warm hospitality in sharing both meals and ideas with me. The strongest influences upon my thoughts remain my close friends, Harry Fox, who has discussed idea after idea with me, and Jacob Neusner, without whose massive studies, arriving almost weekly, I could not have embarked upon this project. While one will find me arguing against some of the approaches of the above scholars, it remains true that without their very valuable work I would have had little stimulation, if any, to carry on this work.

Within only five years of my last work, new translations and studies by major scholars in many countries, have appeared. We are at the beginning of Sifre studies, not at the end. A major merit in the present work is the presentation, for the first time in print, of the Ha'azinu section of a medieval commentary, falsely attributed to Rabbenu Hillel. This entire commentary to Sifre Numbers and Deuteronomy is now being prepared for publication.

My thanks to the Bodleian library in Oxford and the JTS library in New York for permission to use their manuscripts. My thanks also to the Lady Davis Foundation at the Hebrew University in Jerusalem which supported my research for this work and related projects.

Part One

TOPICS IN THE STUDY OF MIDRASH SIFRE HA'AZINU

Chapter 1

TRADITION AND MIDRASH

Jewish exegesis. The academic pursuit of appreciating midrash requires both portrait and landscape views. The fine analysis of the details must be examined before the broader integration of the meaning and place of midrash in Israel's literature can be attempted. In my earlier work, *Midrashic Interpretations of the Song of Moses*[1], I endeavored to provide a thorough exposition of Sifre Ha'azinu. The point was to illustrate how early Jews created midrashic understandings from scriptural verses. I endeavored to get to the utter meaning of midrashic language and technique in Sifre Ha'azinu. The present work is addressed to the broader issues of midrashic study. The body of the present work is devoted to issues of interest in the study of Midrash in general as well as expanded views of Sifre Ha'azinu.

An important feature of this work is a reworked translation of Sifre Ha'azinu. Since my earlier piece three or four other translations have appeared[2]; this indicates the importance of Sifre materials for the understanding of Rabbinic midrash. I regretted not having included the original text in my presentation and this time I include the text as given in B. Ugolino's *Thesaurus Antiquatum Sacrarum Comlectens*, Venice 1753, vol 15, based on the first printed edition of Venice 1546. Of major consequence, a hitherto unpublished medieval commentary, text and translation, is also included here.[3]

Serious midrashic study, on its own terms, is a concept rarely understood in modern academia. The concept connotes a well developed discipline. This discipline is consistent within its own well defined system and claims to discern a profound attempt to uncover the genuine import of Scripture's words. The implication would then be that midrashic method is as capable a method of understanding Scripture for the midrash scholar as is documentary method for the documentary scholar, as is literalism for the fundamentalist scholar, as is Kabbalah for the kabbalistic scholar, as is literary method for the literary scholar, as is historicism for the historian. The point is that each system is more or less discreet. Each one yields results which are satisfying to its system in that it confirms its own postulates and presents a picture of

----

[1] New York and Berne: Peter Lang, 1984.

[2] R. Hammer, *Sifre: A Tannaitic Commentary on the Book of Deuteronomy*, New Haven and London, Yale University Press, 1986. H. Bietenhard, *Sifre Deuteronomium*, Berne, Peter Lang 1984. J. Neusner, *Sifre to Deuteronomy: An Analytical Translation*, Atlanta, Scholars's Press, 1987.

[3] The full text of this commentary on Sifre Numbers and Deuteronomy is now in the final stages of preparation.

Scripture commensurate to the outlook of the particular discipline. One may study all systems but if so, must remain consistently committed to the unique ideals of any particular system during the study of that system. The findings of one system cannot be allowed to interfere, without due cause, with other systems; each system will maintain its own closed truth claims. The study of midrash must be held on the turf of midrash and nowhere else.

Midrash must be seen for what it is, the proposed reality reflected by Scripture. It is meant to reconstruct, as it were, the actuality which Scripture laconically represents.

To appreciate the particular midrashim which have found their way to current times we must appreciate the vast undertaking of exegesis which took place in the time of the Second Temple and earlier. Literary scholars have begun to investigate the early enterprises of biblical exegesis. While their work is not directly germane to the study of midrash it does shed light on the occupation of serious exegesis at the earliest points of recorded evidence. What is germane to our enterprise are the forms of exegesis at the close of the Second Temple period. Extended studies of the works of Apocrypha, Pseudepigrapha, Philo, Josephus, and the Dead Sea Scrolls indicate precise attitudes towards the ways in which the Bible was read. Further evidence from Rabbinic midrash itself shows us that what we have is a method of exegesis accepted throughout the Jewish world. It is therefore useful to indicate some factors which should be taken into account when pondering the formation of midrashic traditions. Let us now proceed to discuss these factors.

To the ancient Jewish mind the world was divided into three spaces-- holy, profane, and impure. God could dwell only in the holiest of surroundings and only the holiest of people could converse with Him. The Temple in Jerusalem had to be kept in an elaborate state of holiness so that the presence of the Divine King could be encountered there. Its premises, furniture and utensils were maintained in states of ritual purity, beyond the bounds of profane human use, so that it could serve as the palace of the Lord. The Land of Israel itself, while available for human use was also ritually hallowed at various periods and so were its fruits. The territory outside of Israel was considered impure territory and it was questionable whether the divine presence could really turn upon it.

People's states were also divided into categories, fit, or unfit. One who was fit could have contact with the holy; unfit persons could not. Israel is told to be a nation of the holy, that is, a nation where God can dwell. To be holy entailed certain physical states of being free from some discharges or diseases and also a moral cleanliness free from sin. Unfit people could not frequent the Temple or even touch hallowed objects. Jewish Temple and Jewish People were to be kept physically and spiritually pure. The "otherness" of the pure, moral and ritual, and the "otherness" of the impure, immoral and sacreligious, were the poles upon which religion turned. Prophet, Priest, and King held sway over moral, ritual, and national fitness. God was the supreme king and the others were functionaries of his institutions.

In the Second Temple period, from roughly 500 BCE to 70 CE, the religious offices of Prophet and King diminished and terminated. The Hasmonean kings, non-Davidic and therefore not religiously sanctioned, were accorded civil powers but their religious office was that of high priests. The latter part of the Era saw a proliferation of groups with programs to restore the sanctity of the Temple, the Land and the People or to project a new era of Heaven on Earth. Such programs were very ancient and date from the dawn of the Biblical period, from the dawn of the people itself. These groups, unlike their ancestors, saw themselves as estranged from the ideal mechanism of Temple, King and Prophet. Redemption meant the ascendancy of the Group's program of fitness over the Jewish nation. In this way, God would truly return as King into the precincts of purity.

Each group developed certain unique teachings but they shared a common legacy of ancient tradition. This legacy has come down through the ages and lies embedded in the literature of the Rabbis. Much of Rabbinic literature is not addressed to the Rabbinic agenda *per se* but to the values all Jews held in common. The Jewish agenda was one of consistency and logic. Scriptures were a three-fold revelation.

First there was the proper lessons to be derived about Israel's beginnings so that its character, its name, would be significant to the Jews. These lessons, as Baruch Halpern points out in his *First Historians*[4], are related in Israel's romantic and lyrical lore and re-interpreted through Israel's narratives as a history of Israel's vicissitudes with much attention to sequential detail. It is not, in the main, a conglomeration of disparate sources, but a library of various genres of writings turned into history and preachings.

If such was the endeavor of the biblical period, we need not be surprised to find that early biblical interpreters tried to explain which texts in Scripture were obscure source texts and which were explicit commentary. Scripture was hazy here and clear there. The Rabbinic literature known as midrash preserves this approach in its most basic format: Obscure biblical text followed by an exegesis which puts it into perspective and context, followed by a clear biblical verse which restates or "proves" the exegesis in another biblical setting. While Halpern is content to see the surrounding narratives of the Song of Deborah as dependent on the Song, the Rabbis find biblical exegesis of Scriptural Songs throughout Scripture. Their citations, introduced by "As Scripture says..." are meant to be real statements of how they saw Scripture reworking the obscure. And they may have been right. Songs are poetic. Prose is history. But if we rework the poetry of the songs we get to the prose message. At times, the Rabbis provide an exegesis that they believe should have appeared in Scripture but did not. Midrash of poetic sections of Scripture is the discovery of how "Prose Scripture" reads "Poetic Scripture" and restructures it for

----

[4] San Francisco: Harper and Row, 1988.

clarity and logic; and in some few cases-- how it should have read it. In this way, Scripture is Torah, a document to be studied and taught so that every word has its explanation, its sense, its definitive teaching.

The second revelation concerns the rules God has given to form his covenant with Israel to be their King. The derivation of these rules, Midrash halakhah, follows the same idea; the reading of Scripture's rules to make sense of an orderly system where all notions mesh consistently. The Rabbis studied various lists of categories of rules. They compared the salient features of like cases and discussed borderline cases that fell between categories. The Rabbis were undoubtedly part of a long process of teachers and their processes seem largely to be stated without any self-awareness that life had functioned in some manner other than theirs in the earlier biblical period.

The third aspect of revelation, is that which provides guidance for the Future Age and the heavenly realms. This aspect, referred to and anticipated in the writings of the Rabbis is nowhere systematically worked out or exegeted but again, Scripture's own processes are distilled and carried into the Rabbinic or even post Rabbinic period. A brief example will suffice. In Scripture, Ezekiel and Daniel are given visions which they do not understand and they must push themselves, somehow, to gain insight into the visions. Now Ezekiel and Daniel were said to have lived in impure regions, in Babylonia, where Temple, prophecy and kingship were not operative. Ezekiel was a Priest who had visions of the angelic abodes and received obscure visions of Israel's restoration:

> It was the appearance of the Form of the divine Glory. And when I saw it, I fell upon my face, and I heard a voice speaking. And it said to me, "Man, stand upon your feet, and I will speak with you." And when he spoke to me, the spirit entered into me and set me upon my feet, and I heard him speaking to me." (Ez. 1:28-2:2).

Ezekiel's prophecy is transmitted by a spirit which props him on his feet-- an idiom for achieving a semi-prophetic state of concentration wherein the unintelligible becomes intelligible. While it is doubtful if Daniel was a Priest, he also had visions of angels and received obscure messages of Israel's restoration.

> But (Gabriel) said to me...As he was speaking to me, I fell into a deep sleep with my face to the ground; but he touched me and set me on my feet. He said, "Behold I will make known to you..." (Dan. 8:17-19).

> Give heed to the words that I speak to you and stand upright...(Dan. 10:11).

When we therefore meet a Rabbinic student, a priest, named Yishmael, who listens to his teacher's obscure descriptions of the angelic abodes and transforms these teachings into actualized and detailed knowledge of the angels and their realms, we can see the progression of composition: Ezeki-el, Dani-el, and Yishma-el.

> Rabbi Yishmael said: When I heard this teaching from Rabbi Nehunia ben Haqanna, my master, I **stood upon my feet** and asked him for all the names of the Angels of Wisdom. And from the very question that I asked I perceived a light in my heart like the clearness of the heavens...and when I stood upon my feet I perceived my face glowing from my wisdom and I began to recite the names of the angels who are in each palace. (*Ma'aseh Merkavah*, ed. Scholem, *Jewish Gnosticism, Merkabah Mysticism and Talmudic Tradition*, New York, 1965, 114).

In all cases, the standing on the feet signals that an obscure message delivered by a heavenly agent is made known. What is interesting in the case of Yishmael is that Nehunia ben Haqanna, a Rabbinic master, is the heavenly agent. Yishmael himself achieves his understanding on his own merits and needs no outside prop. We therefore note that Rabbis are not inferior to angels or prophets. When we now note that certain phrases are used in Daniel which are found in Ezekiel and then applied to Yishmael we can see that each detail of Jewish writing has a component that rests in earlier generations while only in the latter writings is the component clarified. Jewish teaching preserves and carries forward the latent idioms and teachings of Scripture.

Let us demonstrate the integrity of this teaching. The words of Scripture are sacred to Jews. Handed down from antiquity, these words have intrigued Jews for millennia and continue to intrigue them. In Scripture, simple sentences subtly shade in the ancient story of Israel. This is a sacred story intimating the shape of Israel's soul from God's point of view. It is a divine book, a book of theology. For Israel, the writer must be God, or God's spokesman, for who else could quote the ideas and thoughts of God from the vantage of the divine[5]. As a theological work, Scripture is either divine or it is nothing. Were it merely a human document, it could say nothing of divine theology, nothing of divine mystery. The panorama of Israel's heroes dealing with their human, and therefore frail, moral and ethical plights requires the divine vantage. The sinner is not necessarily the one who sins but the one who fails

----

[5] See R. Alter, *The Art of Biblical Narrative*, Basic Books, 1981, 157: "(The narrators,) by a tacit convention in which no attention is paid to their limited human status, can adopt the all-knowing, unfailing perspective of God." If such is the secular view of biblical art; need it surprise anyone that the divine servants in Israel should have taken Scripture for God's very revelation. When the Talmud wants to prove that a work is the product of God's activity, it cites episodes which are given from the divine vantage. E.g. b Megilla 7a shows that the Book of Esther must be taken as the product of divine writing, for, who but God could know what Haman thought.

to cope with the struggle of mending the ruptured; that struggle which was Jacob's and is Israel's. That unique struggle is the story of Torah. As such the Rabbis studied Scripture, God's truth, as Israel's founding document. For them, Scripture is not directed at angels who can study the work of the Infinite at close range but at weak humans. Yet, this supposes a difficulty: As a divine document it lacks the format (to use a term borrowed from the computer age) to be read intelligibly by human Israel.

Israel is not God. Israel's reading of Midrash, its understanding of what lies behind Scripture, its inherited culture which antedates Scripture, needs to restructure the ambiguity of its founding document. The words of Scripture seem indefinite to the human grasp. They need to be studied, set into context, made readable by the unique process of Scripture's living culture, the culture of Israel. Scripture lies buried beneath the weight of Mount Sinai. Yet it is brought to life, resurrected in the suffering and joy of Israel's falling and rising. Scripture lives in the melody of Torah.[6]

Torah, the limiting of Scripture, the defining of how Scripture operates, the defining of the number of its words, the defining of its character, is called *midrash* when it exposes the definitive sense of Scripture. Torah is processed Scripture. The mechanism by which this process is achieved, that is, by which the infinite is rendered finite, by which Mount Sinai is picked up and removed,-- that process is midrash. It is that which releases God from his heavenly prison in Scripture and sets Him, master of Israel, King of the Universe. This is what Torah study does. This is midrash[7]. In sum, it is the forcing of the heavenly into earthly and earthy terms. In midrash, God is merged into the history of Israel. Every word of Scripture is focussed in the left eye to match the focus of every word in the right eye until the depth of Torah emerges. Only the two-eyed are masters of Torah. The measure of the focus of Scripture is in the experienced eyes of Israel. The measures, *mida* or

----

[6] A Talmudic saying (b Meg. 32a) has it that Rabbi Yohanan proclaimed:
  The following verse refers to all who read Scripture without its rhythm
  and recite Mishnah without its melody: *For yea I have given you statutes
  which are not good and laws which are not livable*. (Ez. 20:25)
One who studies without proper inflection cannot discover the truth of God's laws. On the other hand, one who reads with inflection will read the verse to say, *For yea, have I given you statutes which are not good and laws which are unlivable!* For such a one the entire reading of traditional texts will reveal many beautiful laws beneath the simple statements of the texts. Hence, the way in which one chooses to read the verse in Ezekiel indicates one's manner of exegesis and so provides a true indication of what one will find in the Torah: good laws or not good laws.

[7] "The four facets of God" is the rather startling sense of God's speech being "panim el panim" (Deut. 34:10)-- facets to facets, four facets. A rather nice Rabbinic comment occurs in Pesikta Rabbati 21. It illustrates this freeing of God in the midrash: God frowns in Scripture but smiles in Aggada.

mechilta, is the result of human concentration, meditation and speculation upon the divine words.

The words to be measured are physically written in black, bounded by white parchment which is scored into straight lines. The letters are encased by the scoring. These are the divine letters to be measured and reduced to Israel's *talmud torah, talmud lomar*[8], *shene'emar*. These are the words to be given definite meaning, *pesak*, for Israel. *Ka mashma lan*-- Heaven is grasped in the human reach. Torah, the taming of Scripture, is Israel's civilization,

The ancient Rabbis had many ways of talking about their mandate to reduce Scripture to Torah. Torah was that which was "measured". The very name of the compilation which contained midrash was *mekhilta*. It was what was produced through "measuring (*mekhilta*)," the measured rules (*midot*) through which Torah may be sought. It was to be "taken" by boldly grasping the word-- *kehu devarim* this is Torah. That which is then "possessed" is Torah: Talmud, Midrash, Halakhah, Aggada. Thus the ephemeral shadings of Scripture are boldly darkened. The midrash visibly sets and fixes them. Let us note how the Rabbis understood midrash.

> "Possess: QNH emet" (Prov. 23:23):
> I.e. the very substance ("**amita**") of Torah[9] ...which requires lines scored (by a reed-- QNH[10])...and which is meant to be processed through midrash. (y Megilla 1:1)

This possessing (QNH) of the Torah is the act whereby midrashic rules are applied to Scripture through taking the measure (QNH) of The Canon. The "Canon" is the word used by the Church Fathers to designate the set number of books in Scripture. "Kanon", is the Greek word for QANAH, MIDAH,-- a cane, a measuring rod, a reed. Their usage of Canon reflects a Jewish usage of *qanah*.

What is this Canon? It is the raw words, which are bounded by the measured reed, the scoring rule, and through which marking, these words, and these words alone, can be turned into Torah. Torah was defined and bounded, and the boundary was not to be moved. Its double portion for firstborn Israel cloaks Israel. Written Torah is the first portion. It is the divine Scripture reduced to the voice and tenor of human recitation. Oral Torah is the second portion. It is the Scriptures brought to live in Israel's home. What Jew did not possess both portions?

----

[8] I.e. The exegesis is to explain this scripture, "......" to mean: "......"

[9] See Num. Rabba 12:3 for this meaning of "amita shel Torah" as given by *etz yosef umatanot kehuna*.

[10] See y Megilla 1:9.

"When the Most High gave to the nations their inheritance" (Deut. 32:8):
>   When the Holy One, Blessed Be He, gave the Torah to Israel, He stood and looked out and contemplated, as it is said, "He standeth and measureth the earth, He looks and makes the nations to tremble." (Habakkuk 3:6). And there was no nation amongst the nations which was worthy to receive the Torah except Israel: "He specified the boundary of the Nations." (Sifre Deut. piska 311).

Israel's boundary finds its limit in twenty-four books. Twenty-four unknowables to fathom:

>   "Should there be no end to the study of many books; namely to read much and to exhaust one's self?" (Ecclesiastes 12:12):
>   Such study is reserved only for the twenty-four books of Scripture. Others may be read but not exhaustively (y Sanhedrin 1:1 and Ecclesiastes Rabba to Eccl. 12:12).

The Rabbis understood that the Canon was limited and meant to be "measured and ruled" as Israel's defining hegemony, *gevul*. It is not Scripture, as such, that the Jew creates, it is the Torah. The Hellenist Jew Philo also understood this to be so. He, too, took the word "gevul" to refer to Oral traditions[11]. "The one portion granted to Israel is virtue, i.e. "tradition and law". Israel's Torah is a divine portion but it is bounded and part and parcel of Israel. What we find in common between Philo and the Rabbis we posit has earlier roots than either.

Israel is the final stroke of Creation. Redeemed Israel is redeemed creation. What are the defining features of Creation? Torah, Temple and Israel. Torah, exiled and redeemed. Israel, exiled and redeemed. Temple, exiled and redeemed. This is the drama of Justice and Mercy. Where God removes himself, chaos results. Israel is dependent on God for its existence. God's omni-presence is manifested within the limitation of human experience through Torah, Temple-worship, Israel itself-- and through the world He created. Where one story is told all three or four are told. The very opening of the song of Ha'azinu in Scripture shows us the antiquity of this triad. 1) Give ear, O Heavens, and I will speak. 2) May my instruction drop as the rain. 3) For I call upon the name of the Lord. Creation-Israel, Torah, Redemption. What does the Sifre midrash 306 do with this?[12]

----

[11] *Conf.* ch. 128:145. See the discussion in Urbach, *The Sages*, Jerusalem 1975, 291f. He demonstrates that both the Rabbis and Philo understood boundary, gevul, to refer to Torah traditions.

[12] See the detailed discussion of this point in ch. 5 §1.

"And hear the words of my mouth about the earth[13]":
> Consider the earth which I have created to serve you.

"Give ear, concerning the heavens, and I will speak":
> This was said because the Torah was given from the heavens, as it is
said, "Ye, yourselves, have seen that I talked with you from the Heavens."
(Exodus 20:19).
"And concerning the earth, hear the words of my mouth":
> For Israel stood upon it -- And they said: "Of all which the Lord has
spoken we will do and we will hearken." (Exodus 24:7).

Creation (the literal sense of Deut. 32:1) and Torah are brought together
here with the theme of unredeemed Israel who spurns Torah. Now we move to verse
2.

"My instruction shall drop as the rain":
> "Instruction" can only mean "the words of the Torah", as it is said,
"For I give good instruction to you, forsake not My Torah." (Proverbs 4:2).

"As goats upon the grass":
> And for which sin do goats atone? They come for unintentional sins.
So do the words of the Torah atone for unintentional sins.

Here we have the theme of Torah tied to Temple-worship pointing to
redemption, the world of Resurrection. Rabbi Simaye concludes verse 2:

> And Rabbi Simaye also used to say: All creatures who are created to be
> heavenly, their soul and their body is of the heavenly realm. All creatures
> which are to be earthly, their soul and their body are of the earth; except for
> Man. For his soul is of the heavenly realm and his body is of the earthly
> realm. Therefore,if a man learns Torah and does the will of His Father who
> is in heaven, then he is as the creatures of the upper realm, as it is said, "I
> said, ye are godlike beings, and all of you sons of the Most High." (Psalms
> 82:6). If he does not learn Torah and does not do the will of his Father who is
> in heaven then he is like the creatures of the lower realm, as it is said,
> "Nevertheless ye shall die like men." (Psalms 82:7).
> And Rabbi Simaye also used to say: There is no section of Scripture

----

[13] The earth is taken here as the object of the lesson.

which does not refer to the *resurrection of the dead*; however, we do not have the required capability of interpretation, as it is said, "He will call to the Heavens above and to the Earth, that He may judge His people." (Psalms 50:4). "He will call to the Heavens above," -- this refers to the soul; "and to the Earth to judge His people," -- this refers to the body which is judged with it. And from whence do we know that this specifically refers to the resurrection of the dead? As it is said, "Come from the four winds, O wind, and breathe upon these slain...." (Ezekiel 47:9).

The themes of Israel, Torah, Temple-worship and Final Redemption point towards the next verse 3. In chapter 5§1 we will investigate this feature more thoroughly.

"For I will proclaim the name of the Lord, Give praise to our God":
    And from whence do we know that God specifically performed miracles and wonders at the Sea and at the Jordan and at the Valley of Arnon to have His name sanctified in the world? We know it from that which is said, "And it came to pass, when all the kings of the Amorites, that were beyond the Jordan westward and all her kings...." (Joshua 5:1). And likewise did Rahab say to the agents of Joshua, "For we have heard how the Lord dried up the waters of the Red Sea before you." (Joshua 2:10). Thus does Scripture state, "For I will proclaim the name of the Lord."

    And from whence do we know that the Ministering Angels do not mention the name of the Holy One, Blessed Be He, in the heavenly realm, until Israel mentions it in the earthly realm? We know it from that which is said, "Hear, O Israel, the Lord our God, the Lord is One." Deuteronomy 6:4). And Scripture also states, "When the morning stars sang together" (Job 38:7) --and afterwards --"And all the godly ones shouted." "The morning stars" -- These refer to Israel who is compared to stars, as it is said, "I will multiply thy seed as the stars of the heavens," (Genesis 22:17). "And all the godly ones shouted," --These refer to the Ministering Angels; and so does Scripture state, "And the godly ones came to present themselves before the Lord." (Job 1:6).

The theme of redemption and final glory whereby Israel unifies creation, above and below is the theme of Israel now above the angels. They are the morning stars, awakening the dawn of cosmic redemption.

While each verse contains but one element, the midrashist incorporates other elements as well. In potential, Israel, Torah, and Redemption are inseparable. Deuteronomy 32 begins with three verses: Nature, Instruction; Praise. The midrash combines Nature with Instruction and Instruction with Praise and Praise with ultimate Redemption. The midrashist never tires of finding the latent themes in verses where only one is explicitly expressed:

> "That possesses thee --QNH" (Deut. 32:6):
>> This is one of the three which were called "possessions-- QNH". The Torah is called "God's possession", as it is said, "The Lord possessed me as the beginning of his way." (Proverbs 8:22). "Israel is called God's possession", as it is said, "Is He not thy Father that possesses thee." The Temple is called "God's possession", and so does Scripture state, "This mountain, which His right hand had possessed." (Psalms 78:54).

The idea of possession which we noted above is spelled out so clearly that even where QNH has the meaning of "nest" it will still reflect the idea of Torah.

> "As an eagle that stirreth up his nest QNH" (Deut. 32:11):
>> Just as an eagle before coming to his nest, painstakingly with his wings between two trees or two thickets, causes a disturbance for his children, in order that they should be stirred up so as to have the strength to receive him; so when the Holy One, Blessed Be He, came to give the Torah to Israel, He did not come to them from one direction but from four directions, as it is said, "The Lord came from Sinai and rose from Seir unto them...." (Deuteronomy 33:2). Which is the fourth direction? --"God cometh from Teman." (Habakkuk 3:3)

> Another interpretation:
> "As an eagle that stirreth up his nest":
>> This refers to the Future to Come, as it is said, "The voice of my beloved, behold he comes...." (Song of Songs 2:8).

And even where QNH is not present the Rabbis chose to find it. The Nest is still present:

> "He enthroned it (the QNH of Deut. 32:11) on the high places of the earth" (Deut. 32:13):
>> This refers to the Land of Israel which is higher than all the other countries. This is according to the matter of which Scripture states, "We should go up at once and possess it." (Numbers 13:30). And it also states, "So they went up"

> Another interpretation:
> "He enthroned it (the QNH of Deut. 32:11) on the high places of the earth":
>> This refers to the Temple which is higher than the whole world, as it is said, "Then thou shalt arise and get thee up unto the place." (Deuteronomy

17:8).

Another interpretation:
"He enthroned it (the QNH of Deut.32: 11) on the high places of the earth":
> This refers to the Torah, as it is said, "The Lord made me as the beginning of His way." (Proverbs 8:22).

Another interpretation:
"He enthroned it (the Ya'ir of Deut. 32:11) on the high places of the earth":
> This refers to the world, as it is said, "The boar out of the woods (Ya'ar) doth ravage it." (Psalms 80:4).

["And he made him to suck honey out of the crag and oil out of the flinty rock" (Deut.32:13)]..."And the blood of the grape thou drankest foaming wine" (Deut. 32:15):
> On the Future Morrow Israel will inherit their properties and it will be as pleasing to them as oil and as honey.[14]

These passages point to the great themes to be teased out of Scripture through the process of midrash. Although it will not always be so obvious, most midrash deals with some facet of these themes. We may therefore speak of midrashic theme.

Here is another which is found in a number of versions:

Let the beloved come...
The son of the beloved...
And build the beloved...
For the beloved...
In the portion of the beloved...
That the beloveds may be purified there.[15]

There are other versions but the key in all of them seems to be: Israel son of Abraham builds the Temple in the portion of Benjamin for the Holy One. Here is a similar story:

----

[14] This comment obviously originated as part of the cycle of comments attached to Deut. 32:13.

[15] b Menahot 53a, cmp. Sifre Deut. 352, and *Yalkut Shimoni* Deut. 955.

Kiveyakhol[16] God is called first as it says "..."
And Zion is called "first" as it says "..."
And Esau is called "first" as it says "..."
And Messiah is called "first" as it says...

> May God come, who is called "first", and build the Temple,
> that is called "first", and punish Esau, who is called "first".
> Then may The Messiah, who is called "first", come on the first month as
> it is said, "This month is the head of the months."[17]   (Shmot Rabba
> 15:2).

Finally, we again demonstrate the claim that where one of Torah, Israel and the World are present the others are to be considered there. Redemption of one is redemption of all. The Babylonian Talmud[18] has an inexplicable passage which relates that three people are required to read from the Scripture to symbolize a) Torah, Prophets, Writing; b) Priest, Levite, Israelite. We may note that we have here the symbolism of the totality of Canon (the library of Scripture) as well as the totality of Israel (the membership of the people). The point is pushed further. "And what is symbolized by having them read 10 verses?" It is 1) The Ten Commands by which the world was created. 2) The Ten who are permanent residents of the synagogue. 3) The Ten Commandments given at Mount Sinai. These themes are:

   creation,
   the prayer quorum embodying the People of Israel,
   the embodiment of Scriptural teachings.

The motifs are the experienced reality of Israel. They form the lenses through which Torah is produced from Scripture .

----

[16] I.e. in human imagery.

[17] Perhaps the original was, "May the first come and build the first and punish the first and then may the first come." "On the first" may be suspected of being an addition.

[18] b Megilla 21b.

Chapter 2

DESIGN AND STRUCTURE OF MIDRASHIM

1. Generic exegetical forms.

a) *Narrative midrash*. The generic form of biblical exegesis applies to Jewish writings of different groups in the period of the Second Temple. The basic, simple form of exegesis, of which there are several variations, contains three steps. 1) A verse. 2) A supposedly arbitrary statement identifying what the verse is referring to. 3) A statement of proof showing that the identification is correct. In other words we have: the given, the required to prove, and the proof. This form is applicable to exegesis within Scripture, such as dream interpretation, and also to such diverse works as the Dead Sea Scrolls and Philo. There are many variations to this form but ultimately almost every exegesis can be reduced to these three steps. Quite often another verse may supply the proof of the identification and occasionally the identification itself is another verse. Here are some examples:

1- "And our distress." (Deut. 26:7):
2- These are the sons.
3- Of whom it was said, "Every son which is born
you shall cast into the river." (Ex. 1:22).

1- is the given Scripture; 2- is the identification of the event of the Scripture which requires substantiation; 3- is the substantiation. This passage is found in the Haggadah for Passover. In Sifre Deut. piska 301 we find the very same tradition but it omits 2- which is to be understood as trivial once the prooftext is known. The point is that "And our distress" is ambiguous. Scripture itself indicates that its referent is to Pharaoh's order to drown male babies.

Another form merits more discussion. The late J. Heinemann[1] analyzed midrashim where the Torah text was held in abeyance until the end of the midrash. At the end of the midrash, point two, even if unstated, became apparent and the midrash "jelled". The assumption is that these midrashim were composed for expositing Torah. This is probably not the case. The skeletal forms of these midrashim indicate that we have midrashim from the Psalms or Proverbs (only a few from the Prophets) which are enlisted to serve the purpose of introducing a Torah section. Let us consider the following skeletal example from Leviticus Rabba 1:6:

----

[1] J. Heinemann, "The Proem in the Aggadic Midrashim," *Studies in Aggadah and Folk Literature, Scripta Hierosolymita* xxii: (Jerusalem, 1971) 101ff.

1 "And the Lord called to Moses."(Lev. 1:1)[2].
2 [step 2 is absent and held in suspension until 2c]
3 Knowledge is most profitable, (cites Prov. 20,15:)
        1a-"There is Gold,"
        2a-Everyone brought gold offerings to
             the Tent of Assembly.
        3a-"And this is the offering [which you
             shall take from them. Gold..."]
             (Ex. 35:27).

        1b-"And a multiple of jewels,"
        2b-This is the free-will offering of the
             princes.
        3b-"And the princes brought jewels."(Ex. 35:27).

        1c-"But lips speaking knowledge are the most
             valuable ornament."
        2c-Moses' wise words were more
             precious than the metals.
        3c-Thus it says, "And the Lord called
             (only) to Moses."

"Thus it says" indicates this is a sermon which relates to the parashah of Lev.1:1ff. The definitions of context are evident and the verses are supportive. Quite often pth sermons need not refer to a specific verse but could in fact refer to a larger section of Scripture without citing it.

Rabba bar Ofran exegeted terms (pth lh pyth°a) in regards to this parashah (in Esther) from here "And I shall place my Throne in Elam And I shall destroy from there a ruler and ministers." (Jeremiah 49:38). "A ruler"-- this refers to Vashti. "And ministers"-- this refers to Haman and his ten sons. (b Megilla 10b).

Here we have identifications of terms in Jeremiah 49:38 by the obvious matching of the context known from the story of Esther. The match is obvious to the reader and the prooftexts are left unstated. As well second steps may be omitted when they seem trivial. We can conclude that our circular forms are always the result of the same kind of three-step exegesis. They are usually captioned by a lead verse, sometimes with some elaboration, which is then affixed to the pth exegesis.

----

[2] Found at the beginning of the homilies in Lev. R. 1:1 and carried forward.

Let us now return to the midrash on Lev 1:1. In the context of illustrating 2c, Lev. 1:1 is seen as praise for Moses. The sense of the verse, when put into the midrashic context, gains heightened meaning. Lev. 1:1 is subtly given its context by acting as a proof text for Proverbs.

According to J. Heinemann, the beauty of the form is that we have to work our way through the exegesis of a verse in Proverbs until we discover what it is that we are really trying to prove about the lead verse in the Pentateuch. We discover it at the very end of the exegesis of some other verse not in the Pentateuch. Let us look at this more closely.

Were we to put this in some standard intelligible form of Pentateuchal exegesis, we would have to state the reverse.

> 1."And the Lord called to Moses."
> 2. Moses' wise words were more precious offerings
>   than the metals.
> 3. "But lips speaking knowledge are the most
>   valuable ornaments."

As we in fact have it, we seem to have a prooftext (3c) acting as a lead verse (1). Calling it circular should not mean that we have circular reasoning. The given should not also serve as its own prooftext. Good exegesis, we expect, is not circular. Indeed, the notion of a special petichta form is quite recent and is a modern description.

What we really have, and this is not atypical for the petichta form, is a midrash from Proverbs which uses Lev. 1:1 as a proof text. The preacher, or perhaps the redactors, of our midrashim on Torah have simply borrowed the midrashim from Proverbs (or some other Hagiographic work) which have prooftexts (3) from the Torah. The preacher "filed" these midrashim under the Torah verse. The result is a title verse from the Torah followed by a 3 step exegesis utilizing Torah prooftexts to exegete a verse in Proverbs. By removing the lead verse and rearranging the order, we can see that our Leviticus text is one of several cited from the Pentateuch as prooftexts.

> 1- a) "There is Gold,
>   b) and a multiple of jewels,
>   c) but lips speaking knowledge are the most
>   valuable ornament." (Prov. 20:15)

> 2- a) Everyone brought gold offerings to the Tent of
> Assembly.
>   b) This is the free-will offering of the princes.
>   c) Moses' wise words were more precious than the
> metals.

3- a) "And this is the offering which you
          shall take from them. Gold ..."(Ex. 35:27).
   b) "And the princes brought jewels."
          (Ex. 35:27).)
   c) "And the Lord called (only) to
          Moses." (Lev. 1:1).

This is simply a regular midrashic form explaining a verse in Proverbs. The final prooftexts come from the Pentateuch. When the midrash is "transferred" from a Proverb-homily to a Leviticus-homily we find the midrash headed by the verse in Leviticus. In other words, what we consider "petichta" is in fact standard exegetical form and nothing more. That these forms begin with patah is easily explained. The word, as I have indicated elsewhere[3], simply means to explicate one thing in terms of another. That is, it commonly identifies a term in a verse with a term in another verse such that the second reference can then be read back into the first verse. This is the simplest form of three step exegesis and is similar to the Qumran pesher form. Pataḥ simply signifies "exegete" and seems to have been used primarily for the Hagiographa. The term "petichta" in the Land of Israel often "introduced" homilies on lead verses to the sedra. In Babylonia the term was used with greater variety[4]. We have examples in the Talmud (b Meg. 5a) and midrashim[5] of verses from the Hagiographa being exegeted with the term Pataḥ with either no circularity implied or no reference to a Torah verse. Pataḥ, in its most original sense, simply refers to identifying terms in one verse with terms in another verse, another known story, or another known tradition. The form developed a peculiar literary structure in the Land of Israel. However, in all cases, the result is to show the unity of TANAK; all of Scripture is a single cloth.

S.J. Rapoport believed that these midrashim were in fact the openers for synagogue sermons on the Sabbath[6]. The Torah had been read. The Prophets had been read. The *darshan* now began his sermon on the first verse or so of the Torah section by citing a midrash from the Writings. Thus all three sections of TANAK were represented.

----

[3] See H. Basser, "A Distinctive Usage of PTH in Rabbinic Literature," *Hebrew Studies* 20-21 (1979-80): 60-61.

[4] See E. Segal, "The Petihta in Babylonia," *Tarbitz*, 53 (1985), 19-46.

[5] See the examples in H. Fox, " The Circular Proem," *PAAJR*, 49 (1982), 6.

[6] See *Erekh Millin*,vol 1, 1912, s.v. ptḥ. J. Heinemann thought the sermon preceded the Torah reading, hence "opened".

Once we look at the "petichta" midrash without trying to think of the Torah verse as the lead verse we find "three-step exegesis" (or some truncated form of it) and that is all. Nothing is circular in its reasoning. The present forms are circular in that the added introductions (the final prooftext) occasionally state openly what this title verse is going to prove in the body of the midrash. We then wait to see how this prooftext does this. There seems to have been collections of midrashim to Proverbs and Psalms which predate these "petichta" midrashim and were utilized by the preachers. The preachers may have constructed their own midrashim on the verses in the Writings to accomplish these connections. However, the fact that we have midrashim defining words in verses in the Writings with no attempt to connect them to Torah suggests that there did exist separate midrashim on Proverbs and other works. It is quite likely that these midrashim were not promulgated in the synagogue but in the academy. The sermons in the work *Pesikta de Rav Kahana* then would reflect the Synagogue use of exegesis from the academy and, perhaps, transmitted from earlier generations. The pyth³ was not only the definition of terms in a verse, it was also a way of matching one source to correspond with another.

The forms of "pesher" in the Dead Sea Scrolls follow a similar pattern of three steps. Instead of using verses as proofs they offer the experience of the community as prooftext. Thus the history of the group is not offered as an exegesis but, as fact, to prove the identification of a subject in one or another verse.

Quite often the statements of Philo lend themselves to three step analysis whereby the final proof is established by common experience. For example,

1-"And a mixed multitude." (Ex 12:38).
2-If one is to speak in plain terms[7] these are the
irrational doctrines of the soul.
3-Being that they are like cattle.[8]

The claim cannot be made that all exegesis can be reduced to this format but it may be claimed that 99% of midrashic forms are three step in so far as 1- a verse is presented, 2- a middle statement reflects upon the sense of the verse, 3- evidence is brought to resolve the middle. The generic form of simple exegesis is thus established as independent of group or time. It seems to be the reasonable form for any exegesis of a text. It is the particular style in which the three steps are cast which shows the exegesis to be characteristic of any specific group. Moreover, step 3 is usually group specific. The proofs offered are from the unique belief structure of the group so that it may be said that exegesis differs from general commentary in that its

---

[7] See further, sec, #4, for Paul's similar usage of speaking plainly and clearly.

[8] See *The Migration of Abraham* (ch. 27 end) in *Philo*, Volume 4, Loeb classical library, London 1932, 218.

proofs will be accepted only by the specific group which accepts the belief pool from which proofs are offered. Thus in arguments with other groups the structure of argument will conform to the belief pool of the *opposing groups*.

A story in the Mishnah presents an argument between Sadducees and Pharisees[9]. The debate concerns the value of certain books known as Sifre Homoros. The Pharisees tell the Sadducees that they have the value of "bones of a hamor, a donkey". The Pharisees compare their own "beloved" Book to the bones of the "beloved" Sadducean High Priest whose name Yohanan, means beloved of God. This arguing from the others' viewpoint is a common feature of debates in the Gospels and Rabbinic literature. Our observation allows us to identify the intended audience of an exegesis. Arguments dependent upon Christian beliefs are aimed at Christians, if dependent upon Jewish beliefs they are aimed at Jews.

b) *Legal midrash*. A typical form of legal midrash, as found in post 70 sources, is to 1- state a verse. 2- Suggest one and/or another legal sense based on apparent information. 3- Exegete a seemingly trivial particular phrase of an appropriate Scripture to set a specific limit to the legal applicability of the law in question. I suggest that the basic form of the midrash is just 3. The text which indicates this is found below in a citation of Sifra 2:3. Step 2 is rhetorical in that it misdirects in order to show that 3- is a useful exegesis. Such misdirection probably originated as an instructional technique. "Here is a verse. What do you think it means? Could it mean that? (perhaps some people do think so!). No, attentive exegesis shows it has to mean this." Thus, the exegesis is controlled and limited. While, rather simple, the exegesis is shown to conform to elaborate Rabbinic principles (which are, usually in the end, shown not to be applicable). The form of the midrash is now given as three steps. I see no reason to think that such forms could not have been prevalent in Second Temple times. Consider the "antithesis" in Matt. 5:43-4:

1.- ["And thou shalt love thy r ᶜ k." Lev 19:17]

2.- Ye have heard that it hath been said, "Thou shalt love thy neighbor (*reᶜaka*);" and so, thou shalt hate thine enemy.

3.-But I say unto you, Love your enemies...do good to them that hate you and pray for them that spitefully use you, and persecute you, (=*raᶜeka*)....

Here 2- gives us a misdirection based on the traditional pronunciation of the unvocalized letters of the Torah. It might be thought that such refers only to your friend "reᶜaka". 3- supplies a different vocalization, "raᶜeka"-- those who harm you, disproving the suggested exegesis based on a simple reading of the traditional

----

9 Mishnah Yadaim 4:5

pronunciation. The traditional pronunciation (hath been said) is contrasted with Jesus' pronunciation (I say). The same phenomenon occurs throughout the antitheses of Matthew.

Since Scripture can never be trivial, the repetition of a word, or even a letter, can have meaning. This midrash is found in the Passover Haggadah (and Mekhilta to Exodus 13:14):

1. "And you shall interpret for your son on that day: 'Because of this God made for me my exiting from Egypt'". (Ex.13:8)
2. So "on that day"...I might think means... while it is still day.
3. The exegesis of "Because of this" is to explain the point:"Because of this" I distinctly explain as "at the time when *matsa* and *marror* are set before you."

The meaning of *talmud lomar* is not really "Scripture states" as usually rendered but rather "the exegesis of phrase x is to explain this." The formula, "The exegesis is to explain: verse x " is a technical phrase. This is demonstrated in the above example by the rare elaboration. This elaboration paraphrases the formula of *talmud lomar*: "phrase x I distinctly explain as." The point is that the demonstrative "this" tells us that something is being pointed out. It is the *matsa* which is eaten only at night (Ex. 12:18). Hence, we establish the legally set time to explain, to point out the ritual items commemorating the Exodus to the assembled family, is at night. We shall have more to say about the forms in our discussion of Midrash halakhah below.

2. **The antiquity of midrash.** The question of what reflects written sources and what reflects oral sources is always pertinent in the study of midrash. My personal approach is to see that midrashim have sometimes come to us in several forms. Consideration of these forms leads one to see that the form which is more difficult belongs to a compilation which is earlier than the compilation containing the easier form. One might simply think that as time went on the midrash became simplified in retelling so that the phenomenon can be explained as if a process of simplification was at work. Yet, the very opposite may be the case. The simpler forms may represent the earlier forms of the tradition, which were formulated to be transmitted orally while the written forms represent a later form which was set down in writing while the oral form was still current. Since the oral form was current one would know the midrash and appreciate the complications of the written form. Hence the obscure forms were written before the simple oral forms were set down in writing in late compilations. This would explain why later writings still contain very early material. They are independent of the earlier writings and reflect the clearer, oral forms which were current when the first written forms were taking

shape. It is therefore possible that early traditions may appear in the very late sources.

The Egyptian magicians Jannes and Jambres are known through the fragments of an apocryphal book. The book is quoted by the Church Fathers and the names are known to Pagan, Christian and Jewish sources. CD knows them as opponents of Moses (and Aaron) and Tanhuma Ki Tisa 19 alone, of all other sources, preserves the story that "Jonnes" and "Jombres" were in the desert with Moses with 40,000 Egyptians who joined the Exodus. The Damascus document knows of "Johanna and his brother" as opponents of Moses in Chapter 5. "Johanne" and "Mmbrei" are their names in b Men 85a. The name "Johannes" accords with the best traditions in Greek sources as mentioned by M. Stern in EJ[10]. Since the reference in CD assumes the story preserved in Tanhuma, that story must be prior although its compilation into Tanhuma happened many hundreds of years after CD.

The antiquity of many midrashic forms and traditions cannot be dismissed and it is not unreasonable to search midrash for traditions to explain Second Temple period writings.

We can illustrate the antiquity of Rabbinic midrash. Although in early sources the precise exegesis is lacking we can reconstruct it, with a high degree of probability. For instance, Josephus offers us etymologies of the names of the rivers which fed the Garden of Eden, as recorded in Gen. 2:14. These etymologies are not in the biblical versions. Josephus writes that "Hiddekel" means "narrowness and rapidity."[11] b Berachot 59b explains "Hiddekel" to mean ḥad, narrow, and qal, rapid. Were it not for the notice in Josephus we might have thought that the etymology was derived much later than it in fact was. Indeed, we might now posit that such etymologies are very ancient indeed, much before the time of Josephus. It is not likely that the notice in Josephus and the Talmud are simply happy coincidences based on the obvious. The editors of the Loeb edition of Josephus missed the "obvious" point and claimed that Josephus derived the name from ḥad, sharp, and dak, thin, and he left out el. The point is not obvious.

In the case before us we are prevented from arguing that we have a simple coincidence for the shared exegesis. It is not an obvious derivation. The description of the Tigris as "narrowness and rapidity" must actually be based upon the abnormality of a Hebrew root of four letters which is better broken up as two words of two letters. A similar phenomenon is noticed in Philo's derivation of ha-keruvin as if from haker and u-vin, "Recognize and Understand", apparently equal to Goodness and Authority, the powers of the divine Logos.[12] Whether the sense of

----

[10] *Encyclopedia Judaica*, Jerusalem, 1971, s.v. Jannes and Jambres.

[11] Josephus, *Jewish Antiquities*, Bk. 1, Loeb Classical Library, 1930, p. 19.

[12] See Philo's treatise (ed. F. Colson) *On the Life of Moses* 3:8. Colson's note ad loc. relates that this derivation was followed by Clement, Jerome and Augustine.

the Merkavic "Godlo veTuvo" or the Kabbalic "hokhmah and binah" is related to the notion is not our concern here. We do find word division as an exegetical device in the first century, and it is common in Philo and his sources. Hence we may conclude that popular etymologies are likely products of early exegesis and where we can locate identical, unobvious etymologies, a single early tradition may be presumed to be behind both. Folk etymology has very early roots.

Let us now consider another early passage which was absorbed into Rabbinic midrash. This one is from the *Testament of Naphtali*.

> "And you, do not rush to make your deeds evil through lust after gain and to convince yourselves through words of vanity. For should you silence these through pure-heartedness you will know how to become strong in the will of God and to despise the will of Belial.
>
> Sun and moon and stars do not change their order. Thus, you also, do not change the law of God through the disorder of your doings. Gentiles, erring and leaving the Lord, changed their order and followed after wood and stones and spirits of error.
>
> Not so you, my children, who know through the heavens and the earth and the sea and all creation that God has made them in order that you should not be like the Sodomites who perverted their order.
>
> So also did the giants pervert their order such that God cursed them at the time of the Flood and laid waste the earth, on their account, its inhabitants and all that grew upon it.[13]"

Reflection upon the motifs here will allow us to conclude that this passage is based upon an understanding in the 32nd chapter of Deuteronomy.[14] To understand exactly what has been done let us begin by noting the presentation in *The King James Version* of Deut 32:1-7:

> (1)Give ear, O ye heavens, and I will speak; and hear, O, earth, the words of
>   my mouth. 2) My doctrine shall drop as the rain, and my speech
>   shall distill as the dew, as the small rain upon the tender herb, and

----

[13]   *Testament of Naphtali*, 3:1-5. Cf. 1 *Enoch*, 1:1-3. See also H.W. Hollander and M. de Jonge, **The Testaments of the Twelve Patriarchs: A Commentary**, Leiden: Brill, 1985, 305-309.

[14]   Deut 32 refers to "leaving the Lord" (vs 15), "obeying spirits" (vs 17), "disobeying God through lack of wisdom" (vs 28). Lars Hartman, **Asking for a Meaning: A Study of 1 Enoch 1-5** (Coniectanea Biblica, New Testament Series 12: Lund: Gleerup, 1979) connects the midrash on Deut 32, *Sifre Deut* 306, with 1 *Enoch* 2:1-5:3 (see pp 29, 86-7) He also connects this midrash to *T Naph* chs. 3 and 4 (pp 54-5).

as the showers upon the grass: 3) Because I will publish the name
of the Lord: ascribe ye greatness unto our God. 4) He is the Rock,
his work is perfect: for all his ways are judgment: a God of truth
and without iniquity, just and right is he. 5) They have corrupted
themselves, their spot is not the spot of his children: they are a
perverse and crooked generation. 6) Do ye thus requite the Lord,
O foolish people and unwise? is he not thy father that hath bought
thee? hath he not made thee, and established thee?
(7)Remember the days of old, consider the years of many generations: ask
thy father and he will shew thee; thy elders, and they will tell thee.

A quick glance will show us we have two imperatives:"Give ear" and
"Remember". The parallel grammatical forms suggest the same audience; namely,
Israel. Thus (1) can be rendered, "Give ear about the heavens and I will declaim;
and hear the words of my mouth about the earth." Now the passage is more
intelligible. Moses invokes a lesson from nature and a lesson from history to instruct
Israel not to change her order which has been divinely set. The Rabbinic midrash
paraphrases here:

> The Holy One, blessed be He, instructed Moses: Tell Israel, "Consider the
> heavens which I created to serve you. Perhaps it has changed its order....how
> much more so you must not change your order.[15]

The "order" is meant to refer to God's instruction. If we could discover why
the midrashist insisted that the lessons have to do with "changing order" we could
well appreciate that this is not altogether an unreasonable rendering of the passage.
God's instruction is compared to nature's order, rain and dew.

We know Israel is to be instructed through paying attention to the heavens
and the earth (vs.1). What we do not know is what lesson they are to learn from
"the days of old"(vs.7). The Rabbinic midrash is perplexing:

> "Remember what I did....you do not find a generation in which there is not
> the likes of the people of the generation of the Flood nor the likes of the
> Sodomites...[16]"

----

[15] *Sifre Deut* 306, ed. Finkelstein, 332.

[16] *Sifre Deut* 310, ed. Finkelstein, 350. The introductory part of this tradition adds "the
generation of the Dispersion". It appears that, in concert with the predilection of folklore for triads, an
extra villain has crept into the earlier format.

It is not clear why these generations are singled out or indeed where there is any allusion to them in the verse. Inspection of the verse shows us that what was translated above as "many generations" in fact is "generation and generation". Thus the midrashist knew the reference was to two generations. But we also know something else. The reference to "years" is problematic in the biblical text. The word is "shenot". While "years" is a possible translation, "perversions" suits the context much better.[17] The Rabbinic midrash makes no mention of this point in its comment to Deut 32:7. Yet, only if we read Deut 32:7 as "Consider the perversions of the generation and the generation," can we explain the stress the Rabbis put upon "changing order" in their comment to Deut 32:1. At some time the two verses must have been read together as a parallel structure. There is no other way to account for the midrashic comment to Deut 32:1. Moses asked Israel to reflect upon both nature and history to learn the consequences of "changing one's order". Nature taught obedience while history showed what happened in the case of disobedience. This supposition is confirmed through comparing the text of *T. Naph.* to the midrash. Here we also see the instruction of the heavens and the earth which teach one not to change one's order and we also see what happened to the generations of the Flood and Sodom which did change their order. Both the midrash and the pseudepigraphic text refer to "changing one's order."[18] There is no likely way to explain this unless we posit that both sources drew from a common tradition[19] which

----

[17]   See the discussion of *shinah* and *shina* in H. Yalon, Studies in the Hebrew Language, Jerusalem, 1971, pp 150-1. *Shina* is the word used in *1 Enoch* 2:4 (*SNYTN*) which passage is equated with *T Naph* 3 by its author (see *T Naph* 4:1). This is also the sense used in the midrash: *shinah midah* (the reading in ms Vatican, Assemani 32), *shinah seder* (the variant reading in ms Berlin, Acc. Or. 1928, 328 and *Midrash Hakhamim*). While "change order" is quite literal the import of the term is "perversion". The term for "order" is *midah* which is the normal word for "conduct". Thus *j Hag. 2:2* reads "memidah lemidah yatsa", departed from one order to another, while *b Hag* 15a reads "yatsa letarbut ra'ah", departed to evil conduct. In the variant reading in Sifre Deut, that we noted above, we find *seder* can have this sense of "rules of conduct" as demonstrated in *b Ket.* 103b (*sidrei hokhma, sidrei nesi'ut*) and *b Shab.* 53b (*sidrei bereshit*). Gen. Rabba 33:11 refers to the Flood generation: "hem qilqelu silonot shelahem af hamaqom shinah lahem siduro shel olam": They perverted their sexual channels so God **changed the order** of the world. Hartman (**Asking**),55, notes *midah* in the Sifre midrash is paralleled by *taxis* in *T Naph* 3. *Taxis* generally refers to a set order or duty to be performed in good will. This set order is what the evil generations perverted.

[18]   The sense of this phrase is understood by H.C. Kee ("The Ethical Dimensions of the Testaments of the XII as a clue to Provenance," NTS 24, 1978, 262), to refer to the universal natural law of the Stoics. D. Slingerland ("The Nature of Nomos (Law) within the Testaments of the Twelve Patriarchs," JBL 105, 1986, 39-48), disputes Kee's assertion. He claims "the order" referred to is Israel's entire legal corpus (the wider sense of *Torah*). In the view of the midrash, this is certainly the case.

[19] For further examples of commonality between midrash and Pseudepigrapha see J. Klausner, *The Messianic Idea in Israel*, New York, Macmillan, 1955, 342-44 and E. Urbach, *Hazal*, Jerusalem, 1978, 395 n.95, 202 n.44, 147ff.

used exegetical techniques to explicate Deut 32. Hence this exegesis is very ancient.[20]

Moreover the form of the midrash follows what has been identified as first century sermonic form in Greek Jewish writings: the elucidation of a verse, the moral drawn from it concerning the biblical characters, and the lesson for the audience[21]. The indication again is that Rabbinic midrash has roots much more ancient than the Rabbinic periods.

3. **Form criticism.** Here we will utilize the method of "form criticism" to show that traditions found in late sources have roots in very early sources. In the medieval Midrashic compilation of Yalkut Shimoni (Yalkut Balak 766) we find an extraordinary passage which debates whether Christianity is forbidden to everyone or to Jews alone. Once we know that for the Rabbis the Israelite camp measured 60 miles the point becomes clear. The reconstruction of the history of this passage will shed light on the development of midrash in general and Rabbinic views of Christianity in particular.

One of the more questionable techniques for determining the history of midrashic traditions is form criticism. This method depends upon an identifiable form which is exclusive to a certain milieu and period being isolated within texts of unknown dates of composition. By applying common sense to the internal structures of these latter passages one establishes a tradition history.

Proverbs 27:14 is a verse which lends itself without difficulty to the context of Balaam. Balaam was the prophet who arose early in the morning to curse Israel but instead ended up by praising the nation. Proverbs 27:14 states, "He blesses his fellow with a powerful voice, having arisen early in the morning, it is accounted to him as a curse." While everything in the verse points to Balaam, the point of the "powerful voice" requires elucidation. Yalkut Balak 766,*Yalkut Shimoni*, Salonika, 1521:

    I. "He blesses his fellow with a powerful voice,"
       (Proverbs 27:14).

----

[20] *The Testament of the Twelve Patriarchs* originates in the pre-christian period. See A. Kahana, **HaSefarim Haḥitsonim**, Jerusalem, Maqor, 5530, 144-146. Also see J. Kugel, "On Hidden Hatred and Open Reproach: Early Exegesis of Lev. 19:17," **HTR** 80:1 (1987), 55-6. Kugel weighs the premaccabean date of Bickerman against the later but still prechristian dating of Anders Hiltgard and sees it as an early book with later accretions. He notes T. Gade exegetes a verse in line with the exegesis of Sifra to Lev.19:17. Gary Anderson (**HTR** 82:2, 1989,p. 48) finds the exegesis in jubilees 3:2 to reflecxt the very exegesis in Babli Yevamot 63a.

[21] See C. Clifton Black II, "The Rhetorical Form of the Hellenistic Jewish and Early Christian Sermon," **HTR** 81:1 (1988), 1-17.

How far did the voice of Balaam travel?

II.   Rabbi Yohanan says, "Sixty miles." (Only to Israel)

III. Rabbi Joshua ben Levi said, "The seventy nations of the world heard the voice of Balaam."

IV.   Rabbi Elazar HaQappar says:
    1. God endowed his voice with the power to travel from one end of world to the other...
        a) He gazed and saw that the nations   { אומות }   would bow down to the sun, to the moon, to the stars, to trees, and to stones.
        b) He gazed and saw that a man, born of woman, would arise in the future seeking to lead astray the entire world by making himself a god.
        c) It was for this reason He endowed his
            voice with the power (to go from
            end of the earth to the other)--
    2. ...that all the nations of the world
        might hear.

V.   And this is what he warned, "Take care not to follow in error that infamous man." Thus is it written (in the words of Balaam Num. 23:19): "A man cannot be a god so he is lying." -- i.e. anyone who says he is a god is lying. Concerning his future deception by saying that he will ascend and return at the appointed times, (it is written) "This he says but will not do it (he speaks but will not accomplish it)".

VI.   See what is written, "And he pronounced his parable and said: Alas, who will live of making himself a god?" (Num. 24:23)-- i.e Balaam said, "Alas! Who will live from that nation which follows in error [I emend ssm'h, that heard, to st'h since it precedes the word "after". One goes "astray after" but does not "hear after". The very expression was used above.] after that infamous man who made himself a god."

Let us now reconstruct the source material for this passage. We can set aside the statement of Rabbi Yohanan. He simply gives us the dimensions of the Israelite camp in disagreement with Rabbi Joshua. Since Rabbi Yohanan and Rabbi Joshua ben Levi are often in disagreement there is nothing yet to arouse our suspicion that we are dealing with materials of an earlier period here. The same holds true for the next statement in the name of Elazar HaQappar who is contemporaneous with the other two. However, when we proceed to analyze this passage we notice a number of striking irregularities.

1) Why does God have to look twice, once to see that the nations are worshipping idols and again to see that Jesus would arise?

2) Statements of "This is the reason" invariably end midrashim but here the major point is yet to come in the following passage.

3) The printed editions of Yalkut while omitting IVc give the name as Eliezer Haqappar and not Elazar HaQappar. It is true that scribes often mixed up the two but even the careful edition of Brit Abraham, 1650, contains this reading. There never was an Eliezer HaQappar, only an Elazar Haqappar.

4) Midrash Proverbs 27 reads:

> VII. "He blesses his fellow with a powerful voice." This refers to
> Balaam...The Holy One, blessed be He, endowed his voice with the power to
> travel from one end of the world to the other
> a) in order that the nations might hear that he was blessing them [I.e.
> Israel].

We seem to be in touch with a similar tradition here. But why is it so different from the above?

These four questions are best answered by positing the following scenario. We actually have a single statement to which three different explanations have been attached. Taking the common material we can isolate the original passage: God endowed his voice with the power to travel from one end of world to the other.

It is possible "that (all) the nations of the world might hear" belongs to the original strata but I am inclined to see it as an early addition to clarify what happened when Balaam spoke. Thus the much later scholars who reworked the tradition had before them:

> "God endowed his voice with the power to travel from one end of world to
> the other that (all) the nations of the world might hear."

By comparing this statement to the above one in the name of Rabbi Elazar HaQappar we can see that IV 1.,2. is original. a),c) is one gloss, which became internal, and undoubtedly had been separate from b),c), another internal gloss. a),c) exists in the current printed editions as its own unit. Thus what we have is a joining of two separate glosses on the original midrash. VIIa) is a third gloss but did not enter the Yalkut Balak tradition.

Questions 1 and 4 have been answered. The tradition has a life of its own which leads to three commentaries on it:

IVa) and VIIa) maintain that idolatrous nations would now know that Israel's one God defeated the wish of the nations to curse Israel.

IVb) maintains that Balaam warned against the claims of Jesus.

Now comes question 2. Had the commentator IVb) known the rest of the midrash as we now have it, why should he have had to say anything? The answer must be that the passage as we have it now was not in front of him but he knew it from elsewhere. Thus his "lefikhakh" ends his gloss.

Let us return to question 3. The glossator of IVb) maintained the structure of IVa), which he argued against, although he knew the exegesis of Num 23:19[22] that now appears in our text. The glossators of IVa and V11a had other ideas in mind. These are not mere substitutions to avoid the censors for they exist side by side with the Jesus passage in the uncensored *Yalkut Shimoni*, Salonika, 1521. One would be hard pressed to suspect that a censored version somehow became incorporated with an uncensored version; yet, the possibility does exist. One might also note that the passage in Midrash Proverbs lacks any name of a Rabbi. That is the very point to make here. The original statement circulated independently inviting glosses. What was its original setting? The language of the text has the ear marks of the language of Sifre Deut. traditions and may emanate from an Akiban midrash on Numbers.The form of the midrash can be established by looking at the current Sifre Num.

> [Piska 305] "Ascend the top of the height." The verse explains that God showed to Moses distant places as if they were near, hidden places as if they were open, all the settlements of the Land of Israel. This is as it is said, "And the Lord showed him all the land and all Naphtali and the plain."
> [Piska 306] Rabbi Akiba says, "The verse explains that God showed to Moses all the sections the Land of Israel [in an organized fashion] as if they were a set table. This is as it is said, 'And the Lord showed him the whole land...'"
> Rabbi Eliezer says, "He endowed the eyes of Moses with the power to see from one end of the world to the other."
> And this is what you will find concerning the righteous: They can see from one end of the world to the other. And so Scripture states, "Your eyes shall behold the King in his beauty, [you shall the land from far distances]."

The last paragraph is not part of Rabbi Eliezer's statement because the verse explicitly tells Moses to see the land with his eyes. Rabbi Eliezer wanted to point out that this was an exceptional one time endowment. The last paragraph says it was not exceptional but all the righteous have this power. Thus it cannot be part of Eliezer's statement. The last paragraph repeats, "see from one end of the world to the other" in accord with commonplace redactional technique to make it accord with Rabbi Eliezer's statement as if it were the continuation of his statement. Yet Sifre

----

[22] For the early fourth century Christian understanding of this verse see Lactantius, *The Divine Institutes (Catholic University of America Press* , Washington, 1964, 295 (Book 4, ch. 18).

Deut 338 is missing this section. The probability is that the section is secondary and redactionally co-ordinated to suit its current home.

We now must consider whether V., the exegesis, above was an integral part of the original tradition. Let us look at Sifre Deut. 338:

> "And see all the Land of Canaan." Rabbi Eliezer says the finger of the Holy One, blessed be he, became a guide for Moses and showed him all the settlements of the Land of Israel. "Up to here is the territory of Ephraim, up to here is the territory of Menasseh."
>
> Rabbi Joshua says Moses by himself saw it. How was this? He endowed his eyes with the power to see from one end of the world to the other.

There is no difference of opinion here. Both Rabbis say essentially the same thing. The Holy Spirit (or Memra), the subject of God's activity in anthropomorphic images, is called "finger" when it acts the way in which human fingers act (demonstrating, stopping up tubes). See Gen R. 4:3, also compare Luke 11:20 to Matt 12:28. Nevertheless, although no manuscript reads this way, it would seem reasonable that we reverse the names here: Joshua instead of Eliezer and Eliezer instead of Joshua. The original tradition was probably reversed before Sifre was put into writing. The basis of this suggestion is that Sifre Num. knows the "endowment of eyes" as the tradition of Eliezer. Also, I am inclined to emend in Sifre Deut. 'tsmw (by himself) to 'ynyw (with his eyes) because it is clear to me that the midrashist is not arguing against what came before but merely elaborating in his own style upon that tradition. Both Rabbis agree the endowment of spectacular vision was singular. Be that as it may, there is good reason to consider these "endowment" forms as those of the Tannaim in the late Yavne period.

We can now return to our Yalkut passage and reconstruct the history of the tradition based on the results of our form criticism. Rabbi Joshua, the Tanna, or Rabbi Akiba his colleague and teacher, would make a statement concerning someone's special ability and Rabbi Eliezer would gloss it by referring this to a special endowment from God for the occasion. This was not by way of argument, only by way of minimizing the miraculous. Now the statements of Eliezer were supplemented by an editor or editors who added "And this is what you will find..." in way of exegetical explanation, rightly or wrongly.

The tradition of the Yalkut is patterned after this form. If the author inherited the tradition without names we might suppose he chose a form associated with Rabbi Joshua which he attributed to Rabbi Joshua ben Levi and likewise Rabbi Eliezer became Elazar HaQappar (some texts read Eliezer Haqappar). On the other hand, the tradition may have been transmitted in the names of these Tannaim and changed by a scribe who believed that the discussion was occurring at Rabbi Yohanan's academy. He then provided the requisite epithets to the names to show they were Amoraim, as he believed they were. The latter seems to me more plausible. Nevertheless, we may suspect that these words are the most ancient layer:

Rabbi Joshua**** says: "The seventy nations of the world heard the voice of Balaam."

Rabbi Eliezer**** says: God endowed his voice with the power to travel from one end of world to the other.   (That all the nations of the world might hear)

For R. Yohanan, Christianity was preferable to paganism and Yohanan saw the religion as monotheistic enough such that it was suitable for gentiles. He rejected the position that the gentile Nations should have no part of it and were warned to stay away from it.

Section V1. may well have been added after the time of Justinian, when Jews suffered under such decrees, as it reacts against the "Nation which follows in error after that infamous man." The major forms of the tradition were then in existence prior to the middle of the third century. R. Yohanan utilized the tradition as now found in *Yalkut* Balak except that the tradition of sun and moon was probably separate at that time. Because Yohanan's name was associated with the late layer the names of his colleagues entered the tradition. We have now traced the likely route the Yalkut tradition followed from its earliest formulations.

The Balaam tradition of V was also added in the Tannaitic period so as to make clear what the point was. The expression "tenu da'atkhem" is Tannaitic. It appears in Gen. R. 61:3 as the warning of R. Akiba to his students and in 100:2 as the warning of Jacob to his children. The extended note in Theodor-Albeck p.1226 suggests that this tradition, both in its Gen. R formulation and its Tanhuma formulation shows signs of being very early. The phrase also occurs in the Tannaitic midrashim.

Thus a tradition formulated in the early second century had evolved by the middle of the third century to several forms. One of these forms was used by Rabbi Yohanan as a base to hang his own comment. The earlier statement had been to the effect that even gentiles were forbidden to practice Christianity. This might have been the view of the Yavne school in the early second century. Rabbi Yohanan argued that the prohibition concerned Jews only. Hence Balaam's warning was heard by all the Jews at the time but by no one else.

We now turn to the Yerushalmi.

Rabbi Abbahu said: If a man says to you,-- "I am a god" he is lying (**A man cannot be a god so he is lying**); "I am the son of man [Here the title reflects the Son of Man sayings in the NT]."-- at the end he will regret it (**and the son of man so he will regret**); "I will go up to the heavens"-- **this he has said but will not do it**, he spoke but will not accomplish it. (y Ta'anit end 2:1)

This tradition is based upon the verse in Numbers 23:19 but only the last part cites it. I have supplied in bold print those parts of the verse which are being exegeted. The word "establish" (kwm) actually could be taken to mean "ascend"(kwm) and was used by Mandeans in this sense to refer to the ascension of the soul during baptism. The section concerning the Son of Man is preserved in the Yerushalmi but must have fallen out of the source of Yalkut's text simply because it seemed spurious. Why would Jesus claim that he was the son of a man when he was claiming to be divine? Its special usage by Christians was not known by Jews and so it fell out of the sources. Nevertheless the exegesis of Num 23:19 supplied by the Yalkut text is that upon which Yerushalmi is dependent. Rabbi Abbahu was known for his anti-Christian sentiments. From this passage alone we do not know if his objections were only to Jewish Christianity or to gentile Christianity as well.

Since we find no Tannaitic discussion opposing the notion that Balaam warned the whole world against Christianity, we must assume that any distinguishing points of view were not widely entertained, if at all in the Tannaitic period. However, close to the time that Christianity became a state religion we find some positive sentiment towards it. Some Jews saw it as an advance over Roman paganism for the world gentile community.

4. **Midrash halakhah.** We shall now consider the legal midrashim.

We have considered the form of legal midrashim above. Suffice it to say that the Midrash halakhah is the least understood of midrashic forms. The midrashim are cumulative. Information from one exegesis may be exegetically applied to cases mentioned elsewhere. If these other verses are exegeted, without hard limits, we might find a conglomeration of data leading to gross expansions. To avoid "exegesis upon exegesis" as much as possible, fine expositions prevent radical expansions. Thus a common form of Midrash halakhah, extensively used in Sifra, presents 1- a verse and a law, 2- further exegesis is shown to be irrelevant to the expansion of cases of the law, 3- some detail in the original verse establishes the stated law as the maximum that can be exegeted. If 2- would be able to expand the cases in this verse, by some hermeneutic such as analogy, the detail in 3- would lead to megaexpansion or, worse, to abhorrent redundancy. Thus Midrash halakhah is verbal economics. It tries to show that items have to be purchased anew with new words. Old words bought only one item, new words have to buy the others. Thus the expansion is limited and contained. For example we note Sifra 3:5-6:

> 1.- ["If **his offering** is a burnt offering from the herd he shall offer a male without blemish...(Lev. 1:3)":]
>
> 2.- Now from which exegesis do I know that these [blemishes which disqualify burnt offerings] will apply to peace offerings?
>
> - Since Scripture uses analogous conceptions...all of these will apply to it.
>
> [The analogy appears to break down because cheap birds can be used for burnt offerings but only expensive animals are fit for peace offerings.]
>
> I can argue: The burnt offering, for which a bird can be used, is subject to these disqualifications. Hence a peace offering, for which a bird cannot be

used, should certainly be subject to them.

No! (Both arguments fall because peace offerings are more lenient in one respect than burnt offerings and so they cannot be compared to, or argued from, them). How can you compare burnt offerings, where female offerings, unlike males, are not valid, to peace offerings, where females, like males, are valid? Since males and females are valid for peace offerings, we conclude that these disqualifications could not apply to peace offerings

The exegesis is to establish it. "His offering" (an apparently trivial and unnecessary word detail) is to extend the application of the disqualifications to peace offerings (and not further).

To understand this we have to know what came before because Midrash halakhah is a cumulative enterprise which interprets Scripture in a systematically coherent fashion. It had been established in the previous section of Sifra that animals were disqualified from being burnt offerings if they had been used for idolatrous or sexual purposes or if they had gored. Lev. 1:3 contained three trivial and unnecessary details; "if," "burnt offering," "his sacrifice." We had to establish the exact limit of application of these disqualifications before we utilized our "spare" word. The midrash had already pointed out, in its discussion of the first two spare words, that two factors were irrelevant about burnt offerings being subject to the disqualifications. They were that birds could be used, and blemished animals could not be used. The relevant factor seemed to be that burnt offerings could be either free-will or obligatory. They would therefore be analogous to peace offerings. Our use of the final spare word would therefore proceed one step beyond peace offerings. The midrashist wonders if the bird factor was really irrelevant or had only been overruled by one of the trivial words. If, so it would apply and allow us to argue that peace offerings were subject to disqualifications, since they deserve the same if not more respect than burnt offerings. The spare word would then extend the disqualifications to another genre of sacrifice. However we learn that in another way burnt offerings deserve more respect than peace offerings because the former has at least one stricter rule.

Thus the spare coin is utilized. The middle step, "Since Scripture uses analogous conceptions...we conclude that these disqualifications could not apply to peace offerings" seems to be an intrusion. It establishes the correctness of the exegesis. It may well be that it acts as a kind of glossed commentary on older materials by raising objections and settling them. The basic midrash is found in step 3. However misdirection in the middle is prevalent and may be noted to be quite early[23]. However, we do not have simple misdirection here. We have an argument

----

[23] It is also a feature of the later, Babylonian Talmudic style which frequently attempts to associate the name of a Tanna with a mishnah only to dismiss it or to argue a certain application of a mishnah only to dismiss it. The dismissing arguments are then followed by a conclusive statement. The process is one of demonstrating that all possibilities have been considered. The conclusions are thereby rendered iron-clad.

to set the stage for applying step 3. Step 2 including "Since Scripture uses analogous conceptions...we conclude..." demonstrates what the exegesis will accomplish. Some may argue that it misdirects by suggesting alternative exegesis but this is not the same kind of misdirection as suggesting alternative practices. It establishes the basis of the exegesis. This suggests that the exegesis of step 3 already existed. Since the argument of 2 is cast in the rhetorical style attributed to Akiba and his school one may well posit that we have in Sifra reworkings of Temple time materials in the Tannaitic schools of post 70. The example (Sifra 2:3) given below at the beginning of chapter 5:

> "Man" to include converts; "From yourselves" to exclude apostates, what was
> the point of saying thus: "man" to include converts...

substantiates such observations. While the example is specific to that one case, I argue here that it is likely the case throughout much of Sifra.

The form of the midrash in Sifra allows for Rabbinic methods of exegesis to be supported in the face of ancient law. The law is tested against Rabbinic modes which are shown to be in step with the older law. This is accomplished by showing that Rabbinic hermeneutics, if at all applicable, cannot extend the law beyond what was originally stated.

Geiger considered Akiba to have introduced not simply new methods but also new halakhot. Whether or not these halakhot were new, or just had a different provenance than the known ancient halakhot, whether these changes were only in regards to practical law but not Temple ritual etc. are open questions. The structure of much of Sifra seems to indicate that the basic exegeses were known before the middle materials were introduced. The incorporation of Mishnaic materials in the halakhic midrashim is related in sources unknown to the Babli (b Baba Mezia 33a-b) but known to the Yerushalmi (y Shabbat 16:1).

> Rabbi Shimon bar Yohai[24] taught: Whoever studies scripture-- engages in
> some virtue while whoever studies Mishnah-- engages in a rewarding virtue.
> Whoever studies Talmud-- engages in the greatest virtue. Indeed pursue
> Mishnah over Talmud.
>   Said Rabbi Yosi the son of Rabbi Bun: (The incoherence is to be
> explained like this:) The "Mishnah" statement was promulgated (as a

----

[24] The name is not corrupt in the Yerushalmi text. Whether Rabbi Shimon said it or not in point of fact is a separate issue. The Amora claims the final statement was formulated after Rabbi's Mishna was composed. The statement simply incorporated the older view in order to conclude with Rabbi's view which was tacked on. Babli has no name attached to it and seems to understand Gemara or Talmud also as midrash. The   final layer of bavli here is quite complicated and adds nothing to the discussion here.

corrective to Rabbi Shimon's statement) after the Mishnah was composed
but before Rabbi's school had submerged so much of the Mishnah into the
Talmud. (i.e. Shimon bar Yohai's statement was overruled) Once the school
of Rabbi submerged much of Mishnah into it, the emended statement should
be corrected now to say one should pursue Talmud over Mishnah.

The difference between Babli and Yerushalmi seems to be this. The
Yerushalmi thinks that the statement of Shimon bar Yohai gave priority to Talmud
(midrash). When the Mishnah came into being Mishnah was given priority, when
Mishnah was incorporated into Talmud (midrash), Talmud again was given priority
as a major subject of study. Babli agrees that the "Mishnah" statement was added in
the time after the Mishnah had been composed. However it does seem to know the
midrash collections into which much Mishnah had been incorporated. It concludes
that Mishnah study is the best and safest form of study. It appears that the Babli
does not know of the harmonization of Mishnah and Midrash while Yerushalmi
does. Yet Babli knows the names of midrashic works and was produced as a whole
after Yerushalmi. These circumstances indicate that Tannaitic midrashim were
brought to Babylonia before they had reached their final form in the Land of Israel.
They also indicate that we are talking of real compositions and not free-floating
traditions.

The commentators of Babli understood Talmud[25] to refer to the process of
reflecting upon Mishnah. However, it refers to Midrash halakhah. The lists of the
Rabbinic curriculum mentioned in the midrashim separate out Scripture from
Midrash which they refer to as *Talmud*. The study of Scripture entailed the study of
traditional pointing and phrasing, not exegesis. On the other hand "Talmud" in the
sense of Midrash halakhah" was also used in the Babli. This is demonstrated by b
Baba Kama 104b which refers to an exegesis like that of Sifra to Lev. 5:23 by the
term "Talmud".

That is to say that the halakhic midrashim of the Land of Israel, as we now
have them, tend to reflect the wording and the decisions of much Mishnaic
materials. This may mean several things: some conflicting materials were removed
from the original compilations, the wording was adjusted to reflect the Mishnah, the
midrashim were composed anew to fit the Mishnah. The internal structure of the
midrashim in Sifra, as presented above, could fit any of these suggestions. However,
the notice that much of the Mishnah is now embedded in the midrashim suggests
editorial shaping, not new cloth composition. In the talmudic passages cited above,
Talmud, i.e the halakhic midrash, refers to a "text" of study, written or oral, apart
from the Mishnah, which was edited at some point in accordance with the Mishnah.
It seems that "embedding" (šyqᶜ) means "put into a receptacle" as it does in Sifre

---

[25] I.e. "Talmud", as in y Shab., and not "Gemara" as in our editions as a result of the medieval
censor who usually substituted "Gem ara " for "Talmud"

Deut. piska 334. There is nothing to prevent us from seeing here reference to a process with ancient roots and various layers. If the whole process of Midrash halakhah is understood to be post Mishnaic one wonders how the non-Mishnah midrash came to be[26]. Since these forms were apparently current a century before the Mishnah and the layering is observable in the midrashim themselves, we are left to weigh the evidence. The (Tannaitic) midrashim mention Midrash or Talmud (Midrash halakhah) as a subject and the Babli mentions the teaching of Midrash halakhah[27]

Professor Jacob Neusner has argued that the midrashim in Sifra represent a polemic against Mishnah and Tosefta. [28] This does not seem to be case. The present form of Sifra indicates the midrashim incorporate the Mishnah and Tosefta because the midrashim (which must have been well known or why bother) were defeated by them and now had to join forces with them to survive. There is no polemic against methods of one over the other. Mishnah is the authoritative text. Midrash halakhah, in present form, to large extent simply acts as the bridge explaining the scriptural derivation of the mishnaic laws.

In the halakhic midrashim, Professor Neusner sees what I call "setting the stage" as "polemic against classification". In my opinion, we do not have arguments against classification in these passages. Nowhere does it say or imply, "Classification is bad." Setting the stage to exegete a particular phrase is a commonplace in Rabbinic literature. In exegeting Scripture we have *shomea ani, yakhol, ve'im nafshekha lomar, etc.* In exegeting Mishnah we have an abundance of terms to signify that the apparently trivial is ripe with meaning: *peshita, mai lememra, mai lav, mai rabuta, tserikha, mai kamashma lan, hainu hakh* and there are many more phrases. These forms are meant to indicate that mishnaic phrases fill in important blanks in our knowledge, things we could know in no other way. Since the hermeneutic of Mishnah interpretation is not nearly as developed as the hermeneutic of Scriptural interpretation we do not get as sophisticated moves in stage setting. This only shows that Gemara sets its stage by Mishnah hermeneutic while Midrash sets its stage by Scriptural hermeneutic. Scriptural hermeneutic is unconcerned with Mishnah hermeneutic and vice versa. The phrase Professor Neusner thought indicated a polemic against Mishnaic logic is *vehalo din hu*. The phrase is found only in the midrashic midrashim. The technical terms for this device are *teshuva* in midrashic works and *pirkha* in the Gemara (eg. b Baba Kama 5b, see also b Kidd 4b). The Talmudic discussion of b Baba Kama 25b (to Mishnah 5:2) contains examples of the

----

[26] See D. Halivni "Some bring First Fruits," *Bar Ilan Annual*, 1970, 75-77.

[27] See b Kritot 13b. Erring in Talmud does not seem overly serious, on the other hand for b Baba Mezia 33b it is very serious.

[28] See "Sifra's Critique of Mishnaic Logic, 1988, *Hebrew Studies*, 65 n4.

concern with proper hermeneutic both for Mishnah and Torah. Sometimes one Rabbi will maintain the force of a hermeneutical argument while another will refute it. I see no difference in this regard between arguments concerning Mishnah or Midrash. The issue is the halakhah, not the method of expressing it. The hermeneutics are sometimes shown to be insufficient to establish a case, they are never said to be useless. Midrash halakhah itself relies on the hermeneutic of kal vehomer to establish its point. That it sometimes demonstrates the hermeneutic is problematic when applied to a certain case does not mean it dismisses the logic of kal vehomer, only that Midrash halakhah resists expanding laws.

We do find the hermeneutical refutation of a hermeneutical point based on some earlier Scripture. This shows that a hermeneutic applied to the verse under discussion will have to make that point and no other. What we have is the justification for a particular exegesis. We do not have an argument against Mishnaic list logic. Sifra's hermeneutics also depend on similarities and differences, klal and perat, ma matsinu, hekesh and the like. The middle step of these midrashim only establishes that acceptable hermeneutics leave room for a verse to make one point and not another. That is to say, the hermeneutics of Scripture in certain cases are indecisive so that the exegesis of a verse is necessary to establish that point as against another. In fact the final exegesis of these midrashim is rarely, if ever, bare Scripture unaided by a hermeneutic "logic".

The problem of dating our compilations of Sifra deserves an extended note. It is true that the Babli does not know our Sifra as a compilation but here and there we find exegeses in the Sifra which are found in Babli. This has led some to think that Sifra is at least as late as the close of the Babylonian Talmud. The compilers simply took some exegeses from Babli and composed the rest. However, this is hardly likely. Why did they not take vast numbers of midrashim found in b Menahot and b Zevahim? The better argument is the reverse. The Sifra existed prior to the Babli or Yerushalmi. It was knocked out and superseded by the Mishnah which became the major text of study. Only some of its teachings were known and used by the Babli. When the material of the Mishnah was inserted into the midrashim so that the midrashim could once again enter the curriculum of the academy of the Land of Israel, these midrashim became a focus of study. The "sinking" of Mishnah and Tosefta into the midrashim without touching the midrashim in any other way allowed the midrashim to continue their existence. Hence the survival of the midrashim was due to their dependence on Mishnah and Tosefta. Tannaitic Midrash halakhah was more popular in the Land of Israel than in Babylonia. This explanation is provided in the Talmuds.

We might rather see the reverse of Professor Neusner's thinking. Once Mishnah arrives, the derivation of the laws is seen as trivial. What is important is the halakhic discussion that Mishnah's taxonomy can give rise to. When does this apply, when does that apply, how does this differ from that etc. Once we free our thinking from the verse and concentrate on the dynamic of the interaction of the laws we enter a more sophisticated stage of reflecting upon the laws. We form categories, notions of dynamics concerning the behavior of the rules in changing circumstances. This is the halakhic enterprise.

The problems of discussing issues of date of composition and tradition history have been addressed by Jacob Neusner in his *Sifre to Deuteronomy: An Introduction to the Rhetorical, Logical and Topical Program*, Atlanta, Scholar's Press, 1987. Neusner claims that the "authorships" of Jewish works in Late Antiquity did not sign their names and that we are gullible if we accept the names of tradents attached to various dicta in the literature. Neusner finds that the topical program of Sifre is consistent and planned by a single "authorship". We do not know when he lived or who he was. We can only study the internal literary work and describe its contents and views. Neusner catalogues the formal rhetorical features of Sifre Deuteronomy and compares them with other midrashic works.

Why is it "gullible" to accept ascriptions, if they be without reason for complaint, to certain Rabbis? If sayings are attributed to certain sages what is gained by denying the tradition? The name indicates a stance in regards to hermeneutics of halakhah and aggada which are also attributed to those names. Rabbi Akiba has one approach, Rabbi Yishmael another, Rabbi Meir has one outlook, Rabbi Judah another. The names are not infallible indications of who uttered what but they do signal approaches. The ascriptions must be questioned, and indeed always were, when the name and the approach are inconsistent. On the contrary, while we must accept Tannaitic statements as Tannaitic and Amoraic statements as Amoraic, we must not lose sight of the fact that traditions are likely older than the sage reputed to have repeated them. This can be demonstrated over and over.

To further our analysis of Professor Neusner's stance we might note that it appears that there were two versions of the midrash to Deuteronomy: Mekhilta to Deut. and Sifre to Deut. produced by separate schools but incorporating materials from both schools. Our present text of Sifre shows evidence of both schools. It was once thought that, in general, halakhic materials emanated from one school, aggadic materials from another[29]. However, the evidence is far from conclusive and no one theory can account for all rhetorical features. The history of the rhetorical forms can be explained only partially by recourse to documentary hypotheses. The program of concerns is determined by the Scriptural base which guides the topics of concern. The halakhic materials appear to be early. Much of it predates the Mishnah[30]. The

----

[29] See R. Hammer, *Sifre*, New Haven and London, 1986, 5-8 with attention to his notes. Hammer gives a brief overview of various views. See Also D. Hoffman, *Zur Einleitung in die Halachischen Midrashim, Beilage zum Jahresberich des Rabbiner Rabbiner Seminars*, Berlin, 1888; J. N. Epstein, *Introduction to Tannaitic Literature: Mishnah, Tosefta , and Halachic Midrashim*, Jerusalem, 1957; and H. Albeck, *Introduction to the Talmuds*, Tel Aviv 1969, as well as his *Untersuchungen über dir halachischen Midraschim*, Berlin, 1927.

[30] See L. Ginzberg, "The Relation between the Mishnah and the Mekhilta", *Studies in Memory of Moses Schorr*, New York, 1944, 90-95; L. Finkelstein, "Prolegomena to the Sifre," PAAJR (1931-2),

aggadic materials are shaped by exegetical concerns centered upon the thrust of scriptural verses as their understanding had been passed down. Neusner's data is not inconsistent with this approach although his analysis addresses literary rather than historical concerns. Neusner does demonstrate that the concerns of Sifre Deuteronomy and its forms of expression are limited. His work does not preclude the analyses of Hoffman or Epstein but gives us an added appreciation of Rabbinic rhetoric and exegetical faithfulness to Scripture.

We noticed above that, essentially, what demarcates groups is central to their exegesis. Qumran pesher proves its points by appeal to the central myths peculiar to its group. Likewise, New Testament appeals to the central myths of its doctrines to clinch its exegesis. However, the bulk of aggadic midrash of the Rabbis does not appeal to the doctrines of "Oral Tradition" for its proofs but to the written Torah.

We should certainly wonder about this. It would seem that the Rabbis were trying to appeal to all Jews through their midrash, regardless of their affiliations. And indeed one might suggest they were successful in doing this because we find clues that the Rabbinic midrash has made its way to Samaritan exegesis as well. Yet the same evidence can be interpreted in a different way as well. It could suggest that much of what we call Rabbinic is simply generic midrash, preserved by the evidence we have in Rabbinic literature but really, at one time, was the property of all Jews. Sifra, in its current form, far from being a polemic against Mishnaic ways of thinking, may represent a legitimate attempt to make the Mishnah part of generic Judaism[31]. Midrash halakhah, as we have it today, would then seem to indicate that Mishnah began as the bottom line of a universal style of exegesis as practiced in Temple times. This exegesis would be acceptable to all except to the Rabbis who had developed ideas of exegeting details in ways that other groups did not. The pressure was on the Rabbis to defend their exegetical system and this they did by illustrating that the earlier Midrash halakhah and the Mishnah were compatible.

As already noted, the names of midrashic compilations are also known to the Babylonian Talmud[32]. In balance, we could argue that our compilations originate in these midrashim. The alternate claim, that our compilations originate in some hodgepodge fashion from late materials raises the question as to where and how the late traditions came to be in the first place. Then one has to posit still some earlier source and we come full circle to having an earlier midrash on which ours is based. Why should not exegesis of materials relating to the Temple be assigned to Temple

---

39-40.

[31] See J. Neusner, *Paradigms in Passage*, Lanham, New York, London, University Press of America, 132.

[32] See b Kiddushin 49b, Sanhedrin 86a, Shevuot 41b.

times (in the need of a working hypothesis)? The survival of traditions from Temple times is attested. We shall illustrate the point in the next chapter.

Chapter 3

THE ANTIQUITY OF LEGAL MATERIALS

1. **The ancient legacy of the Rabbis.** Abraham Geiger wrote a monograph in which he demonstrated that a number of Rabbi Yishmael's statements preserved in Mekhilta display archaic contents known from the Septuagint and other Second Temple works such as Philo and Josephus. These laws differed from the later halakhah of Akiba and his school.

Geiger adduces many examples. For instance, the early law interpreted Exodus 21:29,30 to mean that if a man's ox (known to be a killer) killed another person the owner was liable to death unless the judges or relatives of the deceased decided that monetary fine would be acceptable as punishment[1]. Mekhilta, dinin par. 10, notes that R. Yishmael maintains such a position. We may note that Josephus knew something like this to be the meaning of the verses[2]. He mentions only the death penalty for the death of a free adult. However, he places this after a notice that judges have the option of demanding monetary payment in lieu of maiming and may intend verse 30 to apply to the law of the talio as well as the goring ox. One notes that, in Scriptures, the option of the "ransom" (verse 30) follows the law of judging the owner of the ox and yet was taken by Josephus to refer to the talio (verse 27). Akiba maintained that Heaven alone could decree the owner 's death and the court was obliged to order monetary fine only[3].

Louis Finkelstein also demonstrated the antiquity of forms attributed to Yishmael and demonstrated how Akiba reflected upon these traditions to form a much expanded exegetical base for ancient midrash. Finkelstein considered that early midrash glossed Scriptures with short comments stating the conclusions of exegesis while Akiba reconstructed the exegesis.

"Man" to include converts;
"From yourselves" to exclude apostates,
   what was the point of saying thus: "man" to include
   converts...(Sifra 2:3).

----

[1] A. Geiger, *Ha-miqra we-targumau*, Hebrew translation by Y. L. Baruch, Jerusalem, 1949, 288.

[2] See *Antiquities*, ed. Whiston, 4:8:36.

[3] Wilna Gaon, *Aderet Eliahu* to Ex. 21, harmonizes a related matter by saying the talio was theoretically an option. He claimed that the practical halakha had determined that only monetary payment could be required, not death.

Here we have an earlier halakhah which is explained by an extensive later gloss in the midrash[4]. The base of Midrash halakhah is a compendium of ancient rulings to which some Tannaim later affixed short lines of analysis to justify the rulings.

We can note that the collections of Rabbinic midrash are not as much the inventions of the Rabbis as many suppose. A large section of these midrashim are not the beginning of new methods of exegesis but rather they indicate a closing point of the Jewish reading of Scripture after hundreds of years. This was recognized by Geiger in the last century and Finkelstein in this century.

Ch. Albeck has demonstrated that although the Tannaim utilized scriptural interpretations to decide rules which had been forgotten or for new situations, the majority of rules in the Sifra were based on the actual practices of the Second Temple[5]. The exegesis was secondary. Accordingly, he would have us suppose a two or threefold development in the composition of Midrash halakhah. First, the statement of the rule itself. This rule was practiced in the time of the Temple but a scriptural origin was not transmitted to the Tannaim. The earliest Tannaim provided Scriptural bases. Thus many rules, originally passed down as a Mishnah form, were only later associated with Scriptures, the exegeses being shown to be both necessary and sufficient. Albeck's position is well argued and concerns many rules which are not clearly rooted in Scripture. We should still keep in mind that Philo, Josephus, and New Testament writings indicate that sophisticated scriptural exegesis of legal materials was prevalent by the end of the Second Temple Era and likely much earlier.

A comparison between Sifra and Sifre type materials in the Babli and the Yerushalmi was undertaken by the present writer and the following result was suggested. The forms in the Talmuds are earlier in their internal logic as they suggest oral components while the midrashic compilations suggest written components. The Talmudic materials are clear, the midrashic ones ambiguous. Once we see the Talmudic formulation we understand the point and the midrashic composition can be understood. This is, I suggest, because oral materials must be clearer than written materials. Oral materials were meant to clarify while written ones were meant to present riddle and art to the reader. They were obscure and required concentration; hence, the injunction against recording oral tradition was not altogether breached. It is not to be thought that the Talmudic materials represent a later commentary to the written ones or a later version. Were that the

---

[4] L. Finkelstein, "Midrash, Halakhot, and Aggadot," *Yitzhak F. Baer Jubilee Volume*, Jerusalem 1960, 46-7.

[5] *Introduction to the Mishnah*, Bialik Institute, Tel Aviv, 1960.

case we should expect the later reworked material to have survived in compilation form rather than the problematic texts we do have.

Finally we might note that Christian sources can be used to show us that both the midrash form of exegesis (using Scripture) and the Mishnah form of teaching were current in the Land of Israel in the first century. Matthew 22:31-33, (Mark 12:18-, Luke 20:27-):

> And concerning the resurrection of the dead have you not read that which was said to you from the mouth of God, "I am the God of Abraham and the God of Isaac and the God of Jacob". (Ex. 3:6). Now God is not the God of the dead but the "God of the living".(Deut. 5:23).

Reflection here shows the exegesis to be as follows: 1. "I am the God of Abraham..." (2. Abraham still lives.) 3. God is "The God of the living." Hence Abraham = living. This is midrash form. On the other hand we might note Matthew 15:5 (Mark 7:11):

> You say, "One who says to his father or to his mother korban is all the benefit which you might derive from me, (behold this is a vow)."

The point is that we have in this passage echoes of teaching forms which predate the Mishnah. We can therefore assert that both the midrashic and the mishnaic form predate the Mishnah. Indeed the Mishnah itself contains both forms. These traditions were noted to be ancient, handed down by the fathers, and this suggests that they were current among the Pharisees in the Second Temple period. The roots of the enterprise we find in Rabbinic literature are certainly more ancient than the recording of that literature.

2. The common conception of the exegetical enterprise. For the Rabbis the old was adapted to the new. Scripture had messages and every work of the Rabbis adapted the traditional study of the Torah to illustrate the precise message of a unit of scripture. For hundreds of years before there were any Rabbis Jewish children studied Scripture, adults analyzed it, and scholars provided guidance from it. There is not much evidence to suggest that it was divergence of exegesis that separated one group of Jews from the next but rather power and politics. Religious differences were exploited in intellectual activities only after breaks occurred for other reasons. Hence it is possible to speak of a common body of exegesis and of common forms although each group molded the body and the forms to its own inner set of what made the group unique. This holds true both of legal and narrative materials.

Let us now take a careful look at the concept of Torah as presented in first century documents and in third century and later midrashic compilations.

"Some things the lawgiver shrewdly veils in enigmas, others he sets forth in
solemn allegory; but wherever straightforward speech was expedient, there
he makes his meaning absolutely plain." (Josephus, Antiquities, 1:24.)

The Introduction to *Genesis Rabba*[6] makes one suspect that Josephus'
introduction is perhaps an older formula than Josephus' work:

"And I was the 'mwn with Him;
And I was Entertaining [daily
         Playing in His presence;
         Playing in His world
         Entertaining with people.[7]]
'mwn means a pedagogue. 'mwn means covered. 'mwn means veiled.[8]"

It appears that the midrashist understands the chiastic form as stressing how
Wisdom is at once the entertainment of the divine realm and whose play there is
mirrored in the human world. To play with the Torah is then *imatatio dei*. From the
human perspective Torah operates on several levels, one of which is veiled in the
divine knowledge (mystical), another hidden in worldly terms (poetical), and
another which is immediate and personal (literal). Josephus progresses in his
description of the art of Torah from that which is veiled to that which is plain. His
order is the same as that in Proverbs 8. The midrash progresses from that which is
plain to that which is hidden. One wonders if Josephus was aware of Pr 8:30 as a
description of the nature of Torah's style, since it too progresses from the hidden to
the plain. That the midrash reverses the order indicates that it has used a
formulation of more logical progression-- from the revealed to the veiled. That
Josephus has the reverse order may well indicate his dependence upon an ancient
exegesis of Proverbs in the manner of the midrashic introduction to *Genesis Rabba*.

The probability of the existence of an ancient introduction to the study of
Torah along these lines is further enhanced by a consideration of Galatians 3. The
composition of Galatians 3 seems to be based on Paul's debates with Jews or Jewish
Christians. His references would then be to Jewish traditions maintained by his
opponents.

----

[6] *Gen. R.* 1:1.

[7] Proverbs 8:30.

[8] See my remarks in JAOS, "Josephus as Exegete," Winter 1987, in which I endeavor to show
that the passage in Gen. R. beginning "Others say" may be a later addition to the text but preserves a
very ancient tradition concerning Alexandrian exegesis.

In 3:20 Paul claims the Torah was given by angels in the hand of a mediator. A mediator is two but God is one. The passage speaks of the Torah being given by angels. Galatians 3:19-25:

> Wherefore then *serveth* the law? It was added because of transgressions till the seed should come to whom the promise was made; *and it was* ordained by angels in the hand of a mediator. Now a mediator is not *a mediator of* one, but God is one. Is the law then against the promises of God? God forbid: for if there had been a law given which could have given life, verily righteousness should have been by the law. But the scripture hath concluded all under sin, that the promise of faith by Jesus Christ might be given to them that believe. But before faith came, we were kept under the law, shut up unto the faith which should afterwards be revealed. wherefore the law was our schoolmaster [pedagogue] *to bring us* unto Christ, that we might be justified by faith. But after that faith is come we are no longer under a schoolmaster.

In 3:24 Paul goes on to mention that the Torah was the Pedagogue but its job was to bring the people to the time of Jesus so that people could experience God directly, not through an intercessor. Moreover, Paul claims the law came because of transgressions. This seems to be a positive statement claiming that the simple sense of the law was to protect one from transgression until the time of faith which would do the same more effectively. Paul has utilized the idea of the Torah as Pedagogue to claim that the Torah, if a pedagogue, loses it function when the child matures. For him the Pedagogue is the slave who accompanies the child to school and who teaches the child the basics. Paul argues against the levels of Jewish interpretation for they miss what is blatant. The law had literal purpose until Christ, now Christ has literal purpose.

It appears that the identification of Torah with the pedagogue is meant to refer to the simple, literal meaning of the text. When one looks beyond Scripture then one is able to comprehend what Scripture really was-- a temporary legal document whose real purpose was to lead to Christ. In an interesting twist he tells us the eyes of the Jews are veiled in their inability to read beyond the front of Scripture to find Jesus at the end. 2Cor. 3:12-4:6 :

> Seeing then that we have such great hope we use great plainness of speech. And not as Moses, which put a veil over his face, that the children of Israel could not steadfastly look to the end of that which is abolished. But their minds were blinded: for until this day remaineth the same veil before their eyes in the reading of the old Testament; which veil is done away in Christ. But even unto this day when Moses is read, the veil is as a covering upon their heart...But we all, without a covering on our faces, do see the glory of our Lord as in a polished mirror, and our image is changed into that image and ascends from glory to glory before the Lord of the Spirit....

But if our gospel be hid, it is hid to them that are lost: In whom the god of this world hath blinded the minds of them which believe not, lest the light of the glorious gospel of Christ, who is the image of God should shine unto them....For God who commanded the light to shine out of the darkness, hath shined in our hearts, to give the light of the knowledge of the glory of God in the face of Jesus Christ.

The passage is very complex. The idea of speaking plainly introduces what is the goal and end of the Torah of Moses. The irony is this. Faith in Christ allows for the plain sense of Exodus 34:25 to emerge. When Moses received the tablets from God he put on a veil. Paul undoubtedly understood this in the sense that first century Judaism took it. The Targumim explain that Moses's face had the radiating splendor of divine glory. LXX has it that the face of Moses was *dedoxastai*, imbued with glory. The "glory of God" represents Gods image, that which emanates from the divine realm. The Rabbis, we saw, understood this to be Torah, the Wisdom of Proverbs. Not for Paul. He can declare the image of Moses putting on the veil over the glory as something else. Moses' face shone and radiated the direct experience of the divine whom he had just encountered. This glory was the goal and underpinning of the entire Law. But the people were blinded by it and Moses put a veil over his face. The purpose of the veil was to accustom the people to looking at the outer layer of his face as a conduit to what lay behind the Law which would be abolished at the proper time. The Jews were unable to remove the veil of the Law and remain ignorant as to the real Glory. The Christian is as Moses. The act of faith is not a written word but a direct knowledge of Christ. Christ is the real glory. The Christian face shines with that glory, transferred to their face, like that of Moses after his face to face encounter with the divine. The greater the belief the closer one approaches the spirit. Christ is the light, the divine glory.

There seems to be a break in the understanding of the first paragraph as opposed to that of the second. In the first it is Moses who put on the veil and this is not criticized. It seems to belong to the idea that the Law served a purpose of conduit until its function was no longer useful-- it was a shield against the light. It was the evolutionary link to the divine glory. In the second paragraph the ground has shifted. Here we have the first inkling of the idea that the Christian gospel is the knowledge of the risen Christ. The Christian doctrine is rooted in the divine realm whereas the Jewish doctrine is rooted in this world and the Jews are misled by the lord of this world who shields them from the light of the true God. In exegetical terms the second paragraph explains the first. The first paragraph relates: 1. Ex. 34:25. 2. In clear speech: This refers to the veil over the heart of the Jews. 3. The Christian who has removed the veil by abolishing the Law participates more and more in the experience of the divine realm. The second paragraph now discards the notion that the Law of Moses had something behind it at its end, as its goal. The fault is no longer that of the blind Jews, it is that of the power of this world. The true divine light is veiled by the scheme of the nefarious lord of this world to keep them from the light of the true divine image. But this explanation ignores the role of the veil, the role of the Law in paragraph 1, and puts the blame for the state of affairs in the realm of the lower god of this world. The gnostic framework of the passage, if it is Pauline, may be Paul's later addition to an earlier synagogue sermon of his to address the Corinthians in their own terms or it may be an interpolation. That is not the point here. The point is that Torah is not ascribed to the glory, to the divine realm. A scripture is exegeted according to the revealed truth of Christian faith which, Paul claims, removes the shield hiding the purpose of the Law. Only in the abolishment of the law can its function be realized since it was meant to be temporary. Moses' face had dual aspects, the glory and the veil. The glory, Christ, was the goal and that goal is lost to the Jews who adhere to the veil, the Law. Paul's allegory is clear. The Jews search Scripture. It is the veil. The real truth is not even in the deepest exegesis of Scripture, it lies historically behind Scripture in a second revelation given directly in Christ.

Paul's understanding of exegetical techniques of allegory is not really similar to those of the Rabbis. Similarly, unlike Rabbinic proof which often relies on various scriptures; Philo's proofs depend upon observation from experience, Qumran relied upon their group history. Paul depends upon his hope, his faith, the Christian experience, to prove his allegories. Whereas the Josephan and Rabbinic notion was that Torah had levels which were hidden but could be revealed to the adept, for Paul the entire Torah hid the greatest truth. First of all, it hid the knowledge of this truth behind its allegories. Secondly, the real truth was not in the Torah at all but in the glory of Christ who was to be known when the Law was removed. The law itself covers the greatest truth. Paul can unlock these hidden notions to reveal what is clear once the law is removed. Thus he can speak in clarity about what the allegories in the Law refer to. Once the Law is removed its meaning is clarified because the simple truth at the end of the law clarifies all. That is the "prooftext" in Paul's exegesis and that is why he can preach only to churches, only to those which will accept his third step. They had to be churches which accepted the importance of the Law as a document to be preached or his sermons would have had little point. He indeed may have used the same sermons in the synagogue but would not have met with success, his final proofs being unacceptable to those who did not already accept Jesus as Christ.

The common vocabulary of all the above statements and their import leads one to think that Paul, Josephus and the Midrash are in touch with an ancient notion concerning the manner in which Torah may be approached. This is the case even though Paul's point is to discredit the Law as efficacious in his time. While for Paul the process was evolutionary, the Law being outmoded to partake directly in the divine, for Jewish mystics and philosophers such as Philo and Maimonides, the dictates of the Law were seen as a primary rung on a chain of being leading to the apprehension of the higher realms. The Law introduced necessary discipline, although insufficient without a properly developed intellect, to apprehend the divine.

We must now note some differences between the approach of Josephus, Philo, Paul and that of the Rabbis. The Ten Commandments represented the words of God whereas the rest of Scripture represented Moses' representation of his communication with God and were meant to be exegeted in accordance with common literary techniques. Josephus claimed that Moses wrote some things in a plain fashion and other things in a less plain fashion. They can therefore be interpreted. For Josephus this is not the case with the Ten Commandments which should not even be translated but may be discussed[9]. Philo mentions that Moses wrote statements which have both admirable literal senses and also symbolic meanings.[10] That is, one statement can have two meanings at the same time. He stresses the Ten Commandments are the very words of God and discusses them in an unusually straightforward manner without any attempt to exegete them as allegory.[11] Paul states, as we noted, that the Law is indirect communication whereas Christ is direct communication with God. For the Rabbis, all Scripture was the very expression of God and could be exegeted. I cannot find evidence that the Ten Commandments were treated differently than any other part of Scripture[12]. They were once read as part of the morning Temple service until the recitation was suspended out of fear that opponents to the Rabbis could use the fact of the recitation against the Rabbis[13]. This observation surely tells us something about the differing attitudes of the Rabbis and other groups of Jews in respect to the theological and exegetical status of the Ten Commandments.

3. **Cross referencing**. There are a number of places in Rabbinic literature where early legal statements subtly refer to traditions which appear in works of much later redaction. One notes the statement in M. Yadaim 4:2 in which ben Azzai relates that he received a tradition from the 72 elders who were present the day Rabbi Elazar ben Azariah was seated as president of the Sanhedrin. The law appears with the same notice in M. Zevahim 1:3. The tradition states that sacrifices which were not offered with the proper intention may be eaten although they do not fulfill one's sacrificial obligation with the exception of the Passover and sin offerings. One wonders what the point of identifying the scholars with Rabbi Elazar ben Azariah might be.

----

[9] See *Antiquities*, ed. Whiston, 3:5:4.

[10] See *On the Confusion of Tongues*, 183-190.

[11] See *On the Decalogue*, 121-78.

[12] See the Mekhilta passage to Ex. 20:18 at the end of ch. 5 below.

[13] See Mishnah Tamid 5:1 and b Berachot 12a.

In b Berachot 27b one finds a well edited pastiche of traditions relating that Rabbi Gamliel was temporarily deposed from his presidency because he insisted that his students had to be as pure in their motives inside as they were in their actions outside. Elazar ben Azariah was appointed in his stead. Finally we discover that Gamliel and Azariah are to alternate weeks according to an agreed upon arrangement. The story in the midrash relates how Rabbi Elazar ben Azariah, although only eighteen years old, suddenly found his hair had turned white. Rabbi Joshua, the esteemed sage, was not recognized because he was a charcoal maker and his face had become black. In other words, the story portrays elements of its theme. Insides and outsides do not match. Now we come to our legal tradition regarding the eating of sacrifices which were not offered with proper intention. We are informed that many of them are fit for consumption by their owners. Again the theme of proper action, improper motivation.

We could not appreciate the reference to the elders who were there on the day that Rabbi Elazar ben Azariah was president unless we knew the story in the midrash. The theme of the particular ruling in M Zevahim occasions the obtuse reference to Rabbi Elazar ben Azariah.

The story of the two Rabbis alternating weeks concludes that this is what was meant by the question, "Whose week was it?" That question is found in a story which recurs in Mekhilta Bo 17, Avot de R. Natan A 18 and Tosefta Sotah 7 and b Hagiga 3a[14]. That story contains the information that all are to come to hear the Torah read (probably for the commandment of assembling the people every seven years to hear the king read the Torah). Woman and children are obliged to come as well. The Torah belongs to all regardless of ability or motivation. Again we have the notion of a law situated in the context of a midrashic story which escapes us if we ignore the reference. b Berachot ended the story of Elazar ben Azariah by referring to other places which are dependent upon this story. The unity of conception behind the story extends into the realm of halakhah, even to the Mishnah itself. The story is of late redaction but, in its essentials, seems to predate the Mishnah and the Mekhilta.

Traditions found in later sources are sometimes reliable guides for the understanding of earlier materials.

----

[14] Rav Nissim Gaon, in his commentary to the story in Berachot mentions that the Yerushalmi mentions that he was made chief judge of the High Court.

Chapter 4

SIFRE'S PRIMACY

1. **The primacy of Sifre's version of the death of Rabbi Hanina ben T'radyon.** We begin this chapter by offering one example to show that Sifre Ha'azinu traditions preserve the earliest form of stories and commentaries. We will also analyze the dynamic by which these early traditions develop.

There are three possible positions available to evaluate the historicity of details in Rabbinic stories: 1) Details in stories are presumed true unless proven otherwise; 2) Details in stories are presumed to be fictitious unless proven otherwise; 3) No presumptions can be made and the burden of proof rests upon the one who makes any positive assertion. The third option seems most logical where no criteria exist for upholding positions 1) or 2). We also note that whatever is said in Rabbinic stories is said on some basis. We must assume that generally some known event generates a story in the first instance even if in the telling names, dates, and surrounding details are completely unhistorical. So it is that we may accept the notion that Rabbi Hanina ben T'radyon was a martyr of the Hadrianic persecutions but question the details of the Rabbinic stories about his death. Was he in fact burned with his Sefer Torah? A. Marmorstein suspects the story is stylized by references to various Roman practices and too romanticized to reflect reality.[1] The images, style and language disclose literary sources, not historical ones. On the other hand S. Lieberman believes only eye-witnesses could have furnished such accurate details as we find in these stories.[2]

Our position here is to admit to the probability of the historicity of the martyrdom of Rabbi Hanina but to vigorously question that he was wrapped in his Torah scroll and burned. The fact that our best and earliest sources mention the burning of a Torah scroll would seem, at first blush, to support Lieberman's position.[3] However, a searching examination of the sources will cast serious doubt upon this position. For a theological perspective of these stories, let us begin by looking at the accounts of the martyrdoms in Higger's edition (Jerusalem, 1960) of *Semachot*.

Following the story of Akiba's martyrdom in *Semachot* 8 we find a parable attributed to Rabbi Meir[4]. He apparently reflects upon the meaning or, perhaps,

---

[1] See A. Marmorstein, *Studies in Jewish Theology*, Oxford, 1950, pp. 142, 167, 174.

[2] See *Jubilee Volume in honor of Salo Baron on the occasion of his eightieth birthday*, Jerusalem, 1975, 218-222.

[3] Sifre Deuteronomy 307, Minor Tractates *Kallah* (end) and *Semachot* 8.

[4] See ed. Higger, p. 156.

more accurately, senselessness of the Hadrianic persecutions. In this parable, the king invites guests to a banquet. Some leave early to go to bed (i.e. die) peacefully before the lights and shops are finished. Others leave later and retire without lights while some shops are still open. Those who stay at the banquet into the night become intoxicated and wound each other; finally there are those who end up by killing each other. At this point, the teller indicates that Meir's parable has been structured in concert with Amos 9:1, "The candelabra knob, strike it (happy are they who have departed before this), and doorways have been obstructed (fortunate they who have already left), their wounding is all at their beginnings while at their ends I kill by the sword." While many Rabbinic stories show a preference to end on a note of consolation, and this one could have also, we have no inkling here of vs.11 which follows the catastrophic announcements of Amos: "In that day I will raise up the booth of David."

The point of Meir's parable is to show that those who tarry in the palace of the king at the royal banquet are doomed to destruction. The "Kafkian-like" parable haunts us. Where is the king? How is such madness permitted in the palace? Yet the focus of the story is not upon the king but upon the guests. The king does not appear. Nevertheless, one is haunted, anxious. Where is this banquet? Is it here, in this world? Why is the consolation verse of Amos 9:11 omitted? In one manuscript we are somewhat relieved of this theological question. "All who are royal servants act by the king's authority such that important people can be purified (punished) by minor officials." The proof text for this assertion is the statement cited from Hosea 6:5, "I have hewn out the prophets, I have killed them by My word." Only by God's authority are prophets killed through lesser agents. The tension caused by Meir's parable's hint of chaos is somewhat relieved in this manuscript by showing that divine authority has sanctioned the deaths of the righteous. This is done by relating the "I kill by the sword" (Amos 9:1) to the Rabbinic tradition exegeting "I have killed them by My word (*imrei fi*)" (Hosea 6:5). Nevertheless, the reason for the king's decree remains problematic. This note of royal sanction is followed by an examination by Rabbi Akiba of various kinds of reactions to inexplicable and apparently unwarranted sufferings.

In the other manuscripts (which are the more numerous) of *Semachot*, we are not given sufficient time to ponder the problem of Rabbi Meir's parable. We are immediately thrust into the story of Hanina ben T'radyon's death and told that he was wrapped in his Torah scroll when he was burned. Only the body and parchment burned, the letters did not. In these manuscripts it is in this story (not in the parable) that we find the assertion that only by the king's authority can the lesser official afflict the greater. Again, the proof text of Hosea 6:5 is attached to this statement to show that all is by the king's authority. The problem we had in the parable, "where is the king", although suspended through the story of Hanina, is defused here to a greater degree than was the case in the manuscripts which deal with the same problem directly at the end of Meir's parable. This is so since the reader can return to the parable after reading the story of Hanina with the conviction that what is true of the Torah is true of the soul. The palace (this world) is not really an essential palace, the affliction is only momentary, and the real banquet is in the future life. For this *Semachot* version, version 1, the prophet is wrapped in the *imrei fi* of Hosea 6:5 (i.e both "by God's command" and "in a Torah scroll"), and is killed. The ending of the verse "your law of light has departed" equates the death of the prophet with the burning of the scroll. This manuscript answers the haunting parable with the story of the martyrdom of Hanina ben T'radyon by highlighting the eternity of the spiritual; and then concludes with Akiba's analysis of suffering. Akiba's point is meant to show that silence (or prayer) is the best answer to Meir's parable. Ultimately we may know that God has willed the suffering of the righteous but what then are we to make of God? The only answer is that of faith, of silence in the face of the inscrutable.

In short, version 2 of *Semachot* introduces the story of Rabbi Hanina ben T'radyon on the heels of the parable so as to provide a theodic notion of the eternity of the soul and Torah. There is a future reward even if there is suffering in this world. Version 1 mildly dilutes the sting of the parable by immediately citing Hosea 6:5 to show that God's authority is the basis of all that happens. The world is not chaotic. We still remain perplexed by the decree of the king. Perhaps we have not really diluted the problem but only shifted its focus. Faith is still needed. The Messiah is not here, the House of David lies in ashes.

In version 1 the parable was completed with the reference to Amos 9:1. Why is Hosea 6:5 also cited there? Do we need new characters in the parable; namely, servants? The cause of the chaos in the parable is the heavy intoxication of the guests, not the servants of the king. Why should we worry about who is killed in the parable, lesser and greater are not issues here. Also Amos 9:1 itself shows God ("I kill") to be the source of the death and destruction. So indeed, what is gained by the citation of Hosea 6:5?

I suspect the statement claiming the king's authority rests in minor officials was originally attached to Hosea 6:5 without regard to Meir's parable. If this statement placing the cause of suffering upon God's will was originally part of Meir's parable, how did it get attached to the martyrdom story of Rabbi Hanina ben T'radyon in the more prevalent *Semachot* texts? We did note that Hosea 6:5 was connected with Amos 9:1 in order to attribute human suffering to God's punishments. Why would editors or scribes connect Hosea 6:5 to the Hanina ben T'radyon martyrdom story unless it originated there. The location of the tradition is problematic in both versions.

I believe it can be argued that the plans of all Rabbi Hanina ben T'radyon martyrdom stories were always associated with Hosea 6:5. The end of the verse, though not quoted in *Semachot*, is really the essential reference (concerning *zidduk hadin*) for *Semachot* and the other versions of Rabbi Hanina's death, as we will see later. The main point of these stories was indeed to justify (although we hardly know the justification) God's permitting great sages to die through torture. Thus Hosea 6:5 which spoke of the death of the prophets by the word of God became important for some Rabbinic views treating the theodicy problems inherent in the Hadrianic persecutions. Meir's parable was assimilated to these views by reference to the whole of this verse. The associations between Hosea 6:5 and the narratives of the death of Rabbi Hanina ben T'radyon will be seriously considered further in this paper.

We are now in a position to evaluate how the general story of Rabbi Hanina ben T'radyon's martyrdom was viewed in theodical theologies. It portrayed a tone of divine justice amid horrendous suffering. Thus all the versions of the story invariably contain references to divine justice, or reasons for his suffering (or punishment), or an indication of his place in the afterlife. The early stories of Akiba's suffering do not present such a view, as E.E. Urbach has demonstrated.[5] The story of Hanina, then, was presented as a contrast to the early stories of Akiba. Later Akiban stories do introduce at least some notion of Akiba's place in the afterlife.[6] These stories allow us to see how the Rabbis used history, Scriptures, and stories in the service of theology and faith in the most difficult of times.

We will now proceed to demonstrate the primacy of the Rabbi Hanina ben T'radyon martyrdom tradition in Sifre to Deut. (ch. 32), piska 307. U. Cassuto illustrated the literary connections between the Book of Hosea and Deut. 32.[7] L. Finkelstein proposed direct influence of some prophetic books upon Sifre materials.[8] I have offered evidence that parts of Sifre to Deut. 32 are dependent upon the language of the Book of Hosea even where such references are unacknowledged in our Sifre texts.[9] My working hypothesis is to ascribe traditions in Sifre 32 which reflect influence of Hosea to the original sources of Sifre. The observation that Deut. 32 and Hosea were associated at an early stage, earlier than Sifre, is supported by a passage in the Dead Sea Scrolls. In Pesher Hosea we are given a passage from Hosea followed by: "Interpreted this means that they ate [and were filled...] but they forgot God who... They cast off his commandments etc." Here the bold represents a version of Deut. 32:15ff. Although it is exceedingly rare for pesher literature to use Scriptural proof texts as opposed to proofs from history, Hosea 2:8 is indeed read in the light of Deut. 32:15.

Where similar non-Sifre, Tannaitic or Amoraic Hanina ben T'radyon stories appear to have been developed beyond the Sifre text by an implicit or acknowledged

----

[5] "Ascesis and Suffering in Talmudic and Midrashic Sources," *Baer Jubilee Volume*, Jerusalem, 1960.

[6] See b Berachot 61b.

[7] U. Cassuto *Biblical and Oriental Studies* vol. 1: Jerusalem, 1973, 79 ff.

[8] L. Finkelstein *New Light from the Prophets* London, 1969.

[9] H. Basser, *Midrashic Interpretations of the Song of Moses* New York, 1984, 285 ff.

exegesis of an operative Hosea verse, I posit the Sifre version to be the source of the other versions and hence prior to them. In the Sifre version we are told that a) Rabbi Hanina's Torah scroll" was burned, b) that his wife was killed and, c) that his daughter was forced to "do duty" in the brothels of Rome. We now note that other versions of the martyrdom story speak of the burning of Rabbi Hanina himself.[10] Now b Sanhedrin calls at least one other Rabbi "a Sefer Torah",[11] and Yerushalmi Moed Katan notes that one who sees a scholar who has died is like who sees a Torah scroll which has been burnt.[12] Hence, we might suspect that here "Sefer Torah" refers to Rabbi Hanina himself. Why call him a Sefer Torah here? Parallel passages directly mention the *kuba shel zonot* and not the euphemistic "do duty" here.[13] Bacher rightly maintains that *kuba* reflects the earliest wording of Sifre tradition.[14] We argue that Hosea 6:5 has directed the flow of the story and its versions. "Therefore I have hewn out the prophets, I have killed them by the words of my mouth, and your law goes out by light (*or = ur*, fire)." I think *imrei fi* would have been understood by the originator of the Sifre story to mean only "by my command" and not "in my Torah scroll" as it does in *Semachot* 8 which I see as a later development. The speaker in Hosea is God: "Your law will be burned." I suspect that the originator of the Rabbi Hanina ben T'radyon narrative found an allusion to the Rabbi here. For him, the Rabbi was alluded to in this verse as "law",[15] hence the midrashist refers to him as (a) "Sefer Torah," as the law.[16] (b) His

---

[10] b Avodah Zarah 17b (the same line appears in *Kallah* (end).

[11] The term was applied to Rabbi Eliezer, b Sanhedrin 101a, b Sota 49b, the sources appear to quote Tannaitic traditions. Cf. S. Lieberman, *Tosefta Kifshutah* VIII, Sota, New York, 1973, 761.

[12] See y Moed Katan 3:7.

[13] Since both *Semachot* 8 and b Avodah Zarah 17b-18a read *kuba* (brothel chamber) we assume it lies behind Sifre's euphemism "do duty". W. Bacher, *Tannaim* Tel Aviv, 1924-5, 116f claims *kuba* is original to the tradition. It appears that Sifre Deut.'s editor was fond of circumlocution and disguising scriptural references, e.g. see Basser, 217(E9), 200(E1).

[14] W. Bacher, *The Legends of the Tannaim*, Tel Aviv, 5682, 116f.

[15] The homilist may well have noticed the wording of the verse "your law" rather than the expected "My law". Thus he saw here an allusion to the human embodiment of the *law* the human container of Rabbi Hanina's body.

[16] See n.11 above. The appellation "Sefer Torah" seems to have been applied to Rabbis who were dead or ill and the intent was to show that there was a real or impending loss of Torah teaching in the world. For the process by which folktales become attached to Biblical verses (often unstated) whose guiding words are associated with other scriptural motifs and for an understanding of how these allusions direct the narrator and influence the formation process of the narratives and the functional moves see D. Noy, *Scripta Hierosolymitana: Studies in Aggadah and Folk-literature* vol. 22, Jerusalem, 1971, 173, 156-6, 184-5, 190-6. See the same volume, 210, for S. Safrai's assertion that Rabbinic Sage-

wife is to be "killed." (c) His daughter is to do duty in *"kuba shel zonot* (chamber of prostitutes)." Hosea 6:5 reads "hewn out"--*hazavti*, while Isaiah 5:2 says, *"yekev hazev bo"*: the hollow shall be dug out in it. Isaiah is speaking of the vat in the vineyard, perhaps taken by the midrashist as a sexual allusion. The major point here is that the word *yekev* contacts consonantly with *kuba*. Thus *hazavti* in Hosea is likely taken midrashically as a reference to *kuba* (that which is hollowed out, i.e. *yekev*).[17] The midrashist in Sifre 307 (this is the case in all versions of Hanina's martyrdom) is interested in showing that even the martyrs recognized the justice in their own suffering; yet, he nowhere in Sifre 307 describes their death scene or the precise reasons for the suffering. This was left an open mystery and others rushed to fill it in.

Thus it is, that other preachers, in want of historical information (I suspect) managed "to locate" Sifre's Biblical source of reference; thus, were able to relate what had happened and why. If the original story was situated in the language of Hosea, further details must be there as well. The martyrdom event had found this verse and I will later demonstrate that the verse continued to reveal further details of the story as now found in the Talmud. Rabbi Hanina ben T'radyon in the post Sifre traditions recorded in the Talmud, became the entire hero of the Hosea verse, he was burned--*hazavti* ("The voice of the Lord hews out [*hazev*] flames of fire according to Psalms 29:7) because he blasphemed. Perhaps *yekev hazev* (Isaiah 5:2) lies behind this version and was understood as in Lev. 24:16, *venokev shem*: "He who blasphemes." Both *hazev* and *nokev* mean to "make hollow." Blaspheming is hollowing, profaning. According to another Talmudic account he was killed because he taught the proscribed Torah[18], likely a midrashic rendering of the *imrei fi* of Hosea 6:5. Still according to another account in *Kallah*, lying behind b Avodah Zarah 117b-118a[19], it was because he changed the use of funds collected for the

---

tales are based on historical facts. And also see here J. Fraenkel's analysis of the function of Biblical verses quoted in such tales (98-9). According to Fraenkel the Rabbis believed that verses could elucidate contemporary history (perhaps we have here a shared notion with Qumran *pesher*). The contentions in my paper will not go beyond any claims that have been cited here. Also see M.D. Herr, "Persecution and Martyrdom in Hadrian's Days" in *Scripta Hierosolymitana* 23, 1972.

[17] The connections between: the Song of the Vineyard in Isaiah, the Book of Hosea; and Sifre to Deut. 32 can be seen in the opening piska, 306, of Sifre to Deut. 32. 13. The point here is that *hazavti* assimilates *yekev* which in turn suggests *kuba*. It is possible that this in turn is read back into Hosea 6:5, "prophets" to refer to brothels of the Roman priest-prophets.

[18] b Avodah Zarah 18a.

[19] See below n.38

celebration Purim.[20] We should not be too far wrong to see the influence of the Song of the Vineyard here as well. Is. 5:24 relates how "the fire consumes straw", "and the ashes fly", a detail recounted in some stories of the martyrdom, because "they despised Torah and the saying[21] of the Holy One of Israel".[22] The very last words of the Isaiah Song 5:30 note, *va'or hashakh b'arifehah*. Since Hosea 6:5 ended by noting "And your law of light (of Purim celebration) went out" [23] and Isaiah 5:30 could be rendered "And the light was monetarily exchanged for darkness," a creative midrashist, believing in measure for measure - "light" for "light" may have found a reference to Purim funds here. That is, burning at the stake is an apt punishment for exchanging Purim funds. First, it should be seen that in Sifre 306, *araf* is rendered as *exchange of money*. Second, the Book of Esther 8:16 refers to Purim celebrations as "light, and happiness and gladness." Purim monies are to be used solely for these purposes according to Tosefta and both Talmuds.[24] Thus we can see how the stories may have developed by preachers connecting verses and traditions to fill in the missing parts of earlier stories. They accentuated the notion of divine justice, Hanina deserved to be punished. Indeed, the Sifre martyrdom verses center upon the idea of God's justice (*mishpat*) as related in Deut. 32:4.[25] "*His mishpat*" again reflects Hosea 6:5 that "your law (judgment) is to go by fire." That is, the decree of fire is just. Thus Sifre 307 seems, indeed, to be tied to Hosea. In the minor tractate of *Semachot* 8, for which I can cautiously allow a Tannaitic date,[26] we find that Torah (and perhaps souls) are indestructible:

> Shall not the Torah consume the fire? Is Torah not a fire-eating fire? In all
> matters of state only through the command of the king the greater can be

----

[20] Minor Tractate *Kallah*, end.

[21] Is. 5:24, "Saying" here seems to suggest pronouncing the Divine Name.

[22] b Avodah Zarah 18a seems here to reinforce the connection between Hosea 6:5 and Isaiah 5:24. The guiding words have found their motif in Isaiah's Son of the Vineyard.

[23] According to a valid translation

[24] See Tosefta Megilla 1 (ed. Zuckermandel 221-222), y Megilla 1:4, b Baba Mezia 78b.

[25] The homilist or redactor of Sifre has attached the tale to Deut. 32:4, "The Rock, his work is perfect, for all his ways are mishpat". It appears that *mishpat* here is associated with *mishpat* in Hosea 6:5 which mentions "your law" or "your decree" by light (fire) will go out. It is related in Sifre and Talmud b Avodah Zarah that Rabbi Judah HaNasi marveled at the aptness of the Deut. verse. Here we have what Noy calls a "guiding word" which has influenced the development of the tale until it reached the form in b Avodah Zarah 18a.

[26] See *Mesechet Semachot*, ed. M. Higger, Jerusalem, 1960, Introduction, 51.

purified (punished) at the hands of the lesser. Surely it is written in Hosea 6:5 "I have killed them (the prophets) by the words of my mouth",(that is the destruction of the scroll,) but, it is also written here, "And your law of fire shall go out."

The point is that the Torah-law-of-fire (and likewise the soul) shall escape harm, while the scroll (and the body) shall be quickly consumed. We are told specifically, according to the *Semachot* midrashist, that the king has not commanded the destruction of the Letters of Torah (so too the soul). Thus Hosea 6:5 belongs to the words of Hanina ben T'radyon in *Semachot* 8. *Imrei fi* has a dual interpretation here alluding to 1) God's command to burn the 2) parchment (*imer*=lamb) of his word, and to let 3) the law of light (the essence) escape.[27]

We have not yet begun to penetrate the complicated textual history of this martyrdom story. We have only considered a possible example of the major operative verses in the dynamic by which such stories are told and retold. Let us now see how Lieberman handled the stories.

In his article about Hadrian's religious persecution of the Jews, Saul Lieberman wrote:

"We cannot make light of post-Talmudic sources which relate, in variant style and additional detail, incidents already known to us from Tannaitic sources. Thus, for example, we read in Sifre Ha'azinu, piska 307 (ed. L. Finkelstein), 345:

"After Rabbi Hanina ben T'radyon was arrested, the decree was issued against him that he was to be burned with his Sefer (Torah). He was told, 'The decree has been issued against you that you are to be burned with your Sefer (Torah)...' His wife was told, 'The decree has been issued against your husband that he is to be burned and against you that you are to be killed....' His daughter was told, 'The decree has been issued against your father that he is to be burned and against your mother that she is to be killed, and against you that you should perform (brothel) duty....' Philosophus[28] opposed his commander saying to him, 'My lord, boast not that you have burned the TORAH, for from the place from which it came, has it returned--to its Father's house.' He replied, 'Tomorrow shall

----

[27] These versions of the tale provide details missing in the Sifre version. The details have been provided by the process of examining "source" verses which were taken to have specific reference to this martyrdom story. Fraenkel (see n. 16 above) attempts to show that the Rabbis seriously took such verses as references which could elucidate contemporary history.

[28] I accept the reading of the Berlin manuscript here "PLWPWS" which I suggest means "praepositor" or supervisor. "Philosopher" makes no sense to my mind.

your judgment be the same as theirs.' He said to him: 'You have pronounced glad tidings to me that on the future morrow my portion may be with them in the Next World.'"[29]

Lieberman further remarked:

"When we examine the details of this story, we find nothing unusual. Everything suits Roman practice. Rabbi Hanina ben T'radyon was sentenced to be burned together with his Sefer Torah because he had taught Torah. His wife was sentenced to be killed according to the usual Roman practice of destroying the entire family of political offenders. His daughter was sentenced to live in a brothel; this was also according to Roman practice. At the end of the story, a certain philosopher expressed some emotionality for the sentenced victim and he, too, was sentenced to death. Everything accords with Roman practice....So in b Avodah Zarah 17b it is related: 'They came to Rabbi Hanina ben T'radyon. They said to him: 'Why are you studying Torah?' He said to them, 'It is as my God commands me.' Immediately they pronounced the decree upon him to be burned and on his wife to be killed, and on his daughter to live in a brothel.'"[30]

Lieberman concluded that the Talmudic version, with perhaps some cited Amoraic interpolations, made it patently clear that the sentence of burning was no mere whim, but the established policy of Rome. His evidence is based on further stories, especially the one in the b Avodah Zarah 18a. The source relates that Rabbi Yosi ben Kisma said to Rabbi Hanina ben T'radyon: "I shall be surprised if they do not burn you and the Sefer Torah with fire." The punishment for teaching Torah was common knowledge. Lieberman summed up his discussion by saying:

"We cannot in any way make light of even Amoraic sources which relate events that occurred decades before that period. Often they were in possession of living traditions passed on by eye witnesses who related facts that they had heard with their ears and seen with their eyes."

----

[29] Here "tomorrow" has two senses. The commander means "the next day", but Philosophus (Lieberman takes this as "philosopher") hears it as a good omen. In Rabbinic terminology "tomorrow" often means "at the end of days--the future world". See Baron volume 218.

[30] The use of *al* with *gozer* simply indicates the object upon whom the sentence is passed and does not mean "(to be burned) *upon him*" but rather "as a decree against him". Urbach cites such a text (*Sages* Jerusalem, 1978, [Heb.], 457) and erroneously gives his source as Finkelstein's Sifre Deut. but this text reads "with his Sefer (Torah)".

All Sifre texts have one common section which will allow us to doubt the correctness of Finkelstein's text. Lieberman correctly quotes that part of Sifre Ha'azinu to which all Sifre manuscripts attest. Philosophus (the reading he accepted and which he took to mean a philosopher) in these texts mentions only the boast of the burning of the "Torah" which in fact returned to its Father's house. A close reading of the source will show how the reference is not to the Torah scroll but to the soul of Hanina ben T'radyon.[31] It is called "the Torah." This, then, is the story which is equivalent to that story cited by Lieberman, b Avodah Zarah 17b, where only the death of the Rabbi is mentioned and there is no mention of burning the Sefer Torah. The upshot of this discussion is that there exists a firm tradition attesting to the death of Rabbi Hanina ben T'radyon by burning. What then shall we make of the *Semachot*, *Kallah*, and Avodah Zarah traditions relating the burning of the Sefer Torah and the Rabbi? It will be shown that this part of the story likely came about through a development which has its roots in the literary expansion and exegeses of two parallel Sifre versions and the exegesis of operative Biblical verses as well.

Our issue here is this. Sifre Deuteronomy reports an early tradition as it misses theodic details which are supplied by other texts. If Sifre knew these other texts it would certainly have mentioned them. Does the best version of our Sifre Deuteronomy text really tell us that Rabbi Hanina ben T'radyon was burned together with his Sefer Torah? Are the texts of Talmud, and minor tractates (*Kallah* and *Semachot*) reliable sources to tell us that the Rabbi was burned with his Torah in actual fact?

Lieberman has read all these sources as one whole story, with greater or lesser detail. All versions fill in each other. Let us now look carefully at the Sifre text, and attempt to recover the most ancient reading and its sense. Unfortunately the Vatican 32 manuscript does not exist for this portion and so we will have to determine the best reading from a critical examination of the various manuscripts. The versions found in the London manuscript and the first printed edition (extant) Venice, 1545, preserve good readings which closely correspond to Vatican 32 in the extant parts.

"After Rabbi Hanina ben T'radyon was arrested, the decree was issued against him that his Sefer (Torah) was to be burned. He was told, 'The decree has been issued against you that your Sefer (Torah) is to be burned.' He recited this verse, 'The Rock, whose deed is perfect.' His wife was told, 'The decree has been issued against your husband, *against him* that his Sefer Torah is to be burned and against you to be killed...' His daughter was told,

----

[31] See the discussion of circumlocutions in E.Z. Melamed in the *Benjamin DeVries Memorial Volume*, Jerusalem, 1968, 138. Also of S. Lieberman, *Hellenism in Jewish Palestine* New York, 1962, p.32.

'The decree has been issued against your father, against him that his Sefer
Torah is to be burned..."'

In accordance with the Sifre to Deut. 32 style, we noted earlier how this
story is couched in terms reminiscent of Hosea 6:5. We also noted that this Biblical
citation actually occurs in the major reading of another Tannaitic source. We also
considered that the Sifre text nowhere mentions the death of the Rabbi outright. It
uses the Hosea reference to "law" as "Torah", indeed, both "Sefer" (body) and
"Torah" (soul) refer to the Rabbi. "And your law shall go out by fire" (Hosea 6:5)
allows for the circumlocution of the Rabbi as "Sefer Torah" here. We have noted
that b Sanhedrin 101a and Yerushalmi Moed Katan 3:7 also note that sages are
called "Sefer Torah." Hanina, according to our Sifre text of London and the first
edition, is not to be burned "with" (*im*) his Torah, rather he has had a decree issued
"against" (*alav*) him. As we have noted, the portion following this account in all
manuscripts of Sifre refers only to "the Torah (soul). It would seem that "Sefer
(Torah)", without mention of the Rabbi, is the better reading of Sifre and is to be
found in the first printed edition and the London manuscript of Sifre.[32]
Nevertheless, it cannot be doubted that the author intended us to understand that
the Rabbi was burnt, for the key part of the Sifre midrash informs us that the Rabbi
sanctified the name of Heaven which always acts justly. By "Sefer Torah" is meant
none other than Rabbi Hanina ben T'radyon, and not his Torah Scroll. *Semahot* 8
presents two scenes. In the first, Hanina is condemned to die at the stake.[33] There is
no mention of his Torah. In the second scene, which seems to be a later addition
within the original Tannaitic *Semahot* layer, he is wrapped in his Torah and
burned[34]. *Semahot* 8 has the original Sifre and preserves the exegetical base, which
we examined above, for scene 2, the burning of the Torah.

We dismiss the implausible but creative comment of Yefeh Eynaim (to
Avodah Zarah 18a) that the Torah was burned on one day "returning to its father's
house" and the Rabbi on the next, i.e., "Tomorrow your fate will be as theirs". It is
more probable that the only story known to the midrashist of Sifre Deuteronomy
related the death of the Rabbi, but not the actual burning of the Torah. Indeed, in

----

[32] Lieberman himself attested to the fine readings in London in his criticism of Finkelstein's
edition, see *Kiryat Sepher* 14, 1937-8, 329. Since the euphemism "Sefer Torah" can be traced to the
influence of a passage from Hosea (a common feature in Sifre Deut. to Deut.32) and the literary
history of the passage suggests that the Babli and minor tractate versions developed out of the Sifre
pattern, the text of London (and the first printed edition) appears to preserve the best readings here.

[33] P. 157. l. 93.

[34] See p. 158, ll. 99-100 where we find an accretion of texts "They wrapped him in a Torah
Scroll and burned him and a Torah Scroll with him." This section seems to be a later one than what
precedes it. The text shows evidence of various readings which are now aglutenated.

Finkelstein's version, the only mention of burning the Rabbi with his Torah scroll is: "After Rabbi Hanina ben T'radyon was arrested, the decree was issued against him that he was to be burned with his Sefer (Torah). He was told, 'The decree was issued against you that you are to be burned with your Sefer (Torah).'" In other references to his death in this same version, only his death is mentioned, without any reference to the burning of a Sefer Torah. Could there not be a scribal interpolation, "with his Torah," in Finkelstein's text describing a double burning. b Avodah Zarah 17b-18a relates one version of the story without any reference at all to the burning of the Torah.

How then is it that b Avodah Zarah 18a records a composite story, incorporating details known to other minor tractates which relate both burning of the Rabbi and the burning of his Sefer Torah? The best explanation is to see that the story circulated in two forms. One story spoke of the death of the Rabbi outright (and this story is evidenced in b Avodah Zarah 17b-18a and the version of Finkelstein, disregarding the first line of the story). The alternate story, attested by Sifre ms. London and the first printed edition, is similar to this but does not speak of the death of the Rabbi outright. It assumes a Biblical reference from Hosea as a circumlocution, "his Sefer (Torah)."[35] The two stories, that of the Rabbi's death and that of the "burning of the Torah", were seen as identical. Due to further speculation upon Hosea 6:5 ("killed in *imrei fi*, the law of light going forth") and natural tendency to harmonize versions into a single fluid story, a version was generated which posited the burning of both Rabbi Hanina ben T'radyon and his Sefer Torah.

The most highly developed story is that version found in b Avodah Zarah 18a:

> "May the Redresser of insult to the Torah redress my humiliation!" His students asked him, 'Master what do you see?' He replied, 'The parchments are burned but the letters are flying.'--'So you also should open your mouth and take in the fire.' He replied, 'Better for He who gave it to take it than for a person to take his own life.'[36]

The complete identification of the Torah scholar with the Torah is here reworked into one of the most poignant martyrdom scenes in Jewish literature. It is little wonder that scribes or preachers readjusted their versions of the Sifre to reflect the story of the burning of Rabbi Hanina ben T'radyon with his Sefer Torah. The idea that the parchment of the Torah Scroll burned but not the letters is directly traceable to the earliest Sifre version in which the "Sefer (Torah) is burned (i.e. the Rabbi) but the "Torah" (his soul) has returned to Heaven. That is, the later authors

----

[35] See above n.11. The references suggest Tannaitic sources.

[36] Compare *Semachot* 8:12.

of the story in *Semachot* and b Avodah Zarah 18a understood the dynamic of the story's growth. What originally referred to the burning of the Rabbi's body was transferred to a literal Torah Scroll. Maharsha's (S. Edels) commentary to b Avodah Zarah 18a correctly accentuates the comparison between the Torah and the Rabbi in the Talmudic version:

> "And (his students) said to him that just as he had noticed not only the burning of the parchment, which is the physical body of the Sefer Torah, but also the upward flight of the letters, which are its spiritual component, so should he emulate it. He should open his mouth, letting the fire enter, so that his physical body would be burned (quickly, to end the torture) even from within, while his soul and spirit would rise and fly upward."

In some sense, the story, even if not factual, reflects the gruesome treatment actually inflicted upon Jews and their sacred literature, as the pious of the faith clung to their ways in the face of horrid persecutions.[37]

Can we date the versions of this story cycle? The end of minor tractate *Kallah* relates that Rabbi Hanina ben T'radyon was wrapped in his Sefer Torah and burned as a punishment for exchanging Purim funds and that the *quaestionarius* joined him in death[38]. Talmud Babli, as well as *Kallah* and *Semachot* know that the scroll was burned. Yet, since the scene describing the death of the Rabbi was omitted in Sifre; and *Semachot* and *Kallah* tell varying stories both of which are reflected in the language of the Babli, one may suspect that Babli here is simply incorporating versions of these texts. These minor tractates are to be dated to the dawn of the Amoraic period and may essentially be considered as Tannaitic texts.[39] It is therefore the case that the burning of the Rabbi and his Scroll was a tradition related around the year 225-250 at the latest. The Tannaitic Sifre text mentions Rabbi Judah the Prince's (c.200) reflections upon the Sifre Tradition. The Sifre Tradition must then date to some time prior to the 225-250 dates.

Did the two traditions (death of Rabbi, burning of Torah) grow side by side or is one dependent upon the other? It is impossible to tell for sure. However, minor tractate *Semachot* 8 relates a solid tradition which will allow us to suspect that both *Semachot* 8:12 and the end of *Kallah* contain amplifications meant to fill in the Sifre versions and that such amplified texts were woven together into the story now found

----

[37] See y Ta'anit 4:5, b Gittin 58a.

[38] The accounts found in b Avodah Zarah 17b-18a which were understood by the medieval commentators, to imply that Rabbi Hanina had rectified the losses from his own pocket, are later versions of the *Kallah* story. That the story was originally seen as negative may be discerned in 17b. The *Kallah* version is apparently earlier than the Talmud but later than Sifre.

[39] See Higger's edition of *Semachot* (Introduction, 51) *Kallah* (Introduction, 13).

in the b Avodah Zarah 18a. *Semachot* 8:12 begins by citing an alternate version, a condensation of Sifre Deut., the version known to b Avodah Zarah 17b, mentioning the burning of the Rabbi but not the burning of the scroll. We then find in *Semachot* what looks like a certain amplification of an earlier notice that Hanina was to be burned. "And when they burned him, they wrapped him in his Sefer Torah and burned him." This text goes on to tell how Rabbi Hanina ben T'radyon understood that only the parchment could be burned, not the Torah itself. We have already noted how Hosea 6:5 has directed this story. The process of growth in the narratives beyond the Sifre version is evident. *Semachot* 8:12, by citing Hosea 6:5, seems to provide a clue to the proof texts which influenced the growth of other stories even if these other stories did not cite the proof texts. People may well have asked "Why did the righteous Rabbi Hanina ben T'radyon suffer by fire?" The answer was found in Hosea 6:5. It was ordained that way by God (*imrei fi*). Later homilists drew out more associations from this verse's vocabulary and from Isaiah's story of the vineyard which used a similar vocabulary and these preachers could then give specific reasons for his death.[40]

In summary, we note that the primary verse in the background of the Sifre 307 was Hosea 6:5. This verse was seen to allude to the burning of the law, the Torah. We find evidence in the Talmuds that early Palestinian Rabbis were called Sefer Torah. It was certainly possible to refer to Rabbi Hanina ben T'radyon as the "Sefer Torah", the "law" of Hosea. We can also see how others later found behind the Sifre version a hint that the Holy Scroll (the *imrei fi* of Hosea) was burned with the Rabbi. Hosea 6:5 could now be read as: "Therefore I decreed against the prophets, I have killed them *with* the Words of my commandments (that is the Rabbi and the Sefer Torah) and your law of fire (in *Semachot*: a fire-eating fire) goes out (it escapes).[41] The verse itself operated as a mechanism to harmonize the two earlier versions of the Sifre story, one which referred to the burning of the Rabbi directly and one which used a euphemism, Torah. The verse was also used to show that these events occurred due to God's commands (*imrei fi*). This

----

[40] The relation of the story of Hanina to Hosea and Isaiah can perhaps be traced through guiding words which speak of "judgment", "law", "fire" and so inform Deut. 32:4. These verses may have been read in unison so as to produce the final version of the tale. Sifre Deut. 306 juxtaposes verses from Hosea and Is. 5 and Machiri to Isaiah 5 relates Isaiah 5 to Sifre Deut. 307. It is possible that Isaiah 5 at one time served as the Haftarah to the opening verses of Deut. 32, see the charts in B. Wacholder's "A history of the Sabbatical readings etc.", in *Prolegomenon to the Bible as Read and Preached in the Old Synagogue* vol.1 (J. Mann), 1971.

[41] After assimilating all the verses to the Hosea verse, the homilist may have been that only the physical letters of the Torah burned while the Torah itself escaped the flames. Indeed, the Sifre darshan already noted that the Torah (soul) had returned to its Father's house. Structural analysis of the story's units will show further the unity of each version as literary creations in their own although the building blocks can be traced in earlier versions.

development may have happened within a few years or after many years of the circulation of the Sifre versions. *Semachot* 8:12 preserves another proof text besides Hosea 6:5. Rabbi Hanina tells his daughter in this version that it is better to die through a raging flame than through an unfanned flame. The text cites Job 20:26: "....the unfanned flame consumes him, it is evil to the remnant of his tent." In the Talmudic version, his students (the remnant of his tent?) plead with him to ingest the flames but the Rabbi refuses. One wonders if Job 20:26 does not somehow lie behind this story as well, especially since the end of the story is that the flames are allowed to rage.

The point is that stories absorb verses which in turn generate new details and then in turn generate new stories. Was Hanina ben T'radyon a martyr? Yes. Was he burned together with his Sefer Torah? Probably not. Lieberman's case rests on showing the primacy of the Finkelstein Sifre reading or the texts of *Semachot*, *Kallah* and Babli. That case is doubtful.[42]

2. **The date of Mekhilta published by Kahana in relation to that of Sifre.** Menahem Kahana has published sections of midrashim which he has identified as the Mekhilta to Deuteronomy.[43] The Mekhilta to Deuteronomy was a work, known in the Middle Ages but since lost, and assumed to have been used by the compiler of the Yemenite, medieval midrash, *Midrash HaGadol*. Kahana has claimed that his fragments contain original forms which later became corrupted in the recording of the Sifre. Indeed, the opposite appears to be the case. His fragments show reworkings of Sifre materials which at times were misunderstood and at times simply "smoothed out". The Sifre origins are sometimes still visible in these "Mekhilta" passages.

נוסח המדרשים

מכילתא (כהנא)   ספרי

ראו...הוא הרי זו תשובה   ראו עתה כי אני אני הוא[44] זו תשובה
לאומר אין מלכות בשמים,   לאומרין אין רשות בשמים.
משיבין אותו   לאומר]יש שתי

----

[42] Finkelstein's text does preserve the non-euphemistic version of Sifre's tale but incorporates a notice that the Rabbi was burned with his Sefer Torah. This notice, in view of our analysis, should be taken as a late scribal gloss.

[43] See M. Kahana, "Pages from the Mekhilta to Deuteronomy Ha'azinu and Vezot Haberakhah," *Tarbits*, 57 (1988), p. 178, n. 73-4.

[44] דב׳ לב:לט

ואומרין לו ואין אלהים עמרי.	רשויות[45 בשמים משיבין אותו ואו' לו ואין
אני אמית ואחיה הרי זו תשובה	אלים עמרי46. או שמא אין יכול לא להחיות
לאום' יש מלכות בשמים אלא שאין	ולא להמית לא להרע ולא להטיב, ת"ל ראו
בו כח לא להמית ולא להחיות לא	עתה (וגו') אני אמית ואחיה 47 וגו' [ואו']
להרע ולא להיטיב, משיבין אותו	כה אמ' יי מלך ישר' וגאלו יי צבאות אני
ואומרין לו אני אמית ואחיה,	ראשון ואני אחרון [ומבלעדי אין אלהים[48.
יכול שהוא ממית את זה ומחיה את	אני אמית ואחיה זה אחר שניתן להן רמז
זה חלמ' לומ' מחצתי ואני ארפא	לתחית המתים...שומע אני מיתה [באחר]
מה מכה ורפואה באחר אף מיתה	וחיים [באחר], ת"ל מחצתי ואני ארפא49 כדרך
וחיים באחר. ד" א ראו...הוא	שמכה ורפואה [באחר] כך מיתה וחיים [באחר].
כענין שנ' כה אמר יי מלך...	
וגאלו וג' ואומ'... .	

The right column represents Sifre piska 329 and the left column represents the Mekhilta. In his presentation Kahana offered the Sifre text according to the Oxford ms:

Sifre: Mekhilta:

"See now I, I, am He...(Deut. 32:39)":
This is the response to those who say
there is no one ruling power in heaven. If
one says there are two powers in heaven,
the answer is given by saying to him,
"There is no god with Me."
   Or perhaps, he is not able to give life
   or to kill, to do harm or to do
   good. The exegesis of "See now I,
   I am He, I kill and I make alive [I
   wound and I heal"] is to explain
   so.
[And Scripture states,] "So says the Lord,
the King of Israel and his redeemer, [the
Lord of hosts, 'I am the first and I am the

"See now I, I, am He...(Deut. 32:39)":
This is the response to those who say
there is no one ruling power in heaven.
The answer is given, "There is no god
with Me."
   "I kill and I make alive...": This is the
response to those who say there is one
ruling power in heaven but he has no
ability to kill or to make alive, to harm or
to benefit. The answer is given, "I kill and
I make alive." I might have thought that
He kills X and gives life to Y. The
exegesis of "I wound and I heal" is to
explain so: Just as wounding and healing
refer to the conditions of X so do death
and life refer to the conditions of X.

----

45 הגרסה על פי כהנא 191-193.

46 רב' לב:לט

47 רב' לב:לט

48 ישע' מד:ו

49 רב' לב:לט

last and besides Me there is no god.']"
(Isaiah 44:6)
"I kill and I make alive.":
This is one of the passages that gives
allusion to the resurrection of the dead...
I might have thought that He kills X and
gives life to Y. The exegesis of "I wound
and I heal" is to explain so: Just as
wounding and healing refer to the
conditions of X so do death and life refer
to the conditions of X.

Another interpretation."See I, I am
He.": This is according to the matter of
which Scripture states, "So says the Lord,
the King of Israel and his redeemer, [the
Lord of hosts, 'I am the first and I am
the last and besides Me there is no god.']
(Isaiah 44:6)....

The editor of the Mekhilta was bothered by an interpolation in the Sifre text which interrupted the monotheistic point, "And there is no god with Me," to state that God is omnipotent: *"Or perhaps, He is not able to kill or to give life (Oxford:to give life or to kill) to do harm or to do good. The exegesis of "See now etc. I kill and I give life..." is to explain so."* He noticed the Sifre midrash then reverted back to the earlier matter of refuting the claims that there are more gods than one: "And Scripture says, 'and besides Me there is no god."[50] The Mekhilta unnecessarily created a new passage in which this prooftext was more directly connected to Deut. 32:39[51].

This Mekhilta editor then reorganized the interpolating passage. In the Sifre, the passage which appears above in italics is intended to teach that God has the ability to make birth ("I make alive") and death ("I kill"), harm ("I wound") and benefit ("I heal"). The midrashist of Sifre simply wanted to illustrate that the verse details God's abilities. Indeed, the Oxford tradition of Sifre here reverses the order of the verse to present the way things happen normally, "to give life or to kill." He is only concerned with God's omnipotence in this world. The order of the words in the verse are not part of his exegesis.

----

[50] The antiquity of joining Isaiah 44:6 to Deut. 32:29 can be demonstrated. The Septuagint and Targums replace "And there is no God with Me (Deut. 32:29)" with "And besides Me there is no God (Isaiah 44:6)". This section is part of the first comment and has been interrupted by an interpolation. Kahana is wrong to suppose the Isaiah verse is connected with life after death and so formed a pericope in Sifre which was separate from the first.

[51] The Mekhilta editor realized that the verse "...and besides Me there is no god" was disjointed in Sifre and put it into its own "another tradition" in his Mekhilta text. This new positioning clairifies that the verse refers to the idea that there is only one God. In Sifre it was somewhat out of place as noted by the author of Zera Avraham in his Sifre commentary. Indeed a similar displacement occurs in piska 308 (ed. Finkelstein 347) and this is smoothed over in Midrash HaGadol. The Mekhilta passages are reworkings of the Sifre.

We now consider the next section of the Sifre. Here we have another voice. This midrashist argues that the verse has another import. The order of the words is crucial. We are not speaking of birth and death but of death and resurrection. We are not merely thinking God kills X and gives birth to Y but he kills X and then gives life to X. The printed edition is based on a tradition which introduces this voice with the words, "Another tradition." Even if such is not the actual reading, the understanding that we have a new voice here is correct.

Let us now see how Kahana's "Mekhilta" presents this material. First of all we note that the material from the first voice (omnipotence) and the second voice (resurrection) are patched together even though the midrashim conflict. The editor removed the interpolated omnipotence passage and moved it below to join a conflicting interpretation. The arguing resurrection passage is based on the word order-- "I kill and I make alive." Here the change in place forces a new sense upon the passage. It must now seem to agree that the verse is speaking of resurrection. Yet the words, which remain from the original Sifre "omnipotence" setting are left dangling in the new context-- *to do harm or to do good*. The evidence of the shift glares at us. The editor who joined these disparate traditions of the original Sifre into a single unit bungled the seam. The patterns do not match.

The point is that later midrashim, like the version of Mekhilta at issue here, reworked earlier ones. Mekhilta is to be seen as a later reworking of Sifre. How much later I do not know but it is certain that the Mekhilta has reworked the Sifre traditions here.

Kahana's claim that it was Sifre which readjusted Mekhilta is not so. He claims that Sifre's "And besides Me there is no god" is supposed to be an integral part of the passage showing God's abilities. Kahana has to force the passsage into its twisted Mekhilta sense. He says this passage actually refers to resurrection. Then he tells us that "And besides Me there is no god" also refers to resurrection in Sifre. There is no indication that the verse does refer to resurrection and every indication that it does not. He has outdone the blunder of the Mekhilta. The Sifre omnipotence passage, by its own testimony, refers to God's abilities in this world. If "And besides Me there is no god", does not revert back to the discussion of monotheism, it would refer to nothing in Sifre. It does not refer to God's power to resurrect people. It is doubtful that the verse could be weighted with this sense. Moreover, there is no discussion of resurrection until the following exegesis. Kahana went as far as claiming that my interpretation of the Sifre passage fit only the Mekhilta which "was unknown" to me. Yet, my interpretation, claiming the verse from Isaiah reverts back to the earlier matter of one God, does fit the Sifre. As for the Mekhilta, its place in the hierarchy of midrashic compilations has been demonstrated to be inferior to Sifre.

We have demonstrated that Sifre Ha'azinu contains very old materials. It preserves much of interest to the scholar who would plumb its depths to understand the workings of midrash.

Chapter 5

FORMAL COMPOSITION

1. **The Song of Moses in Sifre as a unit.** The midrash of Sifre Ha'azinu contains a discreet unit which is a complete entity unto itself. This midrash on the Song of Moses is divided into sections called piska'ot. The first piska of the Song is numbered 306. Generally the units correspond to the separate verses which are being scrutinized but piska 306 is very large and contains information covering three verses. In this way, it resembles Talmud which has a lengthy first chapter that introduces much of the material of the tractate and may even have theological reflections about the subject material as a whole.

2. **The antiquity of the structural understanding of the Song.** The history of the exegesis of the Song requires diligent investigation. We briefly touched upon this complicated exegesis in chapter 1. We will now elaborate more fully.
"Heaven" and "Earth" are addressed in the Song of Moses in Deuteronomy 32:1. We notice that in the first four centuries of the common era that this was understood to refer to the Upper World and the Lower World. Philo understood "Heaven" and "Earth" to refer to all which is above and all which is below. "He convoked a divine assemblage of the elements of all existence and the chiefest parts of the universe, heaven and earth, one the house of the mortals, the other, the house of the immortals."[1] Deuteronomy 32:3 was understood to mean that Moses addressed the mortals and immortals (Heaven and Earth) to join in God's praise. "Hear Heaven and Earth and offer praise". Also Marqah, the Samaritan, tells us, "Moses praised, the angels rejoiced and said '"Praise the Lord' --The glory and all the angels then praised...."[2]
The Sifre midrash, piska 306, subtly touches these themes by laying bare the movement of the entire Song, from rise to fall to rise.

Deut. 32:3-- "For I will proclaim the name of the Lord":
And from whence do we know that the Ministering Angels do not mention the name of the Holy One, Blessed Be He, in the heavenly realm, until Israel mentions it in the earthly realm? We know it from that which is said, "Hear, O Israel, the Lord our God, the Lord is One." Deuteronomy 6:4). And Scripture also states, "When the morning stars sang together" (Job 38:7) --and afterwards --"And all the godly ones shouted." "The morning stars" -- These refer to Israel who is compared to stars, as it is said, "I will multiply thy

----

[1] Philo, ed. Colson, *On Virtues*, ch. 11-12.

[2] *Memar Marqah* 4:7

seed as the stars of the heavens," (Genesis 22:17). "And all the godly ones shouted," --These refer to the Ministering Angels; and so does Scripture state, "And the godly ones came to present themselves before the Lord." (Job 1:6).

There is a consistent theme here which holds together the unity of the exegesis. The first piska of the midrash begins with all in heaven and earth condemning Israel for their rejection of God. It ends with Israel's praise of God together with that of the angels. Israel is the instrument through which God is sanctified. This foreshadows the end of the Song which was also understood to refer to the praise of God coming through Israel.

> Deuteronomy 32:43-- "Clamor, O ye nations because of His people":
> In the Future, the Gentile Nations of the World will rejoice on account of Israel, as it is said, "Rejoice, O ye nations, because of His people". And also the heavens and the earth! As it is said, "Sing, O ye heavens, for the Lord hath done it; Shout, ye lowest parts of the earth." (Isaiah 44:23). From whence do we know that this is so of the mountains and the hills? As it is said, "The mountains and the hills shall break forth before you into singing." (Isaiah 55:12). From whence do we know that this is so of the trees? As it is said, "And all the trees of the field shall clap their hand." (Isaiah 55:12). From whence do we know that this is so of the Patriarchs and the Matriarchs? As it is said, "The *Sela* dwellers will exult, at the head, the mountains will shout." (Isaiah 42:11).[3]

The unity of the Song is portrayed in the midrash and its similarity to the exegesis found in Philo is worthy of note. Philo concludes his description of the Song by noting the praises of the "heavenly choir"[4] This very passage in Philo echoes the way Sifre concludes the Song. For Philo it is a description of

> "Past sins ... **present** admonitions ... exhortations for future ... **happy** fulfillment ... life immortal.

In similar fashion , at the close of the midrash on the Song, Sifre states that the Song:

> "refers to the **present**" ... "refers to the past" ... "refers to the **Future Era**" ..."refers to **This World**" ..."refers to the Coming World"!

---

[3] Piska 333.

[4] *On Virtues* 72-75.

The understanding of the structure of the Song is an ancient one.

Let us now examine the nature of the midrash as a whole. The midrash on the Song begins and ends with traditions in the name of Rabbi Meir. The unit is thus enclosed and portrayed as a document which originated under the guidance of Rabbi Meir. The movement of the midrash follows the movement of the Song in Scripture, from indictment, to punishment, to vindication. This movement is prefigured in the first piska of the Song, piska 306. It comments upon the first three verses of Deut. 32. The first prooftext on the first verse speaks of a righteous Israel witnessing against themselves, and their corruption through nature, while the last prooftext upon this same verse speaks of God witnessing against a corrupt Israel. Here we have the plot: a loved Israel who remains unfaithful. The exposition of the second verse begins with a discussion of Torah-study and ends with the notion of the Resurrection of the dead. Here we have the mechanism of reconciliation and salvation. The third verse is discussed in terms of Moses' and Israel's inferiority to the angels, then in terms of glorifying God's name by bringing the nations to acknowledge God, and concludes with Israel's ultimate superiority, even over the angels. This verse, moving from doom to glory, is taken as the reverse of the first verse. The last verse of the Song, piska 333, is exegeted by noting that those who were to witness against Israel will end by praising them, heavens and earth, mountains and nations. The Septuagint actually records here: "Rejoice ye heavens with him and let all the angels of God worship him." Our midrash mentions the praising of the morning stars here, like Philo, who mentions the divine and earthly assemblages which heard the Song of Moses[5]. Then the final piska concludes with Rabbi Meir, whose name began the midrash on the Song. He promises entrance into the World to Come, the world of resurrected life, to those who dwell in the Land of Israel, read the Shma and speak Hebrew. The final words are "World to Come." This comes full circle to the opening words of the midrash on the Song concerning when Israel was righteous. The note on which the name of Rabbi Meir began is the note on which this same name ends.

The midrash on the Song has a long history. It is to be suspected that the midrash reached near completion, whether written or oral, by the time of the Hadrianic persecutions in 132 CE. The midrash, as we have noted, begins and ends with the name of Rabbi Meir. It would seem plausible that it was he who brought the midrash to the form it is now. His name appears some eight times, matched only by Rabbi Yosi and superseded by Rabbi Yehuda whose name appears 21 times. The date can be fixed from the fact that the name of Rabbi Judah the Prince, 200 CE, appears only in connection with two interpolated glosses reflecting upon the earlier Sifre text. Both occur in the first two piska'ot.

----

[5] *On Virtues*, 73-75.

The first reference illustrates a difficult passage by citing what someone once said to him:

"As the rain winds (שעירים) upon the grass":
Just as the se'irim fall upon the grass and penetrate them so they will not become wormy, so you should pore over the words of the Torah in order that you should not forget them. And so Rabbi Yaacov the son of Hanilai said to Rabbi, "Come and let us pore over (the words of the Torah) the *Halakhot*, in order that they will not become moldy."[6]

The second addition approves of the verses selected by the family of Hanina ben T'radyon:

Said Rabbi: "How great were these righteous people who in their hour of suffering readily specified the three verses which remain unparalleled in all of Scripture for their acknowledgement of God's righteous judgment!"[7]

There is a third recorded occurrence, the originality of which is not certain:

Rabbi says: This refers to the snakes, whose kingdom is specifically that of the dust. (Sifre Deut. 321 to Deut. 32:24).

It is not easy to see the import of this statement. Since it occurs both in the Yemenite Midrash HaGadol and several European manuscripts it seems that it is an early reading. However, The first printed editions of Sifre Deuteronomy and Yalkut Shimoni do not read "RBI 'MR" but "DBR 'HR". That the midrashim in our collection predate Judah the Prince seems certain. That his name occurs at all seems to indicate that it was his school which completed the text, virtually, as it stands before us today.

3 **Biblical verses.** The prooftexts used in the midrash to the Song of Moses appear in approximately the following ratios:

Isaiah 18%; Psalms 16%; Jeremiah 10%; Genesis 8%; Exodus 8%; Ezekiel 8%; Deuteronomy 8%; Job 8%; Minor Prophets, Canticles, Daniel 8%, various historical scriptural books 8%.

----

[6] Piska 306.

[7] Piska 307.

The citations relate to materials concerning God's love of Israel. This is so despite her wayward fidelity to Torah; even in her suffering at the hands of the Gentiles; and especially so in her ultimate glory. Appropriate verses are selected as prooftexts from some ten Scriptural units to illustrate more explicit renderings of verses in Moses' Song. In this way, the Song represents the totality of Biblical theology. The Rabbis did not have to develop any further theology since the one they inherited was perfectly sufficient. It is not true that the Rabbis were blind to theology. They had no need to improve upon the one they inherited from their ancient ancestors.

4. **Midrash and Halakha.** Scriptural verses were read closely by homilists. Nevertheless, some of the Sages thought that syntactical and grammatical considerations should be "bent" to accommodate possible halakhic objections. Here is an example of such a rendering:

> Deuteronomy 32:1-- **Give ear, ye Heavens and I will speak; and let the Earth hear the words of my mouth.**
>> And the Sages say that the matter is not so[8]. Rather, when witnesses come and testify their testimony stands if their words are mutually oriented, and if they are not, then their testimony does not stand. So it was that if Moses had said, "Give ear, ye Heavens" and stopped there, the Heavens would have said, "We only listened by *giving ear*." And had he said, "And let the Earth hear the words of my mouth," the Earth would have said, "I only listened by *listening*."[9] Isaiah came and stated in conjunction with this usage --"Hear, ye Heavens and give ear, ye Earth" in order to apply "giving ear" and "listening" to the Heavens and "giving ear" and "listening" to the Earth. (Sifre Deut. 306)

The Sages argued that halakha dictated the sense of Scripture and not vice-versa. The homilist presented an interpretation of Deut. 32:1 in defense of the rule that witnesses must clearly witness the same event in the same way.[10] The rules of testimony are applied to the way in which Moses charged his witnesses. Our initial tradition intimated (contrary to the halakha) that Moses charged the heavens by asking them to "give ear" (as if he were interested in having Israel's verbal utterances recalled whether they were intelligible or not) while Moses charged the earth to "hear" matters (that were clearly intelligible). Since "give ear" and "hear"

----

[8] That the Heavens and the Earth were addressed separately and differently.

[9] But Moses intended that both Heaven and Earth should each listen and give ear.

[10] b Sanhed. 29a and y Sanhed. 3:9.

may have different meanings it is not clear that the witnesses had understood their duties to be of the same nature and the result would be that their testimonies could not be used to substantiate each other as the halakha requires. The Sages espouse a method of reading the verse refers to as the method of Meir[11] who did not read verses according to the structure in which they are written. The homilist structures the verse to mean that the heavens and the earth were both instructed to "give ear and to hear". He finds confirmation in the words of Isaiah who used "give ear" to charge the earth and "hear" to charge the heavens[12], which is the reverse order of Deut. 32:1. This "proves" that Isaiah understood Moses to have applied equivalent instructions to both heaven and earth since he, Isaiah, undoubtedly based his words upon those of Moses. Thus both the statement of Moses and that of Isaiah are to be read halakhically and not according to their written structure. To both verses we may apply the principle where Scripture contains a word order and its reverse, we consider the terms of equal weight and sharing common circumstance.[13]

In this case, the inherited interpretations of Scripture were scrutinized and found to create halakhic problems. In the 18th and 19th centuries some scholars analyzed both Scripture and Midrash with a watchful eye to reconcile matters with halakhic tradition. The Tannaim preserved ancient tradition but registered halakhic complaint where it was due. The complaint of the Sages exists only in Sifre while the "non-halakhic" interpretations were widely circulated. One may be inclined to conclude from this state of affairs that the realms of aggada and halakha were sufficiently distant that the attempts of some "Sages" to reconcile one with the other were not judged necessary.

5. The manner of composition and compilation. Our present compilation of Sifre Deuteronomy shows that the collections were put into a fixed form and that later additions were interpolated without altering this form. That we have interpolations would tend to indicate that the oral form of midrash continued simultaneously with the written forms. Traditions, originally omitted for one reason or another, were inserted. These insertions are present in all manuscripts and suggest that the process of compiling Sifre Deuteronomy was a long one which ended at the beginning of the fourth century.

Consider the case:
Deut. 32:2-- As שעירים upon the grass:

----

[11] See b Pes. 21b. Cf. Marmorstein, *Old Rabbinic Doctrine 11, Essays in Anthropomorphism*, Oxford, 1950, 108.

[12] Isaiah 2:1.

[13] Mekhilta (ed. Horowitz-Rabin) p. 2 line 11 to Ex. 12:1.

> When a person first goes to study Torah it falls upon him like a se'ir.
> And se'ir specifically means "demon", as it is said, "And the wild-cats shall
> meet with the jackals, and the שעיר shall call to his fellow." (Isaiah
> 34:14). And Scripture also states, "And שעירים flutter there." (Isaiah
> 13:21).

After this we find three interpretations of the beginning of Deut. 32:2: "לקחי shall
יערף as rain", all of them concerning Torah study. The point of the interpolation is
clear and we should not have noticed an interpolation between the above and the
below were it not for the discrepancy between the beginning verse and the
concluding one.

> As שעירים upon the grass:
> When a person first goes to study Torah he does not know what to do
> until he learns two books of Scripture or two sections of Mishnah and
> afterwards it will follow after him like lambs (רביבים). For such reason
> was it said, כרביבים upon the herb."

Why do we begin with se'irim and end with revivim? It must be that the
interpolator went back and took the wrong lead verse. We may suspect that the
early manuscript read something like this:

> "As שעירים upon the grass": When a person first goes to study Torah it falls
> upon him like a se'ir and seir...flutter there.
> "As רביבים upon the herbe": He does not know what to do until he learns
> two books of Scripture or two sections of Mishnah and afterwards it will
> follow after him like lambs.For such reason was it said..."

The interpolation between "like a se'ir..." and "As revivim..." led the
interpolator to recapitulate:

> "As שעירים upon the grass: When a person first goes to study Torah etc."

He then continued, dropping the crucial continuation of the verse (As
רביבים upon the herb):

> "He does not know what to do until he learns two books of Scripture or two
> sections of Mishnah and afterwards it will follow after him like lambs...."

The "etc." was dropped as inconsequential and the whole passage was read
as one pericope. The two read well together. The fact that se'irim is placed, as if a
lead verse, above the revivim passage, enhances the observation that originally there
was a single tradition commenting upon both se'irim and revivim. It was broken by

an interpolation. The latter half of the broken pericope was now introduced by a summary of the earlier half. Thus we see that later materials were added to the early text.

6. **Rabbinic theology and midrash.** The Songs in Scripture are indeed epic poems of Israel's past, present and future. The Mekhilta mentions ten songs which mark turning points in Israel's history beginning with the redemption in Egypt and ending with the final redemption[14]. A more universal version, beginning with the remission of Adam's sin is given at the beginning of the Targum to Canticles. No Song is sung from the days of the early kings of Israel until the ultimate redemption. The midrash to the Song has a concluding statement in Sifre Deut piska 333. It is said in the name of Rabbi Meir that the national (living in the Land of Israel), the ritual (reciting Shma), and the cultural (speaking Hebrew) aspects of Judaism are the mainstays of Jewish existence. Without country, God, and language all is lost. What is astounding is that no mention of the study of the Torah is mentioned. That is the hall mark of the Rabbinic position, the study of Torah outweighs all other merits. That is why our medieval commentator had to find that "Torah" is included in the final words of the Song midrash:

> "And recites the Shma liturgy in the mornings and the evenings: This follows the ruling of the sage who ruled in tractate Menahot 99b-- he thereby fulfills the commandment[15] of *"And you shall speak of them day and night,"* (Josh.1:8). The Shma liturgy is based upon sanctifying His name and committing oneself to His unity and to the yoke of His kingship."

With these words, the commentator notes the parallel structure of the end of the midrash to its beginning: Torah study (Sifre to Deut. 32:2), sanctification of God's unity (Sifre to Deut. 32:3) and the yoke of divine kingship (to Deut. 32:3).

What is blatant is the order of the tradition of Rabbi Meir "mornings and evenings". The order in the Mishnah of reciting the Shma is first "night" and then "day." However, the verse in Joshua which commands the study of the Torah has the order "day" first and then "night." The interpretation of the commentator is not without merit.

7. **Internal design.** The midrash before us, like other midrashim, reads units of Scripture alongside other units which are assumed to be directly related to the passage, thematically and/or semantically. For instance, the mention of Moses, Aaron and Phineas, in piska 326 comes about as a result of the semantic field of

----

[14] *Mekhilta*, shira,1. See the notes in H-R ,118.

[15] Of Torah study.

Deut. 32:36 being directly reflected in Ps. 106. The proof texts do not reflect this rationale and are probably secondary to the original formulations of the midrash. Likewise much of Sifre Ha'azinu is read together with parts of Hosea. Indeed, Qumran's pesher Hosea reverses the process and comments upon Hosea by referring to the Qumran version of Deut. 32. In Pesher Hosea we find the explanation of Hosea 2:8: "Interpreted this means that **they ate [and were filled...]** **but they forgot God who...** They cast off his commandments etc." Deut. 32:15ff is the obvious reference and shows us that the method of synchronic reading is likely earlier than both the Rabbis and the Qumran exegetes.

Another example will illustrate that our midrashim, indeed, are based upon exegeses of verses that are absent from our texts. Our demonstration is based upon a simple observation. When two midrashim appear to be related but contain terms foreign both to their own settings and to each other we can posit that a third verse is responsible for the intrusions. Since, in such cases we can demonstrate that a verse, though unstated, can direct the flow of exegesis we must be open to that possibility in other cases as well. The early commentators were adept at solving problems in the midrash by adducing biblical verses.

Let us now demonstrate that Neh. 8:8 is the missing link between Sifre Deut. 313 and Mekhilta Yitro 9.

Sifre Deut. 313 states:

> "He gave him wisdom" (Deut. 32:10):
>> Through the Ten Commandments. It teaches us here that when the utterance went out from the mouth of the Holy One, Israel could see it and they **gained knowledge** from it and they **knew** how much *Midrash* there is in it, and how much *Halakha* there is in it, and how many *a fortiori* arguments there are in it and how many *arguments by analogy* there are in it.

The material for this comment can be determined by examining the traditions commenting upon "*They saw qolot*"--Exodus 20:18:

וכל העם ראים את הקולת

Mekhilta Yitro para 9 (ed. Horowitz-Rabin, 235) states:

> "Rabbi says: This proclaims the merit of Israel who, when they all stood at Mt. Sinai to receive the Torah, heard the utterance and interpreted it. [This is as it is said, "He compassed him round about, He gave him wisdom (Deut. 32: 10), namely; when they heard the utterance they interpreted it[16].]

---

[16] They clarified its sense.

The section in brackets is absent in the first printed edition, and appears suspect. "He compassed him round about, He gave him wisdom (Deut. 32:10), namely; when they heard the utterance they interpreted it," does not act as a clear prooftext in the usual way. It seems to be a reference, in fact, to something like our Sifre midrash rather than a prooftext. However, the comment, which may have once been a variant of our Sifre, correctly shows that the exegeses of Deut. 32:10 and Ex. 20:18 are connected. Perhaps the "This is as it is said," (שנ׳) is a corruption for "And so" (וכן). The obscure comment drew some notice and Leqah Tov (to Ex. 20:18) preserves an explanation of this "prooftext":

רואים כמו מבינינם שנאמר ולבי ראה הרבה (קהלת א:טז)

"See" means "understand". Nevertheless, even if all of this is the intent of the midrashist[17], we are still at a loss to appreciate the fine connection between "see" and "interpret". Let us now examine Nehemiah 8:8:

ויקראו בספר בתורת האלהים מפרש (interpreting)
ושום שכל ויבינו (attaining wisdom) במקרא.

It is not to be doubted that Nehemiah 8:8, though unstated, is the operative mechanism that links all traditions concerning Ex. 20:18 and Deut. 32:10. We have already noted the midrash stating that יבוננו in Deut. 32:10 refers to Torah study at Sinai. Note well, in this passage, the problematic "משכילין בר" ("gain knowledge") which looks like an intrusion in the Sifre text. Note also the unique usage of the term "מפרשים" in the Mekhilta text. Nehemiah 8:8 is the only verse which contains all three terms: מפרש שכל ויבינו.

Ezra's Torah reading in Neh. 8:8 is understood to be the re-enactment of Sinai and Neh. 8:8 is understood to be the proper interpretation of the Theophany in Exodus and Deuteronomy. These insights came into the hand of the later midrashist who can now tell us that "qolot" are not only "utterances" but are to be understood as "QAL vehomer," etc. etc. Mekhilta's statement in the name of Rabbi, and Sifre Deut. follow some earlier tradition linking Neh. 8:8 to Deut. 32:10 and Exodus 20:18 of which they preserve parts. The relationships are intelligible once we note that the common link is an unstated verse. What is the meaning of the three terms in Sifre Deut. 313"רואים משכלים יורעים" ? They are as follows:

"רואים=מפרש", "משכלים=שכל", "יורעים=ויבינו" .

We note that "see" (Ex. 20:18) = "interpret" (Neh. 8:8) and that is what Mekhilta notes. "Gaining knowledge" is simply gaining "knowledge" and is a total intrusion from Neh.8:8. "Knowing" is "attaining wisdom" (Neh. 8:8) and is likewise

---

[17] One wonders if a prooftext is necessary. Does not "see" mean "clarify" as does "interpret" (PRS).

the "attaining wisdom" in Deut. 32:10. As complicated as it is, this is what the midrash is saying in so many words. Where we find one term present in Scripture we posit the others as well. We know now what this midrashist thought about the wisdom gained when Ezra, the Scribe, read the Torah. That wisdom was derived from midrash, halakha, and Rabbinic hermeneutics[18]. The Rabbinic mode of Torah study is as ancient as the Torah. The original Israelites perceived Torah's depth and immediately began its elucidation. They were able to derive Oral tradition before they received it. We also know how the Rabbis viewed every synagogue Torah reading. Their rules for the reading are indeed patterned both after the accounts of the Sinai Theophany and after Ezra's public reading which accounts they "telescoped" together.

8. **The value of medieval** commentary. In the following pages we will present a hitherto unpublished medieval commentary to a section of midrash. Above we demonstrated the propriety of a commentator adducing verses to explain the obscure. My own comments on the midrash may be located in my earlier work, 1984. Here, we will learn from our commentator who is much more adept than I in adducing Scriptures to explain the processes of midrash. This task is more than warranted; it is obligated. The commentator is also adept at explaining obscure terms, discussing variant readings, and explaining the techniques of midrash.

The general tone of this commentary is in the style of the *Ba'alei HaTosafot*. The scribes of the two manuscripts in our possession attribute the work to Rabbenu Hillel but the commentary is not his. We have his commentary. The 16th century Rabbi Soliman Ohana cites our author with the words "There are those who comment" while Avraham ben Gedaliah (Brit Avraham to *Yalkut Shimoni*, Livorno 1650-), cites him with the words "Thus have I found". The 18th century bibliophile Hayyim Azulai, known by the acronym *hida* ascribed the work to Rabbi Abraham ben David[19], but this ascription is problematic for a number of technical reasons not the least of which is that the mss cite that scholar by name. The author of the commentary is not known to me. His commentary survives in two complete 16th c. manuscripts, in at least one fragment, and is cited anonymously in two commentaries of the 16th and 17th centuries. It appears to have been written before the 15th century since it quotes no one later than the late 13th century. The 1559 Oxford ms. 425 (Mich 376) is corrupt in ways which suggest much prior copying. The later 1587 JTS ms (Boesky 5) contains common errors with Oxford but is the superior of the two. They certainly have a common ancestor with these corruptions

----

[18] See above ch3 for the notice that the Rabbis seem unique in treating the Decalogue as they do the rest of Scripture. We may see here their attempt to affirm their position.

[19] See M. Kahana, "Commentaries to Sifre buried in manuscripts," *Rabbi Isaac Nissim Memorial Volume*, Jerusalem, 1985, 98 n.30.

but JTS is often the better witness. Given the textual history of the commentary we may assume that the work was written in the period designated as late "rishonic" and accord importance to its readings and explanations. We note that all manuscripts and fragments are written in a "Sephardic" or "Eastern hand" and cited by scholars living in Eastern countries. However, the scholars mentioned   are, without exception, North-Western Europeans. Louis Finkelstein identified the text type of the Sifre manuscript used by the author as Italian in the main but it may be noted that the section on Deuteronomy preserves some Sephardic readings. This suggests that it was written by someone schooled in or near France, but who moved to Spain or Spanish communities in the East after he had begun his work. That pages of the work were found in a Yemenite book-binding also suggests that the commentary was known in the East. As well, there appears to be a Spanish word in the text[20] and this further supports the idea of a move.

To date, a number of recent translations of Sifre Deuteronomy have appeared. R. Hammer, *Sifre: A Tannaitic Commentary on the Book of Deuteronomy*, New Haven and London, Yale University Press, 1986. H. Bietenhard, *Sifre Deuteronomium*, Berne, Peter Lang 1984. J. Neusner, *Sifre to Deuteronomy: An Analytical Translation*, Atlanta, Scholars's Press, 1987. Apart from these there is my study of Sifre Ha'azinu, *Rabbinic Interpretations of the Song of Moses*, Berne, 1984 and S. Fraade's current study of Sifre Deuteronomy[21] due to appear this year. All in all, the work of these people could not have proceeded without the benefit of commentaries such as those of Pardo and Lichtstein and even more recent ones like those of Rabbis Berlin or Malbim. Even with them, much remains obscure. The teaching of the commentator, steeped in the tradition, enlightens us as to sources for further consideration of halakhic and aggadic materials, and to readings of manuscripts no longer extant. Furthermore he opens our eyes to the method of study in his times and the life of his community. The commentary, which I hope to reproduce in its entirety within the next year, is provided here in both Hebrew and English.

The text of the commentary itself is based upon citations in Brit Avraham, a 17th century commentary by Avraham ben Gedaliah to *Yalkut Shimoni*, in Soliman Ohana's 16th century commentary to Sifre and upon two complete 16th century manuscripts. The corrupt state of the manuscripts is evident and my sparse annotations are meant to help the reader note difficulties without an elaborate apparatus. An apparatus was prepared but deemed unnecessary since most variants

----

[20] See the discussion of the manuscripts in M. Kahana, "Commentaries to Sifre buried in manuscripts," *Rabbi Isaac Nissim Memorial Volume*, Jerusalem, 1985, 100 n37. Kahana takes the word as French but its spelling shows it to be Spanish.

[21] Fraade's book has the tentative title: *From Tradition to commentary: Torah and Its Interpretation in the Midrash Sifre to Deuteronomy*. He deals at length with selected topics in Deut. 32 and provides his translation of piska 306.

were gross corruptions which could be corrected with a high degree of certainty. The Hebrew Sifre is that of the first edition (Venice, 1546) as reprinted in Ugolino's *Thesaurus*, Venice, 1753. The English translation of the Sifre text is a conjectured reconstruction of the texts used by the author of the commentary using Finkelstein's edition (reprint: New York, 1969) as a guide in conjunction with manuscripts and the commentary itself. No attempt was made to alter the Hebrew text and the reader will note the variants.

Part Two

SIFRE HA'AZINU WITH COMMENTARY (English)

Part Two

SIFRE HA'AZINU

with the commentary of a great sage
printed here for the first time

Abbreviations
O = Oxford manuscript 425 (Mich. 376).

J = JTS manuscript Boesky #5 (reel 56), formerly Sassoon 598/2.

B = Commentary of Brit Avraham to *Yalkut Shimoni*, Livorno, 1650-.

F = Finkelstein's edition of *Sifre on Deuteronomy*: Berlin 1939, reprinted JTSA New York, 1969.

* = See the comment to this passage pp 165ff.

SIFRE HA'AZINU WITH COMMENTARY (English)

PISKA 306

"Give ear, ye heavens, and I will speak...":
Rabbi Meir says:
When Israel was pure they testified about themselves*, as it is said, "And Joshua said unto the people, 'Ye are witnesses to yourselves'." (Joshua 24:22). But then they sinned in regard to themselves, as it is said, "Ephraim compasseth Me about with lies and the House of Israel with deceit."(Hosea 12:1).

So, He notified them they were subject to the witness* of the Tribe(s) of Judah and of Benjamin, as it is said, "And now, O inhabitants of Jerusalem and men of Judah, judge, I pray you, betwixt Me and My vineyard. What could have been done more to My vineyard...." (Isaiah 5:3). Then the tribe of Judah and Benjamin sinned, as it is said, "Judah hath dealt treacherously...." (Malachi 2:11).

So, He notified them they were subject to the witness of the Prophets*, as it is said, "Yet the Lord witnessed to Israel, and Judah by the hand of every prophet (and every seer)...." (2 Kings 17:13). Then they sinned in respect to the Prophets, as it is said, "But they mocked the messengers of God...." (Chronicles 36:16).

So, He notified them they were subject to the witness of the Heavens*, as it is said, "I call heaven and earth to witness to you this day...." (Deuteronomy 30:19). Then they sinned in regard to the Heavens, as it is said, "Seest thou not what they do...." (Jeremiah 7:17). And then it states, "The children gather wood, and the fathers kindle the fire, and women knead the dough, to make cakes for the queen of heaven." (Jeremiah 7:18).

So, He notified them they were subject to the witness of the Earth, as it is said, "Hear, O earth; behold, I will bring evil...." (Jeremiah 6:19). Then they sinned in regard to the Earth, as it is said, "Also their altars are as heaps upon the furrows of the field...." (Hosea 12:12).

So, He notified them they were subject to the witness of the Paths, "Thus saith the Lord; stand ye in the ways and see...." (Jeremiah 6:16). Then they sinned in regard to the Paths, as it is said, "Thou hast built thy lofty place at every head of the path...." (Ezekiel 16:25).

So, He notified them they were subject to the witness of the Gentile Nations, as it is said, "Therefore hear, ye nations, and, know O congregation, what is against them...." (Jeremiah 6:18). Then they sinned in regard to the Gentile Nations, as it is said, "And they mingled themselves with the nations, and learned their works..." (Psalms 106:35).

So, He notified them they were subject to the witness of the Mountains, as it is said, "Hear, O ye mountains the Lord's controversy..." (Micah 6:2). Then they sinned in regard to the Mountains, as it is said, "They sacrifice upon the tops of the mountains...." (Hosea 4:13).

PISKA 306

So, He notified them they were subject to the witness of the Cattle, as it is said, "The ox knoweth his owner (and the ass, his master's crib)...." (Isaiah 1:3). Then they sinned in regard to the Cattle, as it is said, "And they exchanged His Kavod[1] [for the likeness of a calf* that eateth grass....]" (Psalms 106:20).

So, He notified them they were subject to the witness of the birds, as it is said, "Also the stork in the heavens knows her appointed times...." (Jeremiah 8:7). Then they sinned in regard to the cattle, beasts and birds, as it is said, "And I went in and saw; and behold every form of creeping thing and detestable beast...." (Ezekiel 8:10).

So, He notified them they were subject to the witness of the fish, as it is said, "Or speak to the Earth and it shall teach thee; and the fishes of the sea shall declare unto thee...." (Job 12:8). Then they sinned in regard to the fish, as it is said, "And thou makest men as the fishes of the sea..." (Habakkuk 1:14).

So, He notified them they were subject to the witness of the ant, as it is said, "Go to the ant, thou sluggard... she provideth her bread in the summer..." (Proverbs 6:6).

Rabbi Shimon the son of Elazar said: Humbled is the man who should have learned from the ant*[2] --Had he actually taken instruction and acted accordingly he would have been humbled. But he was supposed to take instruction from her ways and, in fact, did not take instruction.

At the time of the Future Judgment, the community of Israel will address the Holy One, blessed be He:

> Master of the Universe, I fear for behold my witnesses exist*, as it is said, "I call heaven and earth to witness against you this day." (Deuteronomy 30:19)

He will say to her:

> Fear not for I will remove them.

This is according to what is said, "For behold I will create a new heaven and a new earth." (Isaiah 65:17).

She will address Him:

> Master of the Universe, I fear for I see places that I have shamed... and I am ashamed.

----

[1] I.e. glory

[2] "Humbled is the man who should have learned from the ant" is a possible translation and our commentator gives the usual understanding of the passage taking *'aluv* as a negative term. More likely is this: "How humble (*'aluv*) would that man have been who was supposed to take instruction from the ant! --Had he actually taken instruction and acted accordingly he would have been humble. But he was supposed to take instruction from her ways and, in fact, did not take instruction." *'aluv* can have a positive sense as in Avot de Rabbi Natan A ch. 23-- *'aluv* like Moses, as it is said, "And the man Moses was very humble." A positive sense works well here.

PISKA 306

This is according to what is said, "See thy way in the valley." (Jeremiah 2:23).
He will say to her:
Fear not, for I will remove them.
This is according to what is said, "Every valley shall be lifted up." (Isaiah 40:4).
She will address Him:
Master of the Universe, I fear for my name exists.
He will say to her:
Fear not, for I will remove it.
This is according to what is said, "And thou shalt be called by a new name." (Isaiah 62:2).
She will address Him:
Master of the Universe, I fear for my name has been associated with the name of the Baals.
He will say to her:
Fear not, for I will remove it.
This is according to what is said, "And I shall remove the name of the Baals..." (Hosea 2:19).
She will address Him:
Master of the Universe, nevertheless the household will mention it.
He will say to her:
"And they shall no more be mentioned by their name."(Hosea 2:19)

Furthermore, on the Future Morrow, at the time of the Future Judgment, she will address Him:
You have yet written, "...saying: If a man put away his wife, and she go from him, and become another man's, may he return unto her again?" (Jeremiah 3:1).
He will say to her:
I wrote nothing other than "a man". Yet has it not been stated, "For I am God and not a man." (Hosea 11:9).

Another interpretation:
--O House of Israel, are you my divorcees? But has it not yet been stated, "Thus saith the Lord: Where is the bill of your mother's divorcement, wherewith I have put her away? Or which of my creditors is it to whom I have sold you?" (Isaiah 50:1).

Another interpretation:
"Let the heavens give ear":

PISKA 306

This may be explained by a parable of a king who entrusted his son to a tutor* to take conscientious care of him. The son declared, "Father, do you think it will do any good to deliver me over to a tutor? I will make sure that he eats and drinks and goes to sleep and then I will go about my own interests." His father said, "I have delivered you over to a tutor from whom you cannot escape."

So did Moses say to Israel, "Perhaps you think that you can escape from beneath the heavens or that you can move away from the presence of the earth!"

And furthermore the Heavens publish, as it is said, "The heavens shall reveal his iniquity." (Job 20:27). And from whence do we know that even the earth informs? As it is said, "And the earth shall rise up against him." (Job 20:27).

At the time of the Future Judgment: the community of Israel will stand in judgment before God and address Him:

"Master of the Universe, I do not know who has subverted whom and who has defied whom³?"

Did Israel sin against God and did God (not) revoke His relationship to Israel?-- Since Scripture says, "And the heavens tell of His righteousness" (Psalms 50:6), it is certainly the case that Israel sinned against God but God did not "revoke His relationship with Israel." And so Scripture says, "For I the Lord revoke not." (Malachi 3:6).

Another interpretation:
"Give ear, ye heavens...":
Rabbi Yehuda says: This may be explained by a parable of a king who had two administrators in the capital city and he entrusted them with everything he had. Then he put his son into their charge and said to them, "Whenever my son fulfills my wishes, thou shalt delight him and indulge him by giving him to eat and by giving him to drink. Whenever my son does not fulfill my wishes he may not taste anything of mine."

So what does Scripture have to say about Israel whenever they fulfill the wishes of God? --"The Lord will open unto thee His good treasure the heavens..." (Deuteronomy 28:12). And what does Scripture have to say about them whenever they do not fulfill the wishes of God? --"And the anger of the Lord will be kindled against you, and He shut up the heavens, so that there shall be no rain, and the ground shall not yield her fruit." (Deuteronomy 11:17).

----

³ For the translation here see H. Yalon, *Studies in The Hebrew Language*, Jerusalem, 1971, 150-54.

PISKA 306

Another interpretation:
"Give ear, ye heavens":
      Rabbi Nehemiah says: This may be explained by a parable of a king whose son fell upon evil ways. He began to complain* about him to his brothers, then he began to complain about him to his friends, then he began to complain about him to his neighbours, then he began to complain about him to his relatives. That father did not leave his constant complaining until he said, "Heavens and Earth! To whom may I complain about you except to these."
      Therefore it is said, "Give ear, ye heavens, and I will speak."

Another interpretation:
"Give ear, ye heavens":
      Rabbi Yehuda says: Is the measure given the righteous at all insufficient! But the world where they live will expand*. For when Israel fulfills the will of God, what is said about them? "The Lord will open unto thee His good treasure the heavens..." (Deut. 28:12). And "opening" is distinctly an expression of "expanding" as it is said, "And He opened her womb." (Genesis 29:31)
      Is the measure given the wicked at all insufficient! But even the world where they live will contract. For when they do not fulfill the will of God, what is said about them? "And Lord's anger be kindled against you and He constrict* the heavens..." (Deut. 11:17). And "constricting" is distinctly an expression of "contracting" as it is said, "For the Lord had fast constricted [the wombs]..." (Genesis 20:18).

Another interpretation:
"Give ear, about[4] the heavens, and I will speak.":
      The Holy One, blessed be He, said to Moses: Tell Israel, "Consider the heavens which I have created to serve you. Perhaps it has changed its custom? Or perhaps the orb of the sun has said, "I will not ascend from the East and light up the entire world."? But this matter is according to that of which it is said, "The sun also ariseth and the sun goeth down." (Ecclesiastes 1:5). And moreover it is happy to do my will, as it is said, "And it is like a bridegroom coming out of his chamber." (Psalms 19:6).

"And hear the words of my mouth about the earth[5]":
----

[4] The midrashist has made the heavens the object of Moses' lesson not the addressee.

[5] The earth is taken here as the object of the lesson.

PISKA 306

Consider the earth which I have created to serve you. Perhaps it has changed its custom? Perhaps you have sown in it and it has not grown? Or perhaps you have sown wheat in it and it brought forth barley? Or perhaps a cow has said, "I will not thresh and I will not plough today."? Or perhaps a donkey has said, "I will not carry the load and I will not go."? And likewise concerning the sea it says, "Fear ye not Me? saith the Lord; will ye not tremble at My presence? Who have placed the sand for the bound of the sea..." (Jeremiah 5:22). For from the time that I set my decree upon it, has it changed its custom and said, "I will arise and drown the world."? But this matter is according to that of which it is said, "And I have prescribed for it My decree and set bars and doors, and said: Thus far thou shalt come, but no further; and here shalt thy proud waves be stayed." (Job 38:10,11). But it is troubled and does not know what to do. The matter is according to that of which it is said, "They toss themselves but they cannot prevail..." (Jeremiah 5:22).

And can it not be argued *a fortiori*:

Since these which are not destined for reward or for deprivation, i.e. if they behave well they receive no reward and if they do ill they receive no punishment, and they care not for the welfare of their sons and their daughters--these have not changed their customs; but you who when behaving well do receive reward and when doing ill receive punishment and you do care for the welfare of your sons and daughters, *a fortiori* you must not change your customs!

Another interpretation:
"Give ear, ye heavens (and I will speak)":

Rabbi Benaya used to say: When a person is found guilty in judgment, only his witnesses may stretch out their hands against him at first, as it is said, "The hand of the witnesses shall be first upon him..." (Deut. 17:7). And gradually, afterwards, that of the people, as it is said, "And afterward the hand of all the people." (Deut. 17:7). So it is that when Israel does not do the will of God, what is said about them? "And the anger of the Lord be kindled against you and he shut up the heaven..." (Deut. 11:17). Gradually afterwards come more ills, as it is said, "And ye perish quickly..." (Deut. 11:17). And when Israel does the will of God what is said about them? "And it shall come to pass in that day, saith the Lord, I will respond with the heavens (and the earth shall respond)..." and then it says, "I will sow her unto Me by the earth." (Hosea 2:23).

Another interpretation:
"Give ear, ye heavens, and I will speak.":

Rabbi Yehuda the son of Hananiah used to say: When Moses said, "Give ear, ye heavens. And I will speak" the Heavens and the utmost Heavens held still*. And

PISKA 306

when he said, "And let the earth hear the words of my mouth," the Earth and everything upon it held still. And if you are bewildered by the matter go out and see that which is said about Joshua: "And he said in the sight of Israel: 'Sun be thou still upon Gibeon; and thou moon, in the valley of Aijalon'. And the sun was still and the moon stayed... And there was no day like that before it...." (Joshua 10:12-14). We find that we have been taught that the righteous have power over the entire universe.

Another interpretation:
"Give ear, ye heavens...":
Since Moses was close to heaven, therefore he said, "Give ear, ye Heavens." And since he was far from the earth he said, "And let the Earth hear the words of my mouth." Isaiah came and stated in conjunction with this usage --"Hear, ye Heavens." (Isaiah 1:2). This was because he was far from heaven. --"And give ear, ye Earth". (Isaiah 1:2). This was because he was close to the earth.

Another interpretation:
Since the *Heavens* are a plurality*-- he specified them in the plural* form»[6]; and since the earth is singular--He specified it by the singular form, "And let the Earth hear[7] the words of my mouth." Isaiah came and stated in conjunction with this usage -- "Hear[8], ye Heavens, and give ear[9], ye Earth." --in order to apply the plural to pluralities and the singular to individuals.

And the Sages say that the matter is not so.* Rather*, when witnesses come and testify their testimony stands if their words are mutually oriented, and if they are not, then their testimony does not stand. So it was that if Moses had said, "Give ear, ye Heavens" and stopped there, the Heavens would have said, "We only listened by *giving ear*." And had he said, "And let the Earth hear the words of my mouth," the Earth would have said, "I only listened by *listening*." Isaiah came and stated in conjunction with this usage --"Hear, ye Heavens and give ear, ye Earth" in order to apply "giving ear" and "listening" to the Heavens and "giving ear" and "listening" to the Earth.

----

[6] I.e. האזינו

[7] I.e. ושמע

[8] I.e. שמעו

[9] I.e. והאזיני

PISKA 306

Another interpretation:
"Give ear, concerning the heavens, and I will speak":
This was said **because the Torah was given from the heavens***, as it is said, "Ye, yourselves, have seen that I talked with you from the Heavens." (Exodus 20:19).

"And concerning the earth hear the words of my mouth":
For Israel stood upon it -- And they said: "Of all which the Lord has spoken we will do and we will hearken." (Exodus 24:7).

Another interpretation:
"Give ear, about the heavens...":
This was said on account of the fact that Israel did not do the commandments, which were given to them, "of the Heavens." And these are the commandments which were given to them, "of the Heavens": **The intercalation of the years*** and the fixing of the months, as it is said, "...and let them be for signs, and for seasons, and for days and years." (Genesis 1:14).

"And hear concerning the earth":
This was said on account of the fact that Israel did not do the commandments which were given to them --"Upon the Earth" and these are the commandments which were given to them "Upon the Earth": the gleanings, the forgotten sheaves, and the corners of the fields; heave offerings and tithes; sabbatical years and jubilee years.

Another interpretation:
"Give ear, about the heavens":
This was said on account of the fact that they did not do all the commandments, which were given to them, "of the Heavens".

"And concerning the earth hear the words of my mouth":
This was said on account of the fact that they did not do the commandments, which were given to them, "of the Earth".

Moses brought to witness against Israel two witnesses which exist eternally and for ever and ever, as it is said, "I call to witness against you this day Heaven and Earth." (Deuteronomy 30:19). And the Holy One, Blessed Be He, brought the *Song* to witness against them, as it is said, "Now therefore write ye this *Song* for you...." (Deuteronomy 31:19). We do not know whose testimony "prevails" --is it the Holy One's, Blessed Be He, or is it Moses'? Since Scripture says, "and this *Song* shall testify before Him as a witness..." (Deuteronomy 31:21).--Thus the Holy One's,

PISKA 306

Blessed Be He, endures overagainst Moses' and Moses' does not endure overagainst the Holy One's.

And for what reason did Moses bring against them two witnesses that live and exist eternally and for ever and ever? He said: "I am flesh and blood, and tomorrow I die. If Israel wanted to say, 'We did not receive the Torah', who could contradict them?" Therefore he brought against them two witnesses that live and exist eternally and for ever and ever.

And the Holy One, Blessed Be He, brought the Song to witness against them. He said: "The *Song* will witness against them from below and I from above." And from where do we know that God is called "a witness"? As it is said, "And I will come near to you in judgment; and I will be a swift witness...." (Malachi 3:5). And Scripture also says: "For I am He who knows and a witness," (Jeremiah 29:23) saith the Lord, and Scripture states "And let the Lord be witness against you, the Lord from His Holy Temple." (Micah 1:2).

2)
"לקחי shall drop ;(יערף) as the rain":

לקחי can only mean "the words of the Torah", as it is said, "For I give good לקח to you, forsake not My Torah." (Proverbs 4:2). **And Scripture further states:** "Take my instruction*, and not silver." (Proverbs 8:10). Now "instruction" distinctly means "the words of the Torah", as it is said, "Hear my son, the *instruction* of thy father, and forsake not the *Torah* of thy mother." (Proverbs 1:8). And Scripture also says, "Hear *instruction* and be wise and refuse it not." (Proverbs 8:33). And likewise Scripture says, "Take fast hold of *instruction*, let her not go." (Proverbs 4:13). Likewise Scripture says, "קחו with you words and return...." (Hosea 4:3). Now "words" distinctly means "the words of the Torah", as it is said, "These *words* the Lord spoke unto all your assembly...." (Deuteronomy 5:19).

"As rain":
Just as rain is life to the world so are the words of the Torah life to the world. But if this is true, then might it not follow:
Just as some of the world is gladdened by rain and some of the world is distressed by it --he whose pit is full of wine and whose threshing floor is readied before him is distressed by it --I might think that such should be the reaction to the words of the Torah!
Therefore Scripture states, "My speech shall distill as the dew,": Just as the whole world is gladdened by dew so is the whole world gladdened by the words of the Torah.

"As the rain winds (שעירים) upon the grass":

PISKA 306

Just as se'irim fall upon the grass and promote their growth*, so do the words of the Torah [raise you and[10]] promote your growth. And so does Scripture say, "Exalt her and she will raise you up." (Proverbs 4:8).

"And as רביבים-drops upon the herb":
Just as rain-drop winds fall upon the grass and make them delightful and fine, so do the words of the Torah make you delightful and fine. And so does Scripture say, "For they shall be a chaplet of grace upon thy head." (Proverbs 1:9) And Scripture also says, "She will give to thy head a chaplet of grace." (Proverbs 4:9)

Another interpretation:
"My teaching (לקחי) shall drop (יערף) as rain":
Rabbi Nehemiah used to say: Indeed **you should accumulate the words of the Torah as general rules***. I might think that just as you are to gather them as general rules you should set them forth as general rules! Yet, Scripture states, "My teaching «לקחי» shall drop «יערף» as rain." And יערף is distinctly a **mercantile term***. For example, one does not say to another, "Break this *sela* into small units for me," but rather "יערף this *sela* for me." So you should accumulate the words of the Torah as general rules and you should break them into smaller units and set them forth as "drops of dew" and not as "drops of rain" which are big units. Rather, you should set them forth as "drops of dew" which are small units.

"As the rain winds (שעירים) upon the grass":
Just as the se'irim fall upon the grass and penetrate them* so they will not become wormy, so you should pore over the words of the Torah in order that you should not forget them. And so Rabbi Yaacov the son of Hanilai said to Rabbi, "Come and let us pore over (the words of the Torah) the *Halachot*, in order that they will not become moldy."

"And as רביבים drops upon the herb":
Just as rain drops fall upon the herbs and cleanse them and enrich them, so you should enrich the words of the Torah by scrutinizing them two, three, four times.

"יערף shall לקחי as rain":
Rabbi Eliezer the son of Rabbi Yosi Hagelili says: "יערף is distinctly an expression of "killing", as it is said, "And they shall break the neck «ערפו» of the

---

[10] These words seem to absent from our commentators text.

PISKA 306

heifer there in the valley." (Deuteronomy 21:4). For which sin does the heifer atone? For bloodshed. And so do the words of the Torah atone for all sins.

"As שעירים upon the grass":
    And for which sin do goats (שעירים) atone? They come for unintentional sins*. So do the words of the Torah atone for unintentional sins.

""And as רביבים upon the herb":
    Just as unblemished lambs (רביבים) are used for the "Tamid"[11] offerings* and atone so do the words of the Torah atone for every sin and transgression.

Another interpretation:
"My teaching shall drop as rain; [תזל My word as dew {טל}]":
    The Sages say: Moses said to Israel, "Perhaps you do not know how much I suffered over the Torah and how much I labored in it and how much I travailed in it."
    --This is according to the matter of which Scripture states: "And he was there with the Lord forty days and forty nights...." (Exodus 34:28). --And Scripture states, "Then I abode in the mount forty days and forty nights." (Deuteronomy 9:9).
    "I entered amongst the angels and I entered amongst the Hayyot and I entered amongst the Seraphim, any one of whom is capable of burning the entire world and its inhabitants." This is according to the matter of which Scripture states, "And above Him stood the Seraphim." (Isaiah 6:2).
    "I have expended my life upon them[12]; I have expended my blood upon them. Just as I learned them in suffering, so you should learn them in suffering."
    But if you say thus, should it not follow that just as you learn them in suffering so you should teach them in suffering*? Therefore Scripture states, "Make cheap «תזל» My word as dew. --You should look upon it as if it is inexpensive, between 1/3 and 1/4 bushels a sela.

"As שעירים upon the grass":
    When a person first goes to study Torah it falls upon him like a se'ir*. And se'ir specifically means "demon", as it is said, "And the wild-cats shall meet with the jackals, and the שעיר shall call to his fellow." (Isaiah 34:14). And Scripture also states, "And שעירים flutter there." (Isaiah 13:21).

----

[11] So reads the Vatican ms (Assemani 32).

[12] Our commentator reads *'alehem* and not *'alehah*.

PISKA 306

Another interpretation:
"יערף לקחי shall as rain":
Rabbi Benaya used to say: If you study the words of the Torah without ulterior motive, the words of the Torah will give you life, as it is said, "For they are life to them that find them." (Proverbs 4:22). But if you do not study the Torah without ulterior motive, they (the words of the Torah) will bring you death, as it is said, "'לקחי shall יערף as rain". And '"Arifah" specifically means killing, as it is said, "And they shall break (ערף) the neck of the heifer there in the valley." (Deuteronomy 21:14). And so does Scripture state, "For she cast down many corpses*; yea, a mighty host are all her slain." (Proverbs 7:26).

Another interpretation:
"יערף לקחי shall as rain":
Rabbi Dostaye son of Yehuda says: If you accumulate the words of the Torah in the way that water accumulates in a cistern, in the end you will merit to behold your Mishna learning, as it is said, "Drink waters out of thine own cistern." (Proverbs 5:15). But if you accumulate the words of the Torah in the way that rain accumulates in a narrow pit, a lengthy ditch, and a spacious cavity, in the end you will water and irrigate others, as it is said, "And running waters out of thine own well." (Proverbs 5:15). And Scripture also states, "Let thy springs be dispersed abroad." (Proverbs 5:16).

Another interpretation:
"יערף לקחי shall as rain":
Rabbi Meir used to say: Indeed, you should accumulate the words of the Torah as general principles. For if you accumulate them as specific cases they will exhaust you and you will not know what to do. This is like the parable of the man who went to Caesarea* and needed 100 or 200 *zuz* for expenses. If he took them in small change it would have exhausted him and he would not have known what to do. Rather, he should combine them and change them into *selaim* and then break these into smaller change which he will spend at every place when he so desires. Likewise, whoever goes to Bet Ilis, to the market, and will need a hundred *manot* or two *ribua* for expenses, if he combines them and changes them into *selaim* they will exhaust him and he will not know what to do. Rather, he should combine them and change them into golden *dinari* and break these into small change which he will spend at every place when he so desires.

"As שעירים upon the grass":

PISKA 306

When a person first goes to study Torah he does not know what to do until he learns two books of Scripture or two sections of Mishna and afterwards it will follow after him like lambs (רביבים). For such reason was it said, כרביבים upon the herb."

Another interpretation:
לקחי shall drop as rain":
Just as the rain falls upon the trees and it **gives delight to each and every one*** according to its specie: to the vine according to its specie, to the olive according to its specie, to the date according to its specie so are the words of the Torah all-inclusive. In it are Scripture, *Mishna*, *Talmud*, *Halachot* and *Haggadot*.

"As שעירים upon the grass":
Just as the rain drop winds fall upon the grass and raise them up, such that there are some grasses which are red, some which are green, some which are black, and some which are white, so do the words of the Torah, such that are some wise people, some honest people, some righteous people, some pious people.

Another interpretation:
Just as you cannot see the rain until it comes --and so it says, "And it came to pass in a little while that the heaven grew black with clouds (and wind)" (1Kings 18:45).---so you cannot recognize a student of the Sages until he teaches *Midrash*, *Halachot* and *Haggadot* or until he is appointed as a public officer over the community.

Another interpretation:
"...shall drop as the rain":
Not like the rain which comes from the south which causes only ruin, causes only disease, and causes only curse, but like the rain which comes from the west* which causes only blessing.
Rabbi Simaye used to say: From whence is it that just as Moses brought the Heavens and the Earth to witness against Israel so he brought the Four Winds of the heavens to witness against them? We know it from that which is said:
לקחי shall drop «יערף» as rain": This describes the west wind which is the strong western back «ערפו» of the world --which causes only blessing.
"It distills as the dew my word": This describes the north wind which makes the sky lambent as gold.
"As שעירים upon the grass": This describes the east wind which renders the sky dark as goats «רביבים».

PISKA 306

"And as רביבים upon the herb": This describes the south wind which spots the sky as goats «רביבים».[13]

Another interpretation:
יערף shall לקחי as rain":
And also did Rabbi Simaye used to say: These four winds were mentioned by Scripture specifically in relationship to the Four Winds of Heaven which blow;
Northern -- in the summer it is beneficial and in the rainy season it is harmful,
Southern -- in the summer it is harmful and in the rainy season it is beneficial,
Eastern -- always harmful,
Western – always difficult*.
The north wind is beneficial to wheat when it is one-third grown and harmful to olives when they are grown. The south wind is harmful to olives when they are one-third grown and beneficial to wheat when it is grown.
And Rabbi Simaye also used to say: All creatures who are created to be heavenly, their soul and their body is of the heavenly realm. All creatures which are to be earthly, their soul and their body are of the earth; except for Man. For his soul is of the heavenly realm and his body is of the earthly realm. Therefore,if a man learns Torah and does the will of His Father who is in heaven, then he is as the creatures of the upper realm, as it is said, "I said, ye are godlike beings, and all of you sons of the Most High." (Psalms 82:6). If he does not learn Torah and does not do the will of his Father who is in heaven then he is like the creatures of the lower realm, as it is said, "Nevertheless ye shall die like men." (Psalms 82:7).
And Rabbi Simaye also used to say: There is no section of Scripture which does not refer to the *resurrection of the dead*; however, we do not have the required capability of interpretation, as it is said, "He will call to the Heavens above and to the Earth, that He may judge His people." (Psalms 50:4). "He will call to the Heavens above," -- this refers to the soul; "and to the Earth to judge His People," -- this refers to the body which is judged with it. And from whence do we know that this specifically refers to the resurrection of the dead*? As it is said, "Come from the four winds, O wind, and breathe upon these slain...." (Ezekiel 47:9).

3)
"For I will proclaim the name of the Lord":
We find that Moses did not mention the name of the Holy One, Blessed Be He, except after twenty-one words*. From whom did he learn this? From the Ministering Angels; for the Ministering Angels do not mention the Name except

----

[13] For the translation here see H. Yalon, *Studies in The Hebrew Language*, Jerusalem, 1971, 163.

PISKA 306

after saying "Holy!" three times, as it is said, "And they called one to the other and said: קָדוֹשׁ קָדוֹשׁ קָדוֹשׁ the Lord of Hosts." (Isaiah 6:3). Moses said, "It is sufficient for me to be reduced one-seventh of the Ministering Angels." And behold the matters should be argued *a fortiori*:

> And just as Moses, who was the wisest of the wise, and the greatest of the great and the father of the prophets did not err by mentioning the name of God but did it after twenty-one words --so it is that he who mentions the name of God in vain does err *a fortiori*.

Rabbi Shimon the son of Yochai says: From whence do we know that one should not say, "To God is this burnt-offering,"; "to God is this meal-offering"; "to God is this peace-offering"; -- but rather, "this burnt-offering is to God"; "this meal-offering is to God"; "this peace-offering is to God"? We know it from the Scripture which states, "An offering to God." (Leviticus 1:2).
Is this not an argument *a fortiori*:

> And just as concerning these offerings, which are hallowed for divine purposes, the Holy One, Blessed Be He, said, "My name shall not be conferred upon them until after they have been hallowed --lest one does wrongly, so does he who mentions the name of the Holy One, Blessed Be He, vainly or in a place of shame all the more so do wrongly.

"For I will proclaim the name of the Lord":

Rabbi Yosi says: From whence do we know that we respond, "Blessed is the Lord who is to be blessed for ever and ever" after they who stand in the synagogue recite, "Bless the Lord who is to be blessed"? We know it from that which is said, "For I will proclaim the name of the Lord --Give praise unto our God".
Rabbi Nehoraye said to him: By Heaven! It is the usual procedure for the soldiers' servant* to stimulate others in regard to war and for the warriors to win."[14]

And from whence do we know that we do not participate in זִמּוּן unless there are three? We know it from that which is said, "For I will proclaim the name of the Lord--give praise to our God."

And from whence do we know that to the one who says ["Bless!" they respond by] "Blessed be the Name[15] whose glorious kingdom is forever"? We know it from

----

[14] Here the reverse is the case. The instigator is the greater one (Moses).

[15] So is the reading in the first printed edition (Venice 1546). It appears to be the correct gloss to an original: From whence do we know to the sayer-- "Blessed be the Name..."

PISKA 306

that which is said, "For I will proclaim the name of the Lord."

And from whence do we know that we say "Amen" after the blesser? We know it from that which is said, "Give praise to our God."

And from whence do we know that we respond, "To eternity and for ever and ever" after they who recite "May His Great Name be blessed." We know it from that which is said, "Give praise to our God."

And from whence* do you say that our ancestors specifically descended to Egypt so that the Holy One, Blessed Be He, could perform miracles and wonders for them and this, so that His Great Name should be sanctified in the world? We know it from that which is said, "And it came to pass in the course of those many days that the king of Egypt died...." (Exodus 2:23). And it further states, "And God heard their groaning and God remembered His covenant." (Exodus 2:24).
And it further states, "When I cry upon the name of the Lord-- Give praise to our God."

And from whence do we know that God specifically brought retribution and specifically brought the Ten Plagues upon Pharaoh and upon Egypt to have His Great Name sanctified in the world? We know it because at the beginning of the episode he stated, "Who is the Lord that I should hearken unto His voice..." (Exodus 5:2), while at the end of the episode he said, "The Lord is righteous and I and my people are wicked." (Exodus 9:27)

And from whence do we know that God specifically performed miracles and wonders at the Sea and at the Jordan and at the Valley of Arnon to have His name sanctified in the world? We know it from that which is said, "And it came to pass, when all the kings of the Amorites, that were beyond the Jordan westward and all her kings...." (Joshua 5:1). And likewise did Rahab say to the agents of Joshua, "For we have heard how the Lord dried up the waters of the Red Sea before you." (Joshua 2:10). Thus does Scripture state, "For I will proclaim the name of the Lord.

And from whence do we know that Daniel specifically descended into the lions' den for the purpose that the Holy One, Blessed Be He, would perform miracles and wonders for him and so that His Great Name would be sanctified in the world? We know it from that which is said, "For I will proclaim the name of the

PISKA 306

Lord." And Scripture also states, "I make a decree, that in all the dominion of my kingdom men tremble and fear before the God of Daniel." (Daniel 6:27).

And from whence do you say that Hananiah, Mishael, and Azaria specifically descended into the fiery furnace so that the Holy One, Blessed Be He, would perform miracles and wonders for them in order that His Great Name would be sanctified in the world? We know it from that which is said, "It hath seemed good unto me to declare the signs and wonders that God the Most High hath wrought toward me." (Daniel 3:32). And Scripture also says, "How great are His signs and how mighty are His wonders." (Daniel 3:33).

And from whence do we know that the Ministering Angels do not mention the name of the Holy One, Blessed Be He, in the heavenly realm, until Israel mentions it in the earthly realm? We know it from that which is said, "Hear, O Israel, the Lord our God, the Lord is One." Deuteronomy 6:4). And Scripture also states, "When the morning stars sang together" (Job 38:7) --and afterwards --"And all the godly ones shouted." "The morning stars" --These refer to Israel who is compared to stars, as it is said, "I will multiply thy seed as the stars of the heavens," (Genesis 22:17). "And all the godly ones shouted," --These refer to the Ministering Angels; and so does Scripture state, "And the godly ones came to present themselves before the Lord." (Job 1:6).

END OF PISKA

PISKA 307

4)
"The Rock (צור)":

I.e. the craftsman (צייר). --For He first fashioned the world and then He formed man within it, as it is said, "And the Lord God crafted (ייצר) the man." (Genesis 2:7).

"His work is perfect*":

His work is perfect in respect to all who have come into the world and none may criticize His works, not even in the least. And none may consider and say, "Would that I had three eyes...," or "Would that I had three hands...," or "Would that I had three feet...," or "Would that I walked upon my head...," or "Would that I had my face turned backwards...", ..."how suitable it would be for me." For Scripture states, "For all His ways are justice." --He sits in judgment in respect of each and every one and provides him with what he deserves.

"A God of אמונה":

For he declared the world worthy (הֶאֱמִין) when he created it*.

"And without iniquity":

For He did not create people to be wicked but to be righteous. And likewise does Scripture state, "Behold, only this I have found that God made man upright, but they have sought out many inventions." (Ecclesiastes 7:29).

"Just and right is He":

He deals uprightly* in respect to all who have come into the world.

Another interpretation:
"The Rock":

I.e. The Mighty One.

"His work is perfect":

His work is perfect in respect to all those who have come into the world and none may criticize His works, not a whit of criticism. And none may consider and say: "How did the people of the Flood Generation deserve* to be drowned in water?" Or, "How did the people at the tower deserve that they should be dispersed from one end of the world to the other?" Or, "How did the people of Sodom deserve to be deluged by fire and brimstone?" Or, "How did Aaron deserve to receive the Priesthood?" Or, "How did David deserve to receive the Kingship?" Or, "How did Korach and his assembly deserve that the earth should swallow them?" For

PISKA 307

Scripture states, "For all his ways are justice." --He sits in judgment of each and every one and gives him what he deserves.

"A God of faithfulness":
    I.e. **The trustee***.

"And without iniquity":
    He collects His debts after meeting His obligations. The manners of the Holy One, Blessed Be He, are not like those of flesh and blood. The manner of flesh and blood is that when one, who owes one hundred, gave his creditor a purse of two hundred in trust and now comes to retrieve his purse --he can be told, "subtracting the hundred that you owe me --here is the rest!". And likewise when a workman, working for his boss to whom he owes a *dinar*, comes to collect his wages --he can be told, "subtracting the *dinar* that you owe me --here is the rest!"
    But "He Who Spoke And The World Was" is not like this; "He is a faithful God" --i.e. the trustee. "And without iniquity." --i.e. He collects his debts after meeting his obligations.

"Just and right is He":
    This is according to the Scripture which states, "For the Lord is righteous, He loveth righteousness." (Psalms 11:7).

Another interpretation:
"The Rock":
    I.e. The Mighty One.

"His work is perfect":
    The dues of those who have come into the world are perfectly administered by Him, the bestowing of reward due the righteous and the placing of punishment due the wicked. The former receive nothing due them in This World and the latter receive nothing due them in This World. And from whence do we know that the righteous receive nothing due them in This World? We know it from that which is said, "O how abundant is thy goodness which thou hast laid up for them that fear thee." (Psalms 31:20). And from whence do we know that the wicked receive nothing due them in This World? We know it from that which is said, "Is this not laid up with Me, sealed up in my treasuries..." (Deuteronomy 32:34). When shall both these and those receive it?

"For all His ways are justice":

PISKA 307

--On the Future Morrow when He sits upon the Throne of Justice in respect to the judgment of each and every one and gives him what he deserves.

"A God of faithfulness":
Just as He pays the completely righteous man in the Next World the reward for the precept fulfilled in This World, so does He pay the completely wicked man in This World the recompense for the light precept done in This World. And just as He exacts punishment from the completely wicke man in the Next World for the sin committed in This World, so does He exact punishment from the completely righteous man in This World for the sin committed in This World.

"And without iniquity":
When a man departs from the world all his deeds come before him to be enumerated and he is told: "Such and such you did on this certain day and such and such you did on that certain day. Do you declare these words to be worthy?" And he says, "Yea!"
He is told: "Sign!" This is as it is said, "By hand, every man shall sign that all men may make known their deed." (Job 37:7).

"Just and right is He":
And he declares the judgment to be righteous by saying: "I have been judged properly." And so does Scripture state, "That thou mayest be justified by thy words." (Psalms 51:6).

Another tradition:
"The Rock His work is perfect":
When Rabbi Hanina the son of Teradyon was apprehended, it was decreed that he should be burned with his scroll.
They said to him: "It has been decreed that you are to be burned with your scroll."
He recited this Scripture, "The Rock, His work is perfect."
They said to his wife: "It has been decreed that your husband is to be burned and that you are to be decapitated.
She recited this Scripture, "A God of faithfulness and without iniquity."
They said to his daughter: "It has been decreed that your father is to be burned and your mother is to be decapitated and that you are to perform *duty*.
She recited this Scripture, "Great in counsel, and mighty in work; whose eyes are open...." (Jeremiah 32:19).

PISKA 307

Said Rabbi: "How great were these righteous people who in their hour of suffering readily specified the three verses which remain unparalleled in all of Scripture for their acknowledgement of God's righteous judgment!"

The three of them directed their hearts and justified the judgment that came upon them.

Philosophus[16] opposed* his commander. He said, "My lord, do not let your mind gloat that you have burned the Torah*, for from the time* it departed it returned to its Father's house." He replied: "Tomorrow, so also may your judgment be* as theirs." He said to him: "You have given me good news* that on the Future Morrow my portion may be with them in the Next World."

Another interpretation:
"The Rock His work is perfect":
When Moses descended from Mount Sinai, Israel gathered about him. They said to him, "Our master Moses, tell us what heavenly justice is like."
He replied to them, "Have I not said we should note the justification of the innocent* and the dues of the guilty? But even should we note the opposite* -- He is a God of faithfulness and without iniquity."
END OF PISKA

----

[16] See the note to the medieval commentary on this passage.

PISKA 308

5)
"Is corruption His? Not (so); His children's is the blemish":
Even though they are full of blemishes they are called "His children". These are the words of Rabbi Meir. --As it is said, "His children's is the blemish." (Deuteronomy 32:4).
Rabbi Yehuda says: They have no blemishes, as it is said, "Not His children's is the blemish."
...And likewise does Scripture state, "A seed of evil-doers, children that deal corruptly." (Isaiah 1:4). If they are called "children" even when they deal corruptly; if they would not deal corruptly how much more so should they be called "children"!

A similar argument to this is:
"They are wise to do evil" (Jeremiah 4:22): And are not these words subject to an *a fortiori* interpretation?
--Since they are called "wise" even when they do evil; if they would do good, how much more so should they be called "wise"!

A similar argument to this is:
"They are sottish children" (Jeremiah 4:22): Since they are called "children", even when they are sottish; if they would be judicious, how much more so should they be called "children"!

A similar argument to this is:
"And they will come unto thee as the people cometh and sitteth before thee as My people and hear thy words" (Ezekiel 33:31): I might think that they will hear and *do* them. But Scripture states, "But do them not...."(Ezekiel 33:31).
And are not these words subject to an *a fortiori* interpretation:
Since they are called "My people", even when they hear but do them not; if they would hear and do them, how much more so should they be called "My people"!

They said in the name of Abba Hadores: Israel became corrupt through all the negative commandments that are in the Torah*! --And why use such an expression* ? --In order to silence potential arguments of the wicked to the effect that whenever we sin before Him, "we" are pained before Him.
To what may the matter be compared? --to one who went to be executed and his father cried for him and his mother threw herself before him. The one said, "Woe is me!" and the other said, "Woe is me!" But this woe is produced only for he

PISKA 308

who goes out to be executed. And likewise does Scripture state, "Woe unto their soul when they have recompensed them with calamity." (Isaiah 3:9).

"A generation crooked and twisted":
    Moses said to Israel, "You are crooked and twisted people* and you will go nowhere except into the fire". --To what may the matter be compared? To one who had in his hand a twisted staff and he gave it to the craftsman to repair. He repairs it by fire*, and if this does not work, then he straightens it by the press, and if this does not work then he chisels it with an adze and he throws it into the fire*. And likewise does Scripture say, "And I will hand thee into the hand of men of burning, skillful to destroy." (Ezekiel 21:36).

Another interpretation:
    Moses said to Israel: "In the way in which you have behaved, I have behaved towards you." --For so does Scripture state, "With the pure thou dost show thyself pure; and with the *crooked* thou dost show thyself *subtle* (עקש תתפל) (2Samuel 22:27) --"A generation crooked and crooked."
    END OF PISKA

PISKA 309

6)
"Do ye thus requite the Lord":

They told a parable: To what may the matter be compared?-- To one who stood in the market place and **reviled* a councilman***. Those who heard him said, "To whom, you common fool, do you stand and hurl insult: against a councilman! What if he wanted to beat you or to tear your garment or to incarcerate you in prison, could you possibly check him? Were he a *centurion*, who is of higher rank than he, how much more so would you be a fool, and were he a councillor, which is of superior rank to both of these, how more so would you be a fool!"

"Do ye thus requite the Lord":

A parable: To what may the matter be compared?--To one who stood in the marketplace and hurled insult against his father. Those who heard him said to him: "You common fool, against whom do you stand and hurl insult! Against your father!! Listen--how much he toiled for you, how much did he labor for you! If in the past you have not honored him you must now honor him lest he inscribe all his property to others."

So Moses spoke to Israel: If you do not remember the miracles and wonders that the Holy One, Blessed Be He, did for you in Egypt, acknowledge how many kindnesses He will ultimately provide for you in the World to Come.

"O foolish people and unwise":

"Foolish -- about that which is past.

"And unwise" -- about the Future to Come.

A similar exegesis is:

"But Israel doth not know" (Isaiah 1:3) -- about the past.

"My people doth not consider" (Isaiah 1:3) -- about the Future.

And what was the cause that made Israel to be foolish and unwise? --They did not gain enlightenment through the words of the Torah. And so does Scripture state, "Is not their tent-cord plucked within them? They die, and that without wisdom." (Job 4:21).

"Is He not thy Father קָנֶךָ":

Shimon the son of Halafta says in his name*: If you were a weak person on top and there was a strong warrior beneath, who would prevail? Could you perhaps subdue him! And all the more so will the upper party prevail when the strong warrior is above and the weak person beneath. And so does Scripture state: "Be not

PISKA 309

rash with thy mouth and let not thy heart be hasty to utter a word before God; for God is in heaven and thou upon earth." (Ecclesiastes 5:1).

"Is He not thy Father that hath gotten thee":
Moses said to Israel: You are his beloveds, you are his acquisition, but you are not His inheritance.
This is comparable to the matter of one whose father bequeathed ten fields to him. He arose and acquired a field of his own and he loved it better than all the fields his father bequeathed him. And likewise it is comparable to the matter of one whose father bequeathed him ten residences and he arose and acquired one residence of his own and he loved that one more than all the residences his father had left him.
So Moses said to Israel, "You are His beloveds; you are His acquisition; you are not his inheritance."

"That possesses thee" (קָנֶךָ):
This is one of the three which were called "possessions* of God" (קִנְיָן). The Torah is called "God's possession", as it is said, "The Lord possessed me as the beginning of his way." (Proverbs 8:22). "Israel is called God's possession", as it is said, "Is He not thy Father that possesses thee." The Temple is called "God's possession", and so does Scripture state, "This mountain, which His right hand had possessed." (Psalms 78:54).

"Hath He not made thee and thy כֵּן":
Rabbi Meir used to say: The till which contains everything*: Priests from its midst, prophets from its midst, sages from its midst, scribes* from its midst. And likewise does Scripture state, "Out of them shall come forth the corner-stone, out of them the stake...." (Zechariah 10:4).
Rabbi Yehuda says: He made you kwin kwin* (--full of cavities).
Rabbi Shimon the son of Yehuda says: He placed you upon your foundation; He nourished you* with the plunder of the Seven Nations. He gave you what He promised you and He bequeathed to you what He promised you. Rabbi Dostaye the son of Yehuda says: He arranged your inner structure to be full of chambers and chambers* such if one of them would infringe upon another, you could not exist.
END OF PISKA

PISKA 310

7)
"Remember the days of old":
   He said to them: Remember what I did to the first Generations, that which I did to the people of the Generation of the Flood, and that which I did to the people of the Generation of the Dispersion and that which I did to the People of Sodom.

"Consider the years of generations and generations":
   You do not find a generation in which there is not the likes of the people of the Generation of the Flood and you do not find a generation in which there is not the likes of the People of Sodom; however, each one is judged according to his deeds.

"Ask thy father and he will declare unto thee":
   This refers to the *Prophets*. It is according to the Scripture which states, "And Elisha saw it and he cried, 'My father, my father....'". (2Kings 2:12).

"Thine elders and they will tell you":
   This refers to the *Elders*. It is according to the Scripture which states, "Gather unto Me seventy men of the Elders of Israel...." (Numbers 11:16).

Another interpretation:
"Remember the days of עולם":
   He said to them: Whenever the Holy One, Blessed Be He, brings suffering upon you, remember how many good things and consolations He will ultimately bestow upon you in the World to Come (עולם).

"Consider the years of generation and generation":
   This refers to the Generation of the Messiah which will have in it three generations, as it is said, "They shall fear you as long as the sun endureth and so long as the moon, throughout generation -- generations." (Psalms 72:5).

"Ask thy Father and He will declare unto thee":
   In the Future Era Israel is destined to see and hear as they who hear from the mouth of the Holy One, Blessed Be He, as it is said, "And thy ears shall hear a word behind thee, saying...." And Scripture also states, **Yet shall not thy teacher be removed anymore*** but thine eyes shall see thy Teacher (Is. 30:20)."

"Thine elders and they will tell you":

PISKA 310

Of that which I showed the Elders on the mountain. This is according to the matter of which Scripture speaks, as it is said, "And unto Moses He said: Come up unto the Lord...." (Exodus 24:1).

END OF PISKA

8)
"When the Most High gave to the nations their inheritance":

Before Father Abraham came, the Holy One, Blessed Be He -- as if it were possible -- judged the world ruthlessly. When the people of the Generation of the Flood sinned, He cast them like bags* upon the surface of the waters. When the People of the Tower sinned He scattered them from one end of the world to the other. When the People of Sodom sinned He destroyed them with brimstone and fire. But when Father Abraham came to the world he merited to receive painful tribulations*. They gradually began to manifest themselves*. This is according to the Scripture which states, "Now there was a famine in the Land and Abram went down to Egypt." (Genesis 12:10).

And if you should ask: Why does suffering come? --Because of the belovedness of Israel: "He specified the boundary of the Nations according to the number of the sons of Israel."

Another tradition:
"When the Most High gave to the nations their inheritance":

When the Most High gave the world to the nations He separated the boundaries of every nation in order that they should not become intermixed. He sent the Gomerians to Gomer, the Magogians to Magog, the Medians to Media, the Yavonites to Yavon, the Tubalites to Tubal. He separated the boundaries of the nations in order that they should not enter the Land of Israel: "He specified the boundary of the Nations*."

Another interpretation:
"When the Most High gave to the nations their inheritance":

When the Holy One, Blessed Be He, gave the Torah to Israel, He stood and looked out and contemplated, as it is said, "He standeth and measureth the earth, He looks and makes the nations to tremble." (Habakkuk 3:6). And there was no nation amongst the nations which was worthy to receive the Torah except Israel: "He specified the boundary of the Nations."

Another interpretation:
"When the Most High gave to the nations their inheritance":

When the Holy One, Blessed Be He, gave the Gentile Nations of the World their inheritance, their portion was in Gehinnom, as it is said: "Assyria is there and all her company..."; "There are the princes of the North and all the Sidonians" (Ezekiel 32:22).

PISKA 311

"There is Edom, her kings...." (Ezekiel 32:29).
And if you should ask: "Who shall take their wealth and their glory?" --I should say, "It is Israel.": "He specified the boundary of the Nations."

Another interpretation:
"When the Most High gave to the nations their inheritance":
When the Holy One, Blessed Be He, gave His inheritance – it was through those nations which were the fearer's of sin and the decent amongst them*.

"When He separated the children of men":
This refers to the Generation of the Dispersion, as it is said, "And from thence did the Lord scatter them abroad upon the face of all the earth." (Genesis 11:9).
Rabbi Eliezer the son of Rabbi Yosi Haglili says: Behold Scripture states, "There are sixty royalties* and eighty concubines* (Song of Songs 6:8)." The sum is one hundred and forty. The number of our ancestors which descended to Egypt was but "seventy souls", as it is said, "Thy father went down into Egypt with three score and ten persons." (Deuteronomy 10:22). And likewise does Scripture state, "The borders of the peoples" -- "גבולי עמים" is not written here but --- "גבולות עמים". The nations merited to take two portions* in relation "to the number of the Children of Israel".

END OF PISKA

9)
"For the portion of the Lord is His people":
This is comparable to the matter of the king who had a field and gave it to tenant farmers. The tenant farmers began to plunder it. He took it from them and gave it to their children who began to be worse than their predecessors. He took it from their children and gave it to their grandchildren. They became much worse than their predecessors. When a son was born to him, he said to them, "Get off my property, I do not want you to be on it. Give me my portion that I may have it identified as mine."

In like fashion, when Father Abraham came into the world there issued from him the dreg of Ishmael and all the children of Ketura. Isaac came into the world -- there issued from him the dreg of Esau and all the chiefs of Edom. They became much worse than their predecessors. When Jacob came no dreg issued from him but all his children were born upright people. This is according to the matter of which Scripture states, "Jacob was a perfect man dwelling in tents." (Genesis 25:27).

From whence does God have His portion identified as His? From Jacob, as it is said, "For the portion of the Lord is His people, Jacob the lot of His inheritance." And the Scripture also states, "For the Lord Jacob hath chosen." (Psalm 135:4). But the matter still remains ambiguous and we do not know whether the Holy One, Blessed Be He, chose Jacob or Jacob chose the Holy One, Blessed Be He. --Scripture states, "Israel, to be His treasured one." (Psalm 135:4). But the matter still remains ambiguous and we do not know if the Holy One, Blessed Be He, chose "Israel to be His treasured one" (Deuteronomy 14:2), or if Israel chose the Holy One, Blessed Be He. --Scripture states, "And the Lord thy God hath chosen thee to be His own treasured people." (Jeremiah 10:16).

And from whence do we know that Jacob also "chose the Lord"? We know it from that which is stated, "Not like these is the portion of Jacob. (Jeremiah 10:16). (For He is the former of all things and Israel is the חבל of His inheritance, the Lord of Hosts is His name)." --"Jacob the חבל of his inheritance": חבל distinctly means "allotment", as it is said, "The allotments (חבלים) are fallen unto me in pleasant places." (Psalms 16:6). And Scripture also states, "And there fell ten allotments (חבלים) to Manasseh," (Joshua 17:5); "Out of the allotments (חבלים) of the Children of Judah was the inheritance of the Children of Simeon." (Joshua 19:9).

Another tradition:
Just as this (Rope[17]-domain)[18] is threefold so was Jacob the third of the

----

[17] *HBL* can mean both rope and domain.

PISKA 312

Patriarchs and received the advantage of all the others. --Concerning Abraham's birth, what does Scripture say? "And a brother is born for adversity[19]*." (Proverbs 17:17).--Concerning Isaac's birth, what does Scripture say? "Two are better than one." (Ecclesiastes 4:9) -- And concerning Jacob's birth, what does it say? "And the three-fold cord* is not quickly broken." (Ecclesiastes 4:12).

END OF PISKA

----

[18] "Domain" is absent in J. and was added between the lines in O. See F. 352.

[19] Heb. "Tsara" read as "Sarah"; i.e. a brother for Sarah who was Abraham's half sister.

PISKA 313

10)
"He found him in a desert land":
This refers to Father Abraham. It is like the parable of the king who went out with his soldiers to the desert. His soldiers left him in a place of unrest, in a place of invaders, in a place of robbers, and they went upon their way. A certain warrior was appointed to him. He said, "My lord King, let not thy heart be faint and have no fears. By thy life, I shall not leave you until you enter your royal residences and sleep upon your bed." --This is according to the matter of which Scripture states, "I, the Lord who brought you out of Ur Casdim." (Genesis 15:7).

"He compasseth him about":
This is according to the matter of which Scripture states, "And the Lord said to Abram, 'Get thee out of thy land'." (Genesis 12:1).

"He instructed him":
Before Father Abraham came into the world, the Holy One, Blessed Be He, -- as if it were possible, was only the king of the heavens, as it is said, "The Lord, the God of heaven, who took me...." (Genesis 24:7). However, when Father Abraham came into the world, he accorded Him dominion over the heavens and over the earth. This is according to the matter of which Scripture states, "And I will make thee swear by the Lord, the God of heaven and the God of earth".(Genesis 24:2).

"He kept him as the apple of his eye":
Even if God had wanted his eyeball he would have given it to Him. And not only his eyeball would he have given but also his soul which was more dear to him than anything, as it is said, "Take I pray thee, your son, your only one, Isaac." (Genesis 22:2). And is it not obvious that this, his son, was his "only one"? -- But it is the soul which is called "the only one", as it is said, "Deliver my *soul* from the sword, mine *only one* from the power of the dog." (Psalms 22:21).

Another interpretation:
"He found him in a desert land":
This refers to Israel, as it is said, "I found Israel like grapes in the wilderness." (Hosea 9:10).

"And in the waste, a howling wilderness":
In a place of distress, in a place of invaders, in a place of robbers.

PISKA 313

"He compassed him round about":
>Before Mount Sinai. This is according to the matter of which Scripture states, "And thou shalt set bounds unto the people round about, saying...." (Exodus 19:12).

"He gave him wisdom*":
>Through the Ten Commandments. It teaches us here that when the utterance went out from the mouth of the Holy One, Israel could see it and they gained knowledge from it and they knew how much *Midrash* there is in it, and how much *Halacha* there is in it, and how many *a fortiori* arguments[20] there are in it and how many *arguments by analogy* there are in it.

"He kept him as the apple of His eye":
>Going twelve *mil* and returning twelve *mil* in conjunction with every utterance, but they were frightened neither by the sounds nor by the torches.

Another interpretation:
"He ascertained for him*":
>Everything was ready-made and prepared for them in the desert. A well arose for them, manna came down for them, quail was prepared for them, The Clouds of Glory surrounded them.

"And in the waste, a howling wilderness":
>In a place of unrest, in a place of invaders (in a place of filth) in a place of robbers.

"He compassed him about":
>With banners -- three on the north, three on the south, three on the east, three on the west.

"He gave him wisdom":
>Through two gifts -- so that when one from the Gentile Nations would extend his hand to misappropriate some manna -- his hand would not receive anything; to fill up with water from the well -- his hand would not receive anything.

"He kept him as אישר ן עינו":
>This is according to the matter of which Scripture states, "Rise up, O Lord, and let thine enemies be scattered: and let them that hate thee flee before thee".

----

[20] See my remarks concerning this passage in ch5.

PISKA 313

(Numbers 10:35).

Another interpretation:
"He found him in a desert land":
This refers to the Future to Come. As it is said, "Therefore, behold I will allure her, and bring her into the wilderness and speak tenderly unto her." (Hosea 2:16).

"And in the waste, a howling wilderness":
These are to the Four Kingdoms*. This is according to the matter of which Scripture states, "Who led thee through the great and dreadful wilderness."(Deuteronomy 8:15).

"He compassed him about ":
Through the Elders.

"He gave him wisdom":
Through the Prophets.

"He kept him as the apple of His eye":
He guarded them from the demons that they should not harm them.
This is according to the matter of which Scripture states, "Surely he that toucheth you toucheth the apple of His eye." (Zechariah 2:12).
END OF PISKA

11)
"As an eagle that stirreth up his nest":
Just as an eagle before coming to his nest, painstakingly with his wings between two trees or two thickets, causes a disturbance for his children, in order that they should be stirred up so as to have the strength to receive him; so when the Holy One, Blessed Be He, came to give the Torah to Israel, He did not come to them from one direction but from four directions, as it is said, "The Lord came from Sinai and rose from Seir unto them...." (Deuteronomy 33:2). Which is the fourth direction? --"God cometh from Teman." (Habakkuk 3:3)

"Spreadeth abroad his wings, taketh them":
This is according to the matter of which Scripture states: "And in the wilderness, where thou hast seen how that the Lord thy God bore thee...."

PISKA 314

(Deuteronomy 1:31)

"Beareth them on his pinions":
    This is according to the matter of which Scripture states:
"And how I bore you on eagles' wings...." (Exodus 19:4).

Another interpretation:
"As an eagle that stirreth up his nest":
    This refers to the Future to Come, as it is said, "The voice of my beloved,
behold he comes...." (Song of Songs 2:8).

"Spreadeth abroad his wings":
    This is according to the verse which states: "I will say to the north: 'Give up',
and to the south: 'Keep not back...'." (Isaiah 43:6).

"Beareth them on his pinions":
    This is according to the matter of which Scripture states: "And they shall
bring their sons in their bosom." (Isaiah 49:22).

END OF PISKA

PISKA 315

12)
"The Lord did set them down alone":
The Holy One, Blessed Be He, said to them, "Just as you have dwelt alone in This World and have no benefit from the Gentile Nations at all, so ultimately will I cause you to dwell alone in the Future and not one of the Gentile Nations shall have benefit from you at all."
"And there was no strange el with him":
--Such that any of the angels of the Gentile Nations may have authority to come and rule over them. This is according to the matter of which Scripture states, "And when I go forth, lo, the angel of Greece shall come" (Daniel 10:20); "But the angel of the kingdom of Persia withstood me" (Daniel 10:13); "Howbeit, I will declare unto thee that which is inscribed in the writing of the truth...." (Daniel 10:21).

Another interpretation:
"The Lord did set them down alone":
Ultimately I am to cause you to inhabit possessions from one end of the world to the other. And so does Scripture state: "...From the east side unto the west side: Asher one portion,"; "...From the east side even unto the west side: Reuben one portion,"; "...From the east side even unto the west side: Judah one portion." (Ezekiel 48:2-7).
What is it that Scripture states: "Dan one,"; "Judah one,"; "Asher one,"*? --It is that ultimately Israel is to take; lengthwise; from the east unto the west, by widthwise: twenty-five thousand rods which measurement is seventy-five mil.
"And there was no strange el with him":
So that there will not be amongst you men who worship idols. And so does Scripture state, "Therefore by this shall the sin of Jacob be expiated...." (Isaiah 27:9).

Another interpretation:
"The Lord did set them down alone":
Ultimately I will cause you to dwell with repose in the world.

"And there was no el נכר with him":
There will not be amongst you men engaged in any type of business, as it is said, "There shall be the fistful of the grain in the earth," (Psalms 72:16) --so that the grains shall produce loaves by the handful; "May his fruit rustle like the Lebanon." (Psalms 72:16) --so that the grains will rub against each other and let their flour

PISKA 315

drop to the ground and you will come and take a handful of it and it will come to provide your sustenance.

END OF PISKA

PISKA 316

13)
"He enthroned it[21] on the high places of the earth":
     This refers to the Land of Israel which is higher than all the other countries.
This is according to the matter of which Scripture states, "We should go up at once
and possess it." (Numbers 13:30). And it also states, "So they went up and spied put
the Land," (Numbers 13:21); "And they went up into the South, and came unto
Hebron." (Numbers 13:22) And it also states, "And they went up out of Egypt (and
they came to the Land of Canaan)." (Genesis 45:25).

"And he did eat of the fruitage of the fields":
     This refers to the fruitage of the Land of Israel which are light to eat*--
lighter than the fruits of all other countries.

"And he made him to suck honey out of the crag":
     For example, in the vicinity of Sachne*. It once happened that Rabbi Yehuda
said to his son, "Go and bring me hardened figs from the barrel." He replied,
"Father, it is of honey!" He said to him, "Dip your hand into it and you will lift out
dried figs from it."

"And oil out of the flinty rock":
     This refers to the olives of Gush Halab. It once happened that Rabbi Yosi
said to his son in Sepphoris, "Go up and bring us olives from the upper story." He
went and found the upper story covered with oil.
                              END OF PISKA

----

[21] The reference is to the nest, QNH, in verse 11.

PISKA 317

14)
"Curd of oxen and milk of sheep":
    This occurred in the days of Solomon, as it is said, "Ten fat oxen, and twenty oxen out of the pastures and a hundred sheep...." (1Kings 5:3).

"With fat of lamb and rams...":
    This occurred in the days of the Ten Tribes, as it is said, "And eat the lambs out of the flock and the calves out of the midst of the stall...." (Amos 6:4).

"With kidney fat of wheat":
    This occurred in the days of Solomon, as it is said, "And Solomon's provision for one day was thirty *kor* of fine flour." (1Kings 5:2).

"And of the blood of the grape thou drankest foaming wine":
    This occurred in the days of the Ten Tribes, as it is said, "That drank wine in bowls...." (Amos 6:6).

Another interpretation:
13)
"He enthroned it[22] on the high places of the earth":
    This refers to the Temple which is higher than the whole world, as it is said, "Then thou shalt arise and get thee up unto the place." (Deuteronomy 17:8). And Scripture also states, "And many peoples shall go and say: 'Come ye, and let us go up to the mountain of the Lord'." (Isaiah 2:3).

"And he did eat of the fruitage of the field":
    This refers to the baskets of the first-fruits.

"And he made him to suck honey out of the crag and oil out of the flinty rock":
    This refers to the libations of oil.

14)
"Curd of oxen and milk of sheep with fat of lambs":
    These refer to the sin-offering, the burnt-offering, peace- offerings, thanks-giving offerings, guilt-offerings and minor sacrifices.

----

[22] The reference is to the nest, QNH, in verse 11.

"With kidney fat of wheat":
> This refers to the dishes of flour.

"And of the blood of the grape thou drankest foaming wine":
> This refers to the libations of wine.

Another interpretation:
"He enthroned it[23] on the high places of the earth":
> This refers to the Torah, as it is said, "The Lord made me as the beginning of His way." (Proverbs 8:22).

"And he did eat of the fruitage of the field":
> This refers to Scripture.

"And he made him to suck honey out of the crag":
> This refers to the *Mishna*.

"And oil out of the flinty rock":
> This refers to the *Talmud*.

"Curd of oxen and milk of sheep with fat of lambs":
> These refer to the **arguments** *a fortiori*, **the arguments by analogy, and comparisons*** and refutations.

"With the kidney fat of wheat":
> These refer to those laws which are the essence of the Torah.

"And of the blood of the grape thou drankest foaming wine":
> This refers to the *Aggadah* which lures man's heart as wine.

Another interpretation:
"**He enthroned it**[24] **on the high places of the earth**":
> **This refers to the world***, as it is said, "The boar out of the woods doth ravage it." (Psalms 80:4).

----

[23] The reference is to the nest, QNH, in verse 11.

[24] The reference is to ya'ir, in verse 11 which resonates with ya'ar here.

PISKA 317

"And he did eat of the fruitage of the field":
    This refers to the Four Kingdoms.

"And he made him to suck honey out of the crag and oil out of the flinty rock":
    These are the vine arrays that are in the Land of Israel[25]*.

"Curd of oxen":
    This refers to their **hypytqin and hegemonim***.

"With kidney fat":
    This refers to the **Kali-riqin***.

"And rams":
    This refers to their centurions.

"Of the breed of bashan":
    This refers to the **pokiron.**

"And he-goats":
    This refers to their senators.

"With kidney fat of wheat":
    This refers to their matrons.

"And the blood of the grape thou drankest foaming wine":
    On the Future Morrow Israel will inherit their properties and it will be as pleasing to them as oil and as honey.[26]

Another interpretation:
"With kidney fat of wheat":

----

[25] It seems that our commentator's text read ATSYN (vine arrays) not MATSYKYM (oppressors) and nothing more, unlike our texts which read, "oppressors who have taken possession of the Land of Israel and it is more difficult to get a penny from them than from a flint. On the Future Morrow, Israel will inherit their properties and it will be as pleasing to them as oil and honey."

[26] The comment has been editorially delayed to this point in order although its real place is above in vs 13.

PISKA 317

In the Future every single grain will be like two kidneys of a large ox - weighing four Sepphorian pounds. And if you should be amazed at this matter, consider the turnip heads. It once happened the weight of a turnip head was thirty Sepphorian pounds. And it once happened that a fox made his nest in a turnip head. It once happened with some plants; there was a mustard stalk which had three twigs on it and one of them **split off*** and they used it to cover a potter's hut. They struck it and they found in it nine *kabim* of mustard. Said Rabbi Shimon the son of Halafta, "There was a cabbage stalk in the middle of my house and I used to go up and down it as one goes up and down a ladder."

Another interpretation:
"And the blood of the grape thou drankest foaming wine":
That you should not become wearied by treading or harvesting but you will bring it in a wagon and stand it in a corner and it will constantly renew the supply that you may drink from it as you drink from a **vat***.

END OF PISKA

PISKA 318

15)
"But Jeshurun waxed fat, and kicked":
    From a sated state they were fit*. And similarly you will find that the people
of the Generation of the Flood rebelled against the Holy One, Blessed Be He,
specifically under circumstances of food and drink, and under circumstances of
tranquillity. And what does Scripture say about them? "Their houses are tranquil
without fear...." (Job 21:9).
    --the rest of the *baraita* is as related in *eleh devarim* etc.[27]
And so we have found that the People of the Tower rebelled against the Holy One,
Blessed Be He, specifically under circumstances of tranquillity, as it is said, "And all
the earth was of one language.*" (Genesis 11:1). And so we have found that the
People of Sodom rebelled specifically under the circumstances of food, as it is said,
"As for the earth, out of it cometh bread..." (Job 28:5) --And the Mishna[28]: -- And
----

[27] PISKA 43:
"Their bull gendereth etc.",(Job 21:10) "They send forth their little ones like a flock etc.", (Job 21:11),
"They spend their days in prosperity etc.",(Job 21:13), --this instigated them: "They said unto God,
Depart from us (Job 21:14)." "What is the Almighty that we should serve Him etc., (Job 21:15), (what
profit should we have?)". They said: It amounts to a drop of rain -- we do not need Him -- "And there
went up a mist from the earth (and watered the whole face of the ground)" (Gen. 2:6).
The Almighty said to them: Through this very goodness with which I graced you,   you lord it over
Me -- through it I will punish you: "And the rain was upon the earth forty days and forty nights." (Gen.
7:12).
Rabbi Yosi ben Dormasqit says: Just as they cast their eyes, the upper and the lower, in order to
perform their lusts so also did the Almighty open upon them the fountains, the upper and the lower, in
order to destroy them, as it is said, "On the same day were all the fountains of the great deep broken
up, and the windows of heaven were opened." (Gen. 7:12).

[28] PISKA 43:
"As for the earth, out of it cometh bread", (Job 28:5). "The stones thereof are the place of sapphires",
(Job 28:6). "That path no bird of prey knoweth", (Job 28:7). "The proud beasts have not trodden it
etc," (Job 28:8). --The People of Sodom said, "We have food! We have silver and gold! Let us arise and
cause the 'Law of Hospitality to Wayfarers' to be eradicated from our land!"
The Almighty said to them, "Through this very goodness with which I graced you, you seek to cause
the 'Law of Hospitality to Wayfarers' to be eradicated from amongst yourselves -- I, then, will cause
you to be eradicated from the world".
What does Scripture say about them? --"He breaketh open a shaft from where men sojourn."; (Job
28:4)."A contemptible brand etc."; (Job 12:5). "The tents of robbers prosper, and they that provoke are
secure." (Job 12:6). This instigated them --"against he whom the Lord brought into their hand." (Job
12:6). And so does Scripture say, "As I liveth saith the Lord God ... Behold this was the iniquity of thy

PISKA 318

likewise Scripture states, "As I live saith the Lord God, if Sodom (thy sister and her daughters) hath done...." (Ezekiel 16:48).

And once Rabbi Gamliel and Rabbi Yehoshua and Rabbi Elazar ben Azaria and Rabbi Akiba entered Rome -- and the rest of this is a *Baraita* in *Eleh Devarim*[29].

And similarly you will find that the People of the Desert rebelled specifically under circumstances of food and drink, as it is said, "And the people sat down to eat and to drink, and rose up to make merry." (Exodus 32:6). What is it the Scripture says about them? "They have turned aside quickly out of the way...." (Exodus 32:8).

The Holy One, Blessed Be He, said to Moses: Tell Israel: When you enter the Land, ultimately you will rebel specifically under circumstances of food and drink and under circumstances of tranquillity, as it is said, "For when I shall have brought them into the Land which I swore unto their fathers, flowing with milk and honey; and they shall have eaten their fill, and waxen fat; and turned unto other gods...." (Deuteronomy 31:20)

So Moses said to Israel: When you enter the Land ultimately you will rebel specifically under circumstances of food and drink and specifically under circumstances of tranquillity, as it is said, "Lest when you have eaten and are

----

sister Sodom: (pride, fullness of bread, and careless ease)". (Ez. 16:48),
So much so -- "Neither did she strengthen the hand of the poor and needy. And they were haughty..." (Ez. 16:50). Similarly you may cite, "For the drink was finished." (Gen. 13:10). What is it that Scripture implies, "And they gave their father wine to drink;" (Gen. 19:33)? And from whence did they have wine in the cave? But it was providentially supplied for the occasion. And so does Scripture state, "And it shall come to pass in that day that the mountains shall drop down sweet wine." (Joel 4:18).
If He bestows such to those who provoke Him, how much more
so will He act kindly towards those who perform His will!

[29] PISKA 43:
And once Rabbi Gamliel and Rabbi Yehoshua and Rabbi Elazar ben Azaria and Rabbi Akiba entered Rome. The reverberating noise of the city could be heard from the Palatium to an extent of one hundred and twenty mils. They began to cry but Rabbi Akiba rejoiced. They said to him, "Akiba, why is it that we cry but you rejoice?" He replied, "Why do you cry?" They said to him, "And should we not lament the fact that the nations which worship idols, sacrifice to gods and prostrate themselves to graven images dwell securely, peacefully and tranquilly while the House of the footstool of our God is a fiery ruin and a den for the beasts of the field." He replied to them, "For that very reason I rejoice: If He grants such beneficence to those who provoke Him, how much more so will He act kindly towards those who perform His will!"

PISKA 318

satiated ... and when thy herds and thy flocks multiply ... then thy heart be lifted up and thou forget the Lord thy God...." (Deuteronomy 8:12-14).

And similarly you will find that the sons and daughters of Job were stricken with punishments specifically under the circumstances of food and drink, as it is said, "While he was yet speaking there came yet another, and said: 'Thy sons and thy daughters were yet eating and drinking wine in their eldest brother's house; and behold, a great wind came..." (Job 12:18-19). And similarly you will find that the Ten Tribes were exiled specifically under circumstances of food, drink, and tranquillity, as it is said, "That lie upon beds of ivory..."; "That drink wine in bowls." (Amos 6:4-7).

"Therefore now shall they go captive at the head of them that go captive."
    And so you will find in regards to the Days of the Messiah* ultimately they will rebel specifically under circumstances of food and drink, as it is said, "But Jeshurun waxed fat and kicked ...and he forsook God who made him."
    This is like the parable of someone who had a calf. He searched out, cut down and fed vetch to it in order that it would be able to plough with him. When the calf grew older, its master placed a yoke upon it. The calf leaped and broke the yoke and severed the end parts of the yoke*. And in this regard does Scripture say, "Thou hast broken the bars of wood but thou shalt make in their stead bars of iron." (Jeremiah 28:13).

"Thou didst wax fat":
    In the days of Jereboam.

"Thou didst grow thick":
    In the days of Ahab.

"Thou didst become gross":
    All this happened in the days of Jehu.

Another interpretation:
"Thou didst wax fat":
    In the days of Ahaz.

"Thou didst grow thick":
    In the days of Menasseh.

"Thou didst become gross":

PISKA 318

All this happened in the days of Zedekiah.

Another interpretation:
"Thou didst wax fat, thou didst grow thick, thou didst become gross":
    When someone is fat in the inside, he causes ridges on the outside. And in this regard does Scripture say, "Because he hath covered his *inside* with his fatness he made collops of fat on his loin *ridges*." (Job 15:27).

Another interpretation:
"Thou didst wax fat, thou didst grow thick...."
    These are the three generations that precede the "Days of the Messiah"*, as it is said, "Their land also is full of horses, neither is there any end of their chariots,"; "Their land also is full of silver and gold neither is there any end of their treasuries,"; "Their land is also full of idols; everyone worshipeth the work of his own hands, that which his own fingers have made." (Isaiah 2:7,8).

"And he forsook the God who made him":
    And in this regard does Scripture say, ("Who hath stretched out the heavens and hath established the earth."), "For My people have committed two evils...." (Jeremiah 2:13). The Holy One, Blessed Be He, said to them: In the measure that you have meted out to Me, have I meted out to you -- "I have abandoned My house, I have forsaken My heritage...." (Jeremiah 12:7; "And he forsook the tabernacle of Shiloh." (Psalms 78:60). And Scripture also states, "For thou hast forsaken thy people the House of Jacob." (Isaiah 2:6).

Another interpretation:
"And he forsook God Who made him":
    This is according to the matter of which Scripture states, "And He brought me into the inner court of the Lord's house, and behold, at the door of the Temple of the Lord, between the porch and the altar, were about five and twenty men, with their backs toward the Temple of the Lord...." (Ezekiel 8:16).
    Rabbi Dostaye the son of Yehuda says: Do not read "And he despised [God Who made him; and he dishonored]" but "And he despised* God Who made him, that the Rock should dishonor his salvation." This is according to the matter of which Scripture states, "Do not contemn us, for Thy name's sake, do not dishonor the throne of Thy glory." (Jeremiah 14:21).

16)
"They roused Him to jealousy with strange gods":

PISKA 318

For they went and made **things pertaining to male organs***. And so does Scripture state, "And also Maacah his mother he removed from being queen because she had made an abominable image for an Asherah." (1Kings 15:13).

"With abominations they did provoke Him":
    This refers to the act of sodomy. And so does Scripture state, "Thou shalt not lie with mankind as with womankind; it is an abomination." (Leviticus 18:22). And Scripture also states, "And also a male prostitute there was in the land." (1Kings 14:24).

17)
"They sacrificed unto demons -- no-gods":
    Had they worshipped the sun and the moon, the stars and the constellations -- things which are necessary for the world since the world derives benefit from them, there would not have been a double jealousy but they worshipped things that were of no benefit to them but were harmful to them.

"Unto demons":
    What is the method of a demon? He enters a person and casts him into a fit.

"Gods that they knew not":
    That even the Gentile Nations of the World are not acquainted with them.

"New gods that came up of late":
    Whenever a gentile sees it he says, "**This is a Jewish image*!**" And so does Scripture state, "As my hand has reached the kingdom of the idols, whose graven images were from Jerusalem and from Samaria." (Isaiah 10:10). This teaches that Jerusalem and Samaria supplied molds to the whole world.

"Your ancestors did not שערו them":
    That the hair (שער) of your ancestors did not stand up in their presence.

Another interpretation:
"Your ancestors did not שערו them":
    For your ancestors did not evaluate (שערו) to know whether or not they had any use.

Another interpretation:
"Your ancestors did not שערום":

PISKA 318

Do not read " שערום (fear them)" but "שעום(regarded them)." For even though they sacrificed and made offerings to them, they did not revere them. This is according to the matter of which Scripture states: "And to Cain and his offering, He did not regard (שעה)." (Genesis 4:5).

END OF PISKA

PISKA 319

18)
"Of the Rock that begot thee thou wast unmindful":
    The Holy One, Blessed Be He, said to them: You have made Me feel as if I were a male who sought to give birth.
    --Were it a recovering woman, sitting upon the birthstool, would she not experience pain? This is according to the matter of which Scripture states, "For the children are come to the birth, and there is not strength to bring forth." (2Kings 19:3).
    --Were it a sick woman who was having her first child, would she not experience pain! This is according to the matter of which Scripture states, "For I have heard a voice as of a woman in travail, the anguish as of her that bringeth forth her first child." (Jeremiah 4:31)
    --Were it that she had two in her womb, would she not experience pain! This is according to the matter of which Scripture states, "And the children struggled together with her." (Genesis 25:22).
    --Were it a man, whose nature is not one of giving birth, who sought to give birth, would the experience of pain not be doubly doubled! This is according to the matter of which Scripture states, "Ask ye now and see whether a man doth travail with child." (Jeremiah 30:6).

Another interpretation:
"Of the Rock that begot thee thou wast unmindful": Would you have me forget about the merit of your ancestors*! And so does Scripture state, "Look unto the rock whence ye were hewn and to the hole of the pit whence ye were digged, (Look unto Abraham your father and unto Sarah that bore you)." (Isaiah 51:1.)

Another interpretation:
"Of the Rock that begot thee thou wast unmindful":
    Whenever I desire to favor you, you weaken the Strength of Heaven:
    You stood by the Sea and said, This is my God and I will adore Him." (Exodus 15:2). --I desired to favor you. Then you reversed yourselves and said, "Let us make a captain and let us return to Egypt." (Numbers 14:4).
    You stood at Mount Sinai and said, "Of all the Lord hath spoken, we will perform and we will hearken." --I desired to favor you. Then you reversed yourselves and said about the Golden Calf, "This is thy god, O Israel." (Exodus 32:4).

PISKA 319

Thus it is that whenever I desire to favor you, you weaken the Strength of Heaven.

"And didst forget the God who gave birth for you*":
> Rabbi Meir said:
The God who experienced pain* (החיל) concerning you. This is according to the matter of which Scripture states, "Pangs (חיל), as of a woman in travail." (Psalms 48:7).
> Rabbi Yehuda says: Who made you full of cavities (מחילים).

Another interpretation:
"And didst forget the God that bore thee (מחוללך)":
> God who caused His name to be associated with you* (הוזיל), yet did not fix it upon any other people or kingdom. And so does Scripture state, "I am the Lord *thy* God who took you out of the Land of Egypt." (Exodus 20:2).

Rabbi Nehemiah says: God who makes you more lowly* than all other peoples when you do not occupy yourselves with Torah. And so does Scripture state, "The voice of the Lord is upon the waters* -- (until)- ...the voice of the Lord makes the "hinds" (אילות) weak (יחולל)". (Psalms 29:3-9).

Another interpretation:
"And didst forget the God that bore thee (מחוללך)":
> The God who forgives you (מוחל לך) concerning all your transgressions.
> END OF PISKA

PISKA 320

19)
"The Lord saw it and spurned":

> Rabbi Yehuda says: "From Moses there descended scorners.*"

Rabbi Meir says: "Because of the provocation of His sons and daughters." And are not such matters to be argued by *a fortiori* arguments:
If even when they provoke, they are called "sons", then how much more so are they to be called "sons" when they do not provoke!

20)
"And He said, 'I will hide My face from them'":

> The Holy One, Blessed Be He, said, "Behold I will remove My Shekina from amongst them."

"I will see what their end will be":

> For I know what is to be their final disposition.

Another interpretation:

> Behold I will deliver them into the hands of the Four Kingdoms so that they will be enslaved by them.

"I will see what their end will be":

> And I will know what they are at their end.

"For they are a generation of upsets":

> --"A perverse generation"? "A generation of perversity"? - -Specifically "A generation of upsets"* is written here: They are upsets and they are rebellious*.

"Children in whom there is no faithfulness":

> You are children in whom there is no constancy. You stood at Mount Sinai and said, "Of all that the Lord hath spoke, we will do and we will hearken". (Exodus 24:7). I responded, "You are heavenly beings". (Psalms 82:6). When you said about the Golden Calf, "This is thy god, O Israel" (Exodus 32:4), so I also said to you, "Then like a man you shall die" (Psalms 82:7). I brought you into the Land (of your ancestors) and built for you the Chosen Temple. I said that you would never be exiled from it. When you said, "We have no portion with David," (2Samuel 20:1) so I also said, "And Israel shall surely be exiled from upon its land." (Amos 7:17).
>
> Rabbi Dostaye the son of Yehuda says: Do not read "in whom there is no faithfulness (אמון)" but "in whom there is no amen". For they did not want to respond "amen" after the prophets when they blessed them. And so does Scripture

PISKA 320

state, "That I perform the oath that I swore unto your fathers, to give them a land flowing with milk and honey, as at this day". (Jeremiah 11:5). And not one of them opened his mouth to say "amen" until Jeremiah himself came and answered "amen", as it is said, "Then I answered and said, 'Amen Lord'." (Jeremiah 11:5).

21)
"They have roused Me to jealousy with a no-god; they have provoked Me with their hot airs":
  You see the case of the man who worships an image -- something which he sees. Yet they worshipped shadows, yea, not only shadows but the very steam that rises from the pot. This is like the matter of which it is said, "They have provoked Me with their hot airs."

"And I will raise them to jealousy with a no-people (עַם בלא)":
  Do not read "by a ל nation" but "by a lvi nation"* (עַם בלוי): This refers to those who come from the nations and the kingdoms and remove them from their houses.

Another interpretation:
  This refers to those who come from Barberia and Mauritania that go naked in the market place. You have no greater example of a shameful, despicable person than he who goes naked in the market place.

"I will provoke them with a vile nation":
  This refers to the *minim*. And so does Scripture state, "The vile person says in his heart, 'There is no God'." (Psalms 14:1)

22)
"For a fire is kindled in my nostril":
  When retribution comes from me, it will come only in "nostril". From where do we know that "nostril" is in Hell? We know it from that which Scripture states, "And burneth unto the depths of the nether-world."

"And it shall devour the land with its produce":
       This refers to the Land of Israel.

"And setteth ablaze the foundations of the mountains":
  This refers to Jerusalem. This is according to the matter of which Scripture states, "Jerusalem -- the mountains are about her (and the Lord is about His people)." (Psalms 125:2).

Another interpretation:

PISKA 320

"And it shall devour the land with its produce":
                    This refers to the world "and the fullness thereof."

"And setteth ablaze the foundations of the mountains":
    This refers to the Four Kingdoms*. And so does Scripture state, "...and behold there came four chariots...." (Zechariah 6:1).
                    END OF PISKA

PISKA 321

23)
"I will gather evils upon them":
　　Behold I will gather together all retributions and bring all of them upon them at one time.

Another interpretation:
　　Behold, I will gather them all together into the net and bring upon them all their retributions -- all at once.

Another interpretation:
　　"I will gather (אסורף) evils upon them" is not written here, but rather "I will bring to an end (אספה)". For all the retributions will be brought to an end but the people will not be brought to an end. And so does Scripture state, "I will bring to an end my arrows upon them," --"My arrows will bring *them* to an end," is not written here, but rather "I will bring to an end *my arrows* upon them". My arrows shall be brought to an end but the people shall not be brought to an end.

Another interpretation:
"I will use up my arrows upon them":
　　This refers to the arrows of famine. And so does Scripture state, "When I shall send upon them the evil arrows of famine." (Ezekiel 5:16)

24)
"The wasting of hunger and the devouring of the fiery bolt":
　　For they shall be **plagued*** by the famine and cast out into the streets. And so does Scripture state, "And people to whom they prophesy shall be cast out in the streets of Jerusalem...." (Jeremiah 14:16).

"And Keteb Meriri...":
　　According to your method you must learn that all who are possessed by a demon do froth.

"And the teeth of cattle..":
　　　　　　　　Do not read: "רשן בהמות אשלח בם" but rather:
"רשן בהמות [נ״ל מהרמות] אשלח בם": that they should become panicky and withdraw from battle [30] on account of the sins.

----

[30] So seems to be the sense of מחזרים. According to Sifre Deut. 197 if one was afraid of the sins in his hand and did not withdraw, he would cause the eventual retreat of all.

PISKA 321

Another interpretation:
    That one of them would become inflamed and pull himself and raise an ulcer so that he gradually die of it.

Another interpretation:
"And the teeth of cattle will I send upon them":
    That his own cow will bite him and he **raise an ulcer*** so that he gradually die of it.
    They said that it once happened that ewes were biting and killing.

"With the venom of crawling things of the dust":
    That they, themselves, would be forced to crawl in the dust. Rabbi says: This refers to the snakes, whose kingdom is specifically that of the dust.

25)
"Without shall the sword bereave":
    From here they said, "In a time of war bring in the foot* and in a time of famine scatter* the foot." And so does Scripture state, "If I go forth into the field, then behold the slain with the sword! And if I enter the city then behold them that are sick with famine." (Jeremiah 14:18). And Scripture also states, "He that is in the field shall die by the sword and he that is in the city, famine and pestilence shall devour him." (Ezekiel 7:15)

"And in the chambers terror":
    One considers the sword as it comes to the marketplace. Even if he fled and escaped from it, then **the chambers of his heart beat within him and he dies***.

Another interpretation:
"Without shall the sword bereave...":
    On account of that which they did in the streets of Jerusalem. And thus does Scripture state, "For according to the number of thy cities are thy gods, O Judah; and according to the number of the streets of Jerusalem have ye set up altars to the shameful thing...." (Jeremiah 11:13).

"And in the chambers terror":
    On account of what they did in the innermost chamber. And so does Scripture state, "Son of man, hast thou seen, what the Elders of the House of Israel do in the dark, every man in his chambers of imagery? For they say: The Lord seeth us not, the Lord hath forsaken the land." (Ezekiel 8:12).

"...also the young man, also the virgin":

PISKA 321

This ("also") **adds to these***: "the suckling with the man of gray hairs." And so does Scripture state, "Also the man with the woman shall be taken, the aged with him that is full of days." (Jeremiah 6:11)

Another interpretation:
"Also the loved one":
   You have caused* Me to harm My loved ones. And so does Scripture state, "And Joshua the son of Nun, the servant of Moses of His beloved ones, answered." (Numbers 11:28).

"Also the virgin":
   This teaches us that they were as clean of sin as a virgin who had never tasted sin in her life.

"Suckling*":
   This teaches us that they would suckle the words of the Torah as a suckling suckles milk from the breasts of his mother.

"With the man of gray hairs (שׁיבה)":
   Do not read "the man of (gray hairs)" but rather "ישׁיבה (great academy)". This teaches us that all of them were worthy to sit in the great academy. And so does Scripture state, "All the mighty, doers of war." (2Kings 24:16).
      Now what "might" can people display who are going into exile? And what "war" can people "do" when they are **bound in fetters*** and put into chains?
Rather:
   "(All the) mighty" --This refers to the mighty ones of the Torah. This is like the matter of which Scripture states, "Bless the Lord, ye angels of His, *mighty* in strength, the *doers of His word*." (Psalms 103:20).

"doers of war" --That they discuss and argue in the war of the Torah, as it is said, "Wherefore it is said in the *Book* of the Wars of the Lord." (Numbers 21:14).

PISKA 321

And Scripture also states, "And all the men of might, and the חרש and the מסגר, a thousand." 2Kings 24:16):

"חרש" --one speaks and all are quiet.

"מסגר" --all sit before him and learn from him.

One פותח and another סוגר to fulfill that of which it is said, "And he shall פתח but not סוגר and he shall סגר but not פותח." (Isaiah 22:22)

END OF PISKA

26)
"I thought I would make an end of them (אפאיהם)":
I thought in *my anger -- where are they* (באפי איה הם).

"I should make their memory cease from among men":
I thought -- they should not be in the world. But what could I do to them -- "(If it had not been the Lord who was for us. Say now Israel:) If it had not been the Lord who was for us when men rose up against us." (Psalms 124:1,2). (If it had not been: "And he said to destroy them...if it had not been for Moses, His beloved...." (Psalms 106:23).)

Another interpretation:
I thought in my anger -- where are they!

"I should make their memory cease from among men":
That they should not be in the world. But what could I do
--"*Except* the Lord of Hosts had left unto us a very small remnant...." (Isaiah 1:9).

Another interpretation:
I would make an end of them -- *were it not* ... as it is said, "And He thought to destroy them were it not that Moses His beloved stood before Him in the breach." (Psalms 106:23).

27)
"Were it not for the accumulated (אוגר) anger of his enemy":
Who caused them to take retribution against these? The anger of the Gentile Nations that had accumulated within their inwards.
"אגור" -- אגור specifically means "accumulated", as it is said, "The words of Agur the son of Jakeh." (Proverbs 30:1). And Scripture also states, "May He incite death against them, let them go down alive into the nether-world; for evil *in their accumulation* (מגורם) is within them." (Psalms 55:16).

"Lest they alienate them in their distresses":
In the time of Israel's distress the Gentile Nations of the World treat them as strangers and pretend that they never knew them. And so we find that when they sought to flee northwards they did not care for them but they **hand them over***. This is like the matter of which it is said, "Thus says the Lord: For three transgressions of Tyre, and for four, I will not turn away the punishment; because they delivered up a whole people to Edom." (Amos 1:9). They sought to flee to the south and they

PISKA 322

delivered them up, as it is said, "Thus says the Lord: For three transgressions of Gaza, and for four, I will not turn away the punishment; because they carried into exile a whole people to deliver them up to Edom." (Amos 1:6). They sought to flee to the east and they delivered them up, as it is said, "Thus says the Lord: For three transgressions of Damascus ...." (Amos 1:3). They sought to flee to the west and they delivered them up, as it is said, "The oracle concerning Arabia, in the thickets in Arabia you will lodge, O caravans of Dedanites...." (Isaiah 21:13-15).

In the time of Israel's fortune, the Gentile Nations of the World flatter* them and pretend to be their brothers. And so did Esau say to Jacob, "I have enough, *my brother*, keep what you have for yourself." (Genesis 33:9). And so did Hiram say to Solomon, "What kind of cities are these which you have given me, my *brother*." (1Kings 9:13).

"Lest they should say, 'Our hand is triumphant, the Lord has not wrought all this'":
Just as those fools said, "Have we not by our own strength taken horns for ourselves." (Amos 6:3).

28)
"For they are a nation devoid of counsel":
Rabbi Yehuda interpreted it to refer to Israel. Rabbi Nehemiah interpreted it to refer to the Gentile Nations of the World. Rabbi Yehuda interpreted it to refer to Israel:
Israel destroyed the good counsel that was given to them. "Counsel" specifically refers to "Torah", as it is said, "I have counsel and Toshia." (Proverbs 8:14).

"And there is no understanding in them...":
There is not one of them who will reflect and say:
Yesterday one person of us could pursue one thousand of the Gentile nations and two could put ten thousand to flight. Yet now one person of the Gentile Nations could pursue one thousand of us and two could put ten thousand to flight ..."unless their Rock had given them."
Rabbi Nehemiah interpreted it to refer to the Gentile Nations:
The Gentile Nations destroyed the Seven Commandments that I gave to them.

"And there is no understanding in them...":
There is not one of them who will reflect and say: Now one of us could chase one thousand of Israel and two could put ten thousand to flight. As for the Messianic Era, could one of Israel pursue one thousand and could two put ten thousand to flight... "unless their Rock had given them!"
It once happened in the war* that Decarion*, on horseback, chased an Israelite man with the intention of killing him but he could not catch him. Before he reached

PISKA 322

him*, a snake had come out and bit the man upon his heel. He said to him: Please say to Polpos*, "Do not think that because we are mighty they have been delivered into our hands..." "Unless their Rock had given them."

END OF PISKA

PISKA 323

29)
"If they were wise they would understand this":

If Israel would reflect upon the words of the Torah that I gave to them, no nation or kingdom could rule over them. And *this* specifically refers to the Torah, as it is said, "And *this* is the Torah which Moses set...." (Deuteronomy 4:44).

Another interpretation:
"If they were wise they would understand this":

If they would have reflected upon what Jacob their father had told them*, no nation or kingdom could have ruled over them. And what did He say to them? "Accept upon yourselves the kingship of Heaven, subdue each other with the fear of Heaven, act charitably towards each other."

30)
"How should one chase a thousand...":

Since you have not fulfilled the Torah, how can I fulfill the promise you sought, that one of you should chase one thousand of the Gentile Nations and two would put to flight ten thousand and now one of the Gentile Nations can chase one thousand of you and two of them put to flight ten thousand.

"Except their Rock had given them over and the Lord had delivered them up":

I do not deliver you up through My own agency but through the agency of others. And there was already an incident in Judah in which the flies delivered them up.

Rabbi Hanina, a citizen of Tibi'in says: This is comparable to one who says to another, "**Consider it bought** and I will deliver it later." -- But I am not so, for I sell and **immediately*** deliver.

Another interpretation:
"And the Lord had delivered them":

I deliver you who are **like the impure into the hands of the pure**; or perhaps, what is meant is that they are like the pure in the hands of the impure! Yet this cannot be for they shut up only those who are defiled, as it is said, "And the priest shall shut up the *plague* for seven days...." (Leviticus 13:4).

31)
"For their צוּר is not as our צוּר":

Not according to the dominion that you give to us do you give to them. For when you give dominion to us we act toward them with the quality of mercy but when you give them dominion they act toward us with the quality of cruelness -- They behead us, they burn us, they crucify us.

PISKA 323

"Even our enemies, themselves, being judges":
> You have written in the Torah that an enemy cannot judge nor testify:
"...and he who is not an enemy," (Numbers 35:23) -- i.e. *he* may testify against him.
"...neither sought to harm him," (Numbers 35:23) -- i.e. *he* may judge him.
And you have appointed over us enemies as witnesses and judges!

32)
"For their vine is the vine of Sodom...":
> Rabbi Yehuda interpreted it in reference to Israel.
Rabbi Nehemiah interpreted it in reference to the Gentile Nations of the World.

> Rabbi Yehuda says:
Are you indeed from the vine of Sodom or from the planting of Gommorah? But surely you are **specifically the holy seed***, as it is said, "Yet I planted thee a noble vine, wholly a right seed." (Jeremiah 2:21).

"Their grapes are grapes of gall":
You are the children of the first Adam whom I punished with the edict of death, placed upon him and his succeeding generations until the end of all generations.

"Their clusters are bitter":
The great ones-- **their bitterness is dispersed amongst them*** as a cluster. And "cluster" specifically refers to "great one", as it is said, "There is no cluster to eat nor first ripe fig which my soul desireth...." (Micah 7:1).

33)
"Their wine is the venom of serpents":
Those angers of the pious ones and reverers of Heaven amongst you are as serpents.

"And the head of asps which is cruel":
For the chief ones amongst you are like the asp which is cruel.

Another interpretation:
"Their wine (יינם) is the anger of serpents":
The anger of the humble (והמתונים) and reverers of Heaven amongst you, is as that of serpents.

"And the head of asps which is cruel":
The chief ones among you are like the asp which is cruel.
> Rabbi Nehemiah interpreted it in reference to the Gentile Nations of the World:

PISKA 323

And it is certain that you are of the vine of Sodom and of the planting of Gommorah. You are the disciples of the primordial serpent who corrupted Adam and Eve.

32)
"Their clusters are bitter":
For the bitterness of the great ones among you is spread out among them as a serpent.

"Their clusters are bitter":
And "cluster" specifically refers to a "great one", as it is said, "There is no cluster to eat (nor first ripe fig which my soul desireth.)" (Micah 7:1).

END OF PISKA

PISKA 324

34)
"Is this not laid up in store with Me":
Rabbi Eliezer the son of Yosi Hagelili says:
Concerning the cup which has been as a (sima)* store and a (mhwsr)* hoard, it might be thought that it would have become weak, so Scripture stated, "strong wine"*. (Psalms 75:9). I might have thought that it would be only half full, so Scripture says, "*full* of mixture". (Psalms 75:9). I might have thought that it wouldn't lack even a single drop, so Scripture says, "And He *poureth* out of the same," (Psalms 75:9):

From that very drop there drank the Generation of the Flood, and the Generation of the Dispersion, and the People of Sodom and Pharaoh and all of his troops, Sisera and all his hordes, Sennacherib and all his devotees, Nebuchadnezzar and all his troops -- and from that very drop, all those who have come into the world will drink in the future, until the end of all generations. And so does Scripture state, "And in this mountain will the Lord of Hosts make unto all peoples a feast of fat things, a feast of wines on the lees, fats full of marrow, lees well refined and death shall be swallowed forever and the Lord God shall wipe away the tears from every face and the shame of His people He shall remove from off the face of the whole earth, for the mouth of the Lord hath spoken." (Isaiah 25:6).

I might have thought that "fat" refers to things that are of benefit and that "lees" refers to things that are of no benefit at all, so Scripture states "fats full of marrow*...lees well refined." (Isaiah 25:6). It refers to fats which contain nothing but refuse.

And so does Scripture state, "Babylon hath been a golden cup in the Lord's hand, that made all the earth drunken. Jeremiah 51:7). (And Scripture also states, "The cup of your sister you shall drink--deep and wide; she shall be for a mockery and a derision--much for it to contain". (Ezekiel 23:32)): Just as it is normal that once golden things are broken they can be restored; so too, once the retributions cease from the Gentile Nations, in the Future the retributions will be reestablished upon them.

Concerning the time when the retributions arrive upon Israel--what is stated in Scripture? "Thou shall drink it and drain it, and thou shalt crunch the sherd, thereof" (Ezekiel 23:34).:

Just as it is normal that once sherds are broken they cannot be restored; so too, once the retributions cease from Israel, in the Future the retributions will not be reestablished upon them.

"Sealed up in my treasuries":
Just as a treasury is sealed and does not permit interest to accrue; so too, the deeds of the wicked do not permit interest to accrue.

PISKA 324

If you would say they do*, they would have destroyed the world.
And so does Scripture state, "Woe to the wicked, it shall be ill with him; only the work of his hands shall be done him." (Isaiah 3:11). But the deeds of the righteous permit interest to accrue and interest on interest. And so does Scripture state, "Say ye of the righteous, that it shall be well with him; for they eat the interest of their doings." (Isaiah 3:10).

Another interpretation:
Just as a treasury is sealed and is not depleted of anything; so too, the righteous do not receive their due in This World. And from whence do we know that the righteous do not receive in This World what is due them? --As Scripture states, "How great is Thy goodness which you have stored away for those who fear You." (Psalms 31:20). And from whence do we know that the wicked do not receive in This World what is due them? --As Scripture states, "Is this not laid up in store with Me?" When do these and those receive their due? In the future when redemption comes to Israel, as is said, "Vengeance is Mine and recompense."

END OF PISKA

PISKA 325

35)
"Vengeance is Mine and recompense":
    I will punish them Myself, not through an angel and not through a sent one, according to the matter of which Scripture states, "Come now and I will send thee to Pharaoh." (Exodus 3:10). And Scripture also states, "And the angel of the Lord went forth and smote in the camp of the Assyrians...." (2Kings 19:35).

Another interpretation:
    "Vengeance is Mine and I will recompense it" is not written here but rather, "and recompense"* -- I recompensed in This World the reward of the deeds that your fathers did before Me. And so does Scripture state, "I will not keep silent except I have recompensed." (Isaiah 65:6). And Scripture also states, "And first I recompensed their iniquity and their sin double." (Jeremiah 16:18).

"Against the time when their foot shall slip":
    This is according to the matter of which Scripture states, "The foot shall tread it down, even the feet of the poor and the steps of the needy." (Isaiah 26:6).

"For the day of their calamity is at hand"*:
    Rabbi Yosi said: If retribution is still coming slowly towards those of whom Scripture says, "For the day of their calamity is at hand", then how much more slowly shall it come towards those of whom Scripture states, "And after many days shall they be punished." (Isaiah 24:22).

"And the things that are to come upon them will make haste":
    When the Holy One, Blessed Be He, brings retribution upon the Gentile Nations, He causes the world to quake upon them. And so does Scripture state, "They fly as a vulture that hasteneth to devour." Habakkuk 1:8). And Scripture also states, "That say: 'Let Him make speed, let Him hasten His work, that we may see it; and let the counsel of the Holy One of Israel draw nigh and come." (Isaiah 5:19). Yet when the Holy One, Blessed Be He, brings punishments upon Israel He does not do so abruptly but He prolongs it. How does He do this? -- He hands them over to the Four Kingdoms that they should be subjugated by them. And so does Scripture state, "Fear not for I am with thee, saith the Lord, to deliver you." (Jeremiah 30:11).
                    END OF PISKA

PISKA 326

36)
"For the Lord will judge His people":
   When the Holy One, Blessed Be He, judges the Gentile Nations He is joyful, as it is said, "When the Lord will judge His people (and repent Himself for His servants)." But when the Holy One, Blessed Be He, judges Israel, He -- as if it were possible -- feels remorse*, as it is said, "And repent Himself for His servants". Now "repentance" specifically means "remorse", as it is said, "For it repenteth Me that I have made them." (Genesis 6:7). And Scripture also states, "It repenteth Me that I have set up Saul to be King." (1Samuel 15:11).

"When He sees that their hand is gone":
   When He sees that all walk before Him* while they wither in the Exile.

Another interpretation:
                     When they abandon hope of redemption.

Another interpretation:
"When He sees their hand* is gone, and there is none remaining to shut up or left at large":
   When He sees that the peruta coin has perished from the wallet, as it is said, "And when they have made an end of emptying the hand of the holy people, all these things shall be finished." (Daniel 12:7).

Another interpretation:
"When He sees that their hand is gone":
   When He sees they no longer have men like Moses* who pray for them, as it is said, "And He thought to destroy them were it not for Moses, His loved one." (Psalms 106:23).

Another interpretation:
"When He sees...":
   When He sees that they no longer have men like Aaron* to pray for them, as it is said, "And he stood between the dead and the living and the plague ceased." (Numbers 17:13).

Another interpretation:
"When He sees...":
   When He sees that they no longer have men like Phineas* to pray for them, as it is said, "And Phineas stood and prayed." (Psalms 106:30).

PISKA 326

Another interpretation:
"When He sees that their hand is gone, and there is none remaining, shut up or left at large":

"There is none shut up and there is none left at large -- and there is no deliverer of Israel." (2Kings 14:26).

END OF PISKA

PISKA 327

37)
"And he will say: 'Where are their *princes*...'":
     Rabbi Yehuda interpreted it in reference to Israel while Rabbi Nehemiah interpreted it in reference to the Gentile Nations of the World.
     Rabbi Yehuda says: In the future it will be that **Israel will say to the Nations of the World***, "Where are your councillors and your consuls."
                    END OF PISKA

PISKA 328

38)
"Who did eat the fat of their sacrifices...":
    For we would give them **Asponit***, and present them with **Donativa*** and bestow upon them **Salania*.**"

"Let them rise up and help you":
    It is not written here "Let them rise up and let them help yourselves* (ויעזרו אתכם)" but specifically "Let them rise up and **let them help you*** (ויעזרוכם)".

Rabbi Nehemiah says:
This refers to evil Titus, the son of Vespasian's wife, who entered the Holy of Holies and slashed two curtains with a sword and said, "If He be God let Him come and oppose this!"

"Who did eat of the fat of their sacrifices..."
He said: Moses led these ones astray by telling them, "Build an altar, and offer burnt sacrifices upon it, and pour libations over it," according to the matter of which it is said, "The one lamb thou shalt offer in the morning and the other lamb thou shalt offer at dusk ... and the drink offering thereof". (Numbers 28:4).

"Let Him rise up and help you, let Him be your protection":
    The Holy One, Blessed Be He, is forgiving towards everything. He exacts immediate punishment for the desecration of His name.

END OF PISKA

PISKA 329

39)
"See now that I, I am He":

This refutes those who say there is no heavenly rulership. As for he who says there are two heavenly rulerships, we refute him by citing, "And yet has it not been written, 'And there is no God with Me.'" (Isaiah 44:6).

Or concerning the declarations that He has not the power to kill nor the power to give life, not the power to cause injury nor the power to give benefit, Scripture states, "See now that I, I, am He, I will kill and I will make alive...." And Scripture also states, "Thus saith the Lord, the King of Israel, and his Redeemer, the Lord of Hosts, I am the first and I am the last and besides Me There is no other God." (Isaiah 44:6).

Another interpretation:
"I will kill and I will make alive":

This is one of the four assurances which contain an allusion to the *Resurrection of the Dead*: "I will kill and I will make alive,"; "My soul will die the death of the righteous" (Numbers 23:10); "Reuben will live and will not die" (Deuteronomy 33:6); "After two days He will revive us." (Hosea 6:2).

I might understand that the reference to "death" applies to one person while the reference to "life" applies to another, so Scripture states, "I wound and I heal": Just as it is only feasible that the references to "wounding" and "healing" apply to the same person; so too, do the references to "death" and "life" refer to the same person.

"And there is none that can deliver from my hand":

Fathers do not deliver their sons: Abraham does not deliver Ishmael and Isaac does not deliver Esau. I only know from here that fathers do not deliver their sons. From whence do I know that brothers do not deliver brothers? I know it from the Scripture which states, "Truly no man can redeem his brother." (Psalms 49:8). - - Isaac does not deliver Ishmael and Jacob does not deliver Esau. And even should a person give Him all the money in the world, he is not permitted to be ransomed, as it is said, "Truly no man can redeem his brother (or give to God his ransom); for the redemption of their soul is priceless." (Psalms 49:8,9). The soul is so priceless that when a person sins against it there is no price which may restore it.

END OF PISKA

PISKA 330

40)
"For I lifted up My hand to heaven (and I said, 'as I live forever')":
When the Holy One, Blessed Be He, created the world He purposely created it by means of command and -not-[31] by means of an oath. And who caused Him to take oath? It was those who lacked faith who caused Him to take oath, as it is said, "And He lifted up His hand concerning them, to cast them down in the desert (and to cast their seed down amongst the nations)" (Psalms 102:26); "I have lifted up my hand, concerning the nations." (Ezekiel 36:7).

"And I said, 'As I live forever'":
For the response of the Holy One, Blessed Be He, is not as the response of one Who is made of flesh and blood. The response of one who is made of flesh and blood is as follows: The **Hpkti*** **enters into the province***[32]. **If he can exact retribution from the officer***, he exacts it[33], and if not, then he is unable to exact punishment. But He Who Spoke and The World Existed is not so. If He does not exact retribution from the living, He exacts it from the dead. If He does not exact it in This World, He exacts it in the World to Come.

END OF PISKA

----

[31] The word "not" is the reading of the better manuscripts.

[32] To plunder it.

[33] I.e. if the king is able to locate the officer before he dies.

PISKA 331

41)
"When I whet My lightning sword":

When retribution goes out from before Me, it is as fleeting as lightning. Nevertheless -- "And My hand shall take hold on judgment; I will render vengeance to My adversaries," --This is one-- "And will recompense them that hate Me," --And this is two*.

Another interpretation:
"I will render vengeance to צרי":

This refers to the Samaritans, as it is said, "When the צרי of Judah and Benjamin (heard of the exiles building the temple)." (Ezra 4:1).

"And will recompense them that hate Me":

This refers to the *minim*. And likewise does Scripture state, "Do not I hate them, O Lord, that hate Thee? And I do strive against those that rise up against Thee; (the end of their hatred is that they become my enemies)." (Psalms 129:31).

END OF PISKA

42)
"I will make Mine arrows drunk with blood":
   Now is it possible for arrows to be drunk with blood! Rather, it means "Behold I will **make others drunk*** from that which my arrows accomplish."

"And My sword shall devour flesh":
   Now is it possible for a sword to devour flesh! Rather it means, "Behold I will feed other creatures from that which My sword accomplishes". And so does Scripture state, "And thou son of man, speak unto the birds of every sort (and to all the birds of the Heavens: 'Gather and come to My sacrifice which I offer')." (Ezekiel 39:18). And Scripture states, "That ye may eat fat abundantly and drink blood (to drunkenness.)" (Ezekiel 39:18). And it states, "The flesh of the mighty shall ye eat ...(and the blood of the princes of the earth you will drink)." (Ezekiel 39:18). And Scripture continues, "And ye shall be filled at My table with horses and horsemen..." (Ezekiel 39:20). And Scripture says, "The sword of the Lord is filled with blood, it is made with fatness," (Isaiah 34:6) -- on what account?-- "for the Lord hath a sacrifice in Bozrah, and a great slaughter in the Land of Edom." (Isaiah 34:6).

"With the blood of the slain and the captives":
   On account of that which they did to the slain of My people. And so does Scripture state, "O that My head were waters, and Mine eyes a fountain of tears, that I might weep day and night for the slain of the daughter of My people." Jeremiah 8:23).

"And the captives":
   On account of that which they did to the captivity of My people. And so does Scripture state, "And they shall take them captive, whose captives they were; and they shall rule over their oppressors." (Isaiah 14:2).

"From the head is the פרעות of the enemy":
   When the Holy One, Blessed Be He, brings retribution (פורענות) upon the Gentile Nations, He does not bring it upon them for their own crimes alone but for these as well as those of their ancestors from Nimrod on. When He brings blessings upon Israel He brings upon them both those which they themselves have earned and also those of their ancestors from Abraham on.

Another interpretation:
"From the head of פרעות, the enemy":
   Why was it suitable to hang upon the head of Pharaoh all the **retributions***? It was on account of the fact that he was the first to enslave Israel.
                              END OF PISKA

PISKA 333

43)
"Clamor, O ye nations, because of His people":
    In the Future when the Holy One, Blessed Be He, brings redemption to Israel, the Gentile Nations of the World will be angered before Him. And this would not be their first time for they already were enraged at an earlier occasion. This is according to the matter of which Scripture states, "The nations heard, they were angered." (Exodus 15:14).

Another interpretation:
"Clamor, O ye nations because of His people":
    In the Future, the Gentile Nations of the World will rejoice on account of Israel, as it is said, "Rejoice, O ye nations, because of His people". And also the heavens and the earth! As it is said, "Sing, O ye heavens, for the Lord hath done it; Shout, ye lowest parts of the earth." (Isaiah 44:23). From whence do we know that this is so of the mountains and the hills? As it is said, "The mountains and the hills shall break forth before you into singing." (Isaiah 55:12). From whence do we know that this is so of the trees? As it is said, "And all the trees of the field shall clap their hand." (Isaiah 55:12). From whence do we know that this is so of the Patriarchs and the Matriarchs? As it is said, "The *Sela* dwellers will exult, at the head, the mountains will shout." (Isaiah 42:11).

"For He doth avenge the blood of His servants, and doth render vengeance to His adversaries":
    Two vengeances: He takes vengeance on murder and he takes vengeance on theft. And from whence do we know that all thefts which the Gentile Nations of the World committed against Israel are accounted unto them as if they had spilled innocent blood? As it is said, "I will gather all the nations and will bring them down into the valley of Jehoshaphat, and I will enter into judgment with them there for My people Israel," (Joel 4:2); "Egypt shall be a desolation, and Edom shall be a desolate wilderness, for the *theft* against the children of Judah, because they have shed innocent blood in their land." (Joel 4:19). --At the very moment: "But Judah shall be inhabited forever, and Jerusalem from generation to generation," (Joel 4:20); "And I will hold as innocent their blood that I have not held as innocent; and the Lord dwelleth in Zion." (Joel 4:21).

"And אדמתו[34] doth make expiation for His people":

----

[34] The sequence of the verse reads "By the spilled blood of his servants...doth make expiation." Then אדמתו is from the root "דם", blood.

PISKA 333

From whence do we know that the slaughter of Israel at the hands of the Gentile Nations of the World is **atonement for them*** in the World to Come? We know it from that which is said, "A Psalm of Asaph. The heathen are come into thine inheritance," (Psalms 79:1); "They have given the dead bodies of Thy servants..." (Psalms 79:2). "They have shed their blood like water." (Psalms 79:3)

Another interpretation:
"And אדמתו doth make expiation for His people":
From whence do you say that the descent of the wicked into Gehinnom effects expiation for them? It is said from that which is stated, "I have granted thy expiation; Egypt, Ethiopia and Seba are beneath you," (Isaiah 43:3); "Since thou are precious in My sight and honorable, and I have loved thee (and I have put אדם[35] in thy nether places)." (Isaiah 43:4).

Rabbi Meir used to say: "The Land of Israel expiates for whoever dwells upon it, as it is said, "As for the nation that dwells in her, its sin is נשוא." (Isaiah 33:24).
--Still, the exegesis hangs upon that which itself is unsupported, ("For the land is filled --the Holy One of Israel." But still the exegesis hangs upon that which is unsupported,) for we do not know if the sense is that their sins will be *razed* upon the land or whether their sins will be *raised* upon it! Since Scripture states, "And His land *expiates* for His people," we see that **they remove*** their sins upon it and not that **they bear*** them upon it.
And similarly was Rabbi Meir wont to say: All who live in the Land of Israel*, and recite the Shma liturgy in the mornings and the evenings*, and speak in the holy language*, will be a citizen in the World to Come.

You have attested: How notable is This Song! For we find in it "that which refers to the present" and we find in it "that which was refers to the past" and we find in it "that which refers to the **Future Era**[36]*" and we find in it "that which refers to **This World***" and we find in it "that which refers to the **Coming World**[37]"!
(END OF THE SONG)
END OF PISKA

----

[35] I.e. the nations.

[36] The time when the Messiah is to arrive.

[37] After the Messiah has come and the dead are ressurected.

44)
"And Moses came":
　　Here it states, "And Moses came" while elsewhere it is stated, "And Moses went." (Deuteronomy 31:1). It is impossible to say, "And Moses came"* while it yet states, "And Moses went." And it is impossible to state, "And Moses went," while it yet states, "And Moses came." You must conclude from this: there came his **Diatikos***: **And authority was given*** into the hand of another.

"And he spoke all the words of this song into the ears of the nation":
　　This teaches that he submerged them into their ears.

"He and Hosea the son of Nun":
　　Why do I require these words, **for yet it has already stated***, "And Moses called to Hosea the son of Nun, 'Joshua,'" (Numbers 13:16)? What is the import of the Scripture which states, "He and Hosea the son of Nun"? --It is to inform one of the righteous behavior of Joshua. I might have thought that when he was granted authority his opinion of himself became inflated! Scripture therefore states, "He and Hosea the son of Nun" --he, Hosea remained the righteous one. Even though he was granted the position of being the overseer of Israel, he was still *Hosea* in respect to his righteous behavior.

A similar case to this you may cite:
"And Joseph was in Egypt" (Exodus 1:5):
　　And do we not know that Joseph was in Egypt! It is to inform one of the righteousness of Joseph who used to shepherd his father's sheep. Now even though he was granted the position of a king in Egypt, he was still *Joseph* in respect to his righteous behavior.

A similar case to this you may cite:
"And David was the youngest" (1Samuel 13:14):
　　And do we not know that David was the youngest! It is to inform you of the righteousness of David who used to shepherd his father's sheep. Now even though he was granted the position of King over Israel, he was still *David* in respect to his "youngest" types of behavior.

END OF PISKA

PISKA 335

46)
"And he said unto them: 'Set your heart unto all the words wherewith I testify
against you this day'":
It is incumbent that a person should have his heart, his eyes, his ears concentrated
upon the words of the Torah. And so does Scripture state, "Son of man, behold with
thine eyes and hear with your ears (and set your heart to) that which I declare unto
thee,"; "And set your heart unto the entering in of the House...(into the exiting out of
the Temple...)" (Ezekiel 44:5). --The argument is *a fortiori*:
Now if a person must have his heart, his eyes, and his ears concentrated upon the
Temple which was visible to the eyes and was measured by the hand, how much
more so is such concentration necessary in respect to the words of the Torah which
are like mountains suspended by a hair!

"That ye may charge your children therewith to observe":
He said to them: Just as I offer you strong thanks so that you will sustain the Torah
after I am gone. So, to your children you also must offer strong thanks* so that they
will sustain the Torah after you have gone.

There is a story: Our master had come from Laodicea wehn Rabbi Yosi the son of
Rabbi Yehuda and Rabbi Elazar the son of Yehuda entered and sat down before
him. He said to them, "Come closer, I must hold it to your credit that you will
sustain the Torah after I am gone. So, you also must hold it to your children's credit
that they will sustain the Torah after you have gone".

Were Moses not so great and there were another. And suppose we had accepted his
Torah. Would it not have had value*? How much more is the value of Moses'. For
this reason is it stated, "That ye may charge your children WITH THEM[38] ."
END OF PISKA

----

[38] I.e with all the things which I warn you about this day to keep the words of this Torah . See Deut.
32:46.

PISKA 336

47)
"For it is no vain thing from you":
   There is nothing so empty in the Torah that if you interpret it you would not receive the benefit of some reward in This World while the principal is maintained for you in the World to Come. Know that this is so, for they said: Why is it written, "And the sister of Lotan is Timna," (Genesis 36:22); "And Timna was a concubine"? (Genesis 36:12).
   --This was written because she said, "I am not sufficiently worthy to be his wife so I will be his concubine!" And why should we care so much? But it is to inform you of the belovedness of Abraham. There were some who did not desire to be of kingship and of royalty but ran to be attached to him. And are not these matters to be argued, *a fortiori*:
   Since kings and royalty ran to be attached to Esau who had only one fulfilled commandment in his possession; namely, that he had honored his father, how much more so were they running to become attached to Jacob, the righteous one, who kept the entire Torah, as it is said, "And Jacob was a perfect man dwelling in tents." (Genesis 25:27).

"And by this word* ye shall prolong your days (upon the earth)":
   This is one of the things that he who does them eats of their fruits in This World while there is "length of days" for him in the World to Come. And it is stated explicitly here in reference to Torah study.
   From whence do we know that this is also the case in reference to the honoring of father and of mother*? We know it since Scripture states, "Honor your father and your mother in order that your days may be prolonged..." (Exodus 20:12). --For the sending away of the mother bird? It is written, "You shall surely send away the mother, and the children you may take for yourself in order that it may be good for you and that you may prolong your days," (Deuteronomy 22:7). --For the making of peace? It is written "And all thy children shall be taught of the Lord; and great shall be the peace of your children." (Isaiah 54:13).
                              END OF PISKA

PISKA 337

48)
"And the Lord spoke unto Moses at the very height of this day (saying).":
In three places it is stated "at the very height of this day":
It is stated "at the very height of this day" (Genesis 7:13) in reference to Noah? This teaches us that the generation of Noah said: "We swear -- may such befall from such, if, when we sense his movement, we let him be! And furthermore we shall take axes and hatchets and chop up the ark in front of him." So the Holy One, Blessed Be He, said, "Behold I will bring him in at noon and whoever is able to oppose, let him come forward and oppose!"

And why was it fitting to say in reference to Egypt "At the very height of this day all the hosts of the Lord departed"? Exodus 12:17).
This was because the Egyptians said: "We swear, may such befall from such, if, when we sense their movement, we let them be! And furthermore we shall take swords and sabers and kill them with these." So the Holy One, Blessed Be He, said, "Behold I will take them out at noon and whoever is able to oppose, let him come forward and oppose!"

And what did He see to say here (in reference to Moses) "At the very height of this day"?
This was because Israel said: We swear, may such befall from such, if when we sense his movement, we let him be! We will not abandon the man who took us out of Egypt and split the sea for us, and (brought down the Torah for us and) brought down the manna for us, and brought across the quail for us and performed miracles and wonders for us." So the Holy One, Blessed Be He, said: "Behold, I will bring him into the cave at noon and whoever is able to oppose, let him come forward and oppose!"
--For this reason it is stated, "And the Lord spoke unto Moses at the very height of this day, saying..."

END OF PISKA

PISKA 338

49)
"Ascend unto this mountain of Abarim":
> It is an "ascent for you and not a "descent".

"(Unto) This mountain of Abarim":
> For it was called by four titles: "Mountain of Abarim"; "Mount Nebo*"; Hor HaHar"; "Rosh HaPisgah". Why was it called the "Mountain of Nebo"? It was called such since there were buried within it these three prophets whose deaths were not caused by sin. And these are they: Moses, Aaron and Miriam.

"Which (אשר) is in the Land of Moab":
> This teaches us that He showed him the succession (שלשלת) of kings which were in the future to arise from Ruth the Moabite.

"Which (אשר) is over against Jericho":
> This teaches us that He showed him by succession (שלשלת) of prophets which were in the future to arise from Rahab the prostitute.

"And see all the Land of Canaan":
> Rabbi Eliezer says: The finger of the Holy One, Blessed Be He, became a *metatron* for Moses which showed him all the settlements of the Land of Israel. "Until here is the boundary of Ephraim; until here is the boundary of Menasseh."
>
> Rabbi Yehoshua says: Moses himself saw it. How was this accomplished? He put such power into the eyes of Moses that he saw from one end of the world unto the other.

END OF PISKA

PISKA 339

50)
"And die in the mount whither thou goest up":
He said to Him: Master of the Universe, why should I die? Is it not better that they should say "Blessed is Moses" from sight than that they should say "Blessed is Moses" from report? Is it not better that they should say "This is Moses who took us out of Egypt, and split the sea for us, (brought down the Torah for us) and brought down the manna for us, and performed miracles and wonders for us" than that they should say, "Such and such was Moses, such and such did Moses"?

He replied to him: "Cease, Moses, it is My decree which is apportioned equally to all people, as it is said, "This is the *law of a man*: that he dies -- in a tent...." (Numbers 19:14). And Scripture also states, "And this is the *law of the man* of the Lord God." (2Samuel 7:19).

The Ministering Angels said to the Holy One, Blessed Be He: "Master of the Universe, why did the first Adam die?"

He replied to them, "Because he did not perform my commandments."

They said to Him: "And behold Moses has performed your commandments!"

He replied to them: "It is my decree apportioned equally to all people," as it is said, "This is the law of the man: that he dies -- in a tent...." ("and this is the law of the man of the Lord.") "And be gathered unto thy people":

Near Abraham, Isaac and Jacob; (your fathers); near Amram and Kehath; (your fathers); near Miriam and Aaron your brother.
"As Aaron thy brother died":
This is the type of death that you desired.

And from whence did Moses desire the type of death that Aaron had had? When the Holy One, Blessed Be He, said, "Take Aaron and Eleazar his son..." (Numbers 20:25); "And strip Aaron of his garments". (Numbers 20:26). --This refers to the priestly garments. "And he put them on Eleazar." (Numbers 20:28). And so the second and so the third. He said to him: "Enter the cave!" And he entered. "Go up on the bier!" And he went up. "Stretch out your hands!" And he stretched. "Stretch out your feet!" And he stretched out. "Close your mouth!" And he closed. "Shut your eyes!" And he shut. At that time Moses declared, "Happy is he who dies by this type of death!" For this reason is it stated, "As Aaron thy brother died." -- It is the type of death that you desired.

END OF PISKA

PISKA 340

51)
"Because ye trespassed against Me":
>   It was you who caused them to trespass against Me.

"Because ye sanctified Me not":
>   It was you who caused them not to sanctify Me.

"Because ye rebelled against My commandment" (Numbers 27:14):
>   It was you who caused them to rebel against my commandment.

The Holy One, Blessed Be He, said to Moses: Did I not say the following to you: "What is that in your hand?" (Exodus 4:2); "Cast it upon the ground!" (Exodus 4:3). -- and you cast it (from your hand). Now you did not complain concerning these miracles which were due to that which had been in your hand, so why should you have complained concerning this light word*!"

And from whence do we know that Moses did not depart from the world until the Holy One, Blessed Be He, wrapped him in His wings? We know it from that which is said, "Therefore ye shall not bring this assembly...." (Numbers 20:12).

END OF PISKA

PISKA 341

52)
"For from afar thou shalt see the land, but thither thou shalt not come":

It is stated here, "but thither thou shalt not come." And it is stated further on, "But thither thou shalt not pass." (Deuteronomy 34:4). It is impossible to state, "But thither thou shalt not pass" for it has yet stated "But thither thou shalt not come." And it is impossible to state "But thither thou shalt not come" for it yet states, "But thither thou shalt not pass"! (And why does Scripture state, "But thither thou shalt not come", "But thither thou shalt not pass"?)--Moses said to the Holy One, Blessed Be He: "(Master of the Universe) If I cannot enter it as a king so I will enter it as a commoner. If I cannot enter it alive so I will enter it dead." --The Holy One, Blessed Be He, replied: "But thither thou shalt not come... but thither thou shalt not pass. Neither as king nor as commoner, neither alive nor dead."

END OF PISKA
END OF SIDRA

A

Medieval Commentary

to

Sifre Ha'azinu

2
Song and Commentary

Parashat Ha'azinu Hashamayim

Piska 306

They testified about themselves: I.e. they testified that God truly exists, is omnipotent, and is continually performing miracles for them.

He notified them they were subject to the witness[1]: He warned them-- The sense of warning them is that they then became legally liable to receive deserved sanctions.

He notified them they were subject to the witness of the Prophets : So that they should repent.

He notified them they were subject to witness of the Heavens : Specifically, in accordance with the injunction that *"The hand of the witnesses would administer punishment"*(Deut. 17:7) it meant that the Heavens were to hold back dew and rain. Similarly they were notified that they were subject to the Earth's withholding produce. Indeed, in specific allusion to this liability we note the subsequent statement, "They sinned in regard to the Heavens". This means they sinned through the Heavenly Host in that they worshipped them. (They made it impossible for the Heavens to punish them) since the law is that just as the star worshiper is penalized so is the object of the worship penalized (Gen. R. 96:1)[2]. The understanding of all the cases in this passage is in the same pattern.

And they exchanged His Kavod[3] **[for the likeness of a calf]** (Ps. 106:20): Even though the midrashist exegetes the verse here only in terms of the Golden Calf it also refers to the calves of Jeroboam and Ahab[4].

Humbled is the man who should have learned from the ant : I.e. Man has an intelligence superior to all creatures and properly all creatures should learn from him. Thus, if a man is required to learn from an ant he is humbled; and especially if he was required to do so and in fact did not learn from it.

Behold my witnesses exist : I.e. I am ashamed of myself and fear them.

Tutor: Guardian; namely, Heaven and Earth.

Complain: Gripe and protest.

Expand: Increase.

And constrict: They constrict and become smaller.

Hold still: They keep quiet.

In the plural: *"You are all to give ear."*

----

[1] The prooftext concerning the witness of the prophets is 2Kings 17:13, "And the Lord testified...by all the prophets etc." Our author sees here the model of understanding all the units in the passage.

[2] See *Bereschit Rabba* (ed. Theodor-Albeck) p. 1196, n.6. See also Tanh. Vayehi 3, Emor 2, y. Hag. 2:1. The introductory formula, *shaninu*, may indicate a tannaitic source.

[3] Lit: "Their kavod" but this is likely a euphemism for His Kavod-- His royal manifestation. See Sifre Num. 84.

[4] See 1Kings 12:28 for the calves of Jeroboam. As for Ahab, see 1Kings 16:3I and the comments of Kimhi (Radak) and Rashi on the verse.

For the Heavens are a plurality: As it states in b Hagiga: There are seven heavens. We may dismiss as irrelevant the midrash (Gen. R. 29:9, PRE 18, Shohar Tob Ps. 92) which mentions seven grounds (or "earths") for it appears that the heavens are discreetly separate, one above the other, whereas the grounds are not layered separately but are all on the same plane, only that some places are qualitatively inferior to others.

And the Sages say that the matter is not so: It seems to me that the Rabbis are not disputing the statement that the Heavens are a plurality. They dispute only the conclusion which was drawn; namely, that to illustrate the point of plurality Isaiah reversed the terminology.

Rather: It was to ensure that the testimonies of the witnesses would be in agreement.

Because the Torah was given from the heavens: The point here is to show that the Heavens were not exclusively "spoken to" nor the Earth only "talked to".

The intercalation of years: It is dependent upon sighting the moon which is in the heavens.

And Scripture further states *"Take my instruction"* (Prov. 8:10): We should strike this *And Scripture further states...* from the text. The main midrash itself is simply an embellishment. The obvious usage of "to take" in Scripture frequently refers to Torah. Certainly there is no sense in seeking here reasons for further Scriptural proofs.

Just as se'irim fall upon the grass and promote their growth: Here se'irim is explained as "rain". Perhaps it is so because they fall during a "sa'arah", a storm. Concerning raindrops the midrashist says they promote delight because they fall gently.

You should accumulate the laws of the Torah as general rules: The exegesis is based upon the order of Scripture. It first says *"upon the grass"* which is a general category for many varieties of grasses. It follows this by *"upon the herb"* which implies each type of herb; namely, it is a specific category.

A mercantile term: The point is the mercantile term means "break into small units". That is, that one should take precise account of each small unit and each letter in the Torah.

Just as the se'irim...and penetrate them: Here se'irim is explained as "wind" like its Aramaic rendering ,"rain winds".

They come for unintentional sins: For example: the goat of Pilgrimage Festivals, of New Moons, and of the Day of Atonement-- "se'ir" here is taken as in the term "se'ir 'izim", goats (Lev. 4:23).

Are used for the Tamid offerings: Here "revivim" is explained as "fats" like the Aramaic rendering for fat, "tarba"(Lev. 3:3).

So you should teach them in suffering: This means that you might not explain the words of the Torah until the questioner had gone through suffering himself; therefore Scripture states etc.

Falls upon him like a se'ir: This is another word for a demon which people fear; likewise when a person is young we force him to go to school for he fears the strap.

'"Arifah" specifically means killing...And so does Scripture state, *"For she cast down many corpses"* (Prov. 7:26): In a previous passage, Rabbi [Eliezer the son of Rabbi[1]] Yosi the Galilean also explained '"arifah" as "killing". Nevertheless, there are major differences between their interpretations. Namely Rabbi [Eliezer the son of Rabbi] Yosi the Galilean considers the term positively in reference to one who

---

[1] Absent in mss of commentary but present in mss of Sifre.

studies for the sake of Heaven, an act which atones like the 'arufa calf'. On the other hand Rabbi Bana'ah considers the term negatively as an expression of cautioning them that if they do not study for the sake of Heaven their necks will be broken ('arof); and in support we find *"For she cast down many corpses."*

To Caesarea: This is the name of a place which is distant and Bet Ilis is one which is extremely distant.

It gives delight to each and every one: This is the correct reading. Here "matoq"[1] is explained like its Aramaic rendering, "It rendered it pleasant." (Ex. 15:25).

Which comes from the west: Here "'oref" is explained "as showing the rear of the neck" which means to face backwards which indeed is to the West[2].

Spots the sky as goats: This is the correct reading.

In the summer it is difficult: In sum, this expresses ruin and disease as mentioned above.

Western-- always difficult: This poses a problem since above we said it was entirely for blessing. Perhaps the solution is that the former case considers a gentle shower while the latter considers a turbulent storm, for a like solution was given in Baba Batra 25b to solve the discrepancy in reports about the South wind.

And from whence do we know that it specifically refers to the resurrection of the dead: "It" refers to Deut. 32:2 in which Scripture mentions the Four Winds.

Except after twenty-one words: This is the number of words from *"Give ear"* until the divine name is reached.

The soldier's servant: This refers to the one leading the prayers, and "warriors" refers to those who respond "Blessed..." for they recite the more complete praise.

And from where do we know that to the one who says ["Bless!"] they respond by] "Blessed be the Name etc."[3]: That there is a call for such response[4] is deduced from *"Praise the greatness (of infinite existence)"*, and the sense that *"I call"* means to use a metonym is deduced from *"And he called"*. Here it says *"For I will call out the name of the Lord"*, And elsewhere, *"And Jacob called out-- the name of the Maqom (i.e. God)"*(Gen. 28:19)[5].

The preferred reading is-- And from where do we know that they specifically went down to Egypt that He might perform miracles and wonders for them to have His name sanctified in the world? It is as Scripture states, *"Then I called out to the name of the Lord."*: The verse is interpreted to mean that Moses said it in reference to the servitude. The proof is given in that Scripture states, a) *"And the children of Israel groaned from the work and they cried out..."*(Ex. 2:23,4) which is why, *"Then I called out to the name of the Lord."*; b) *"And Israel saw the hand which was*

----

[1] It would seem that the commenator read here "yoreh" ("to rain" but also "to show", "to teach") and likely his text provided the verse "...and the Lord showed him a tree which he cast into the water and the waters were rendered pleasant, there he gave him a law etc." (Exodus 15:25)

[2] Since the sun rises at the earth's front and sets at its back, East is front and West is back.

[3] The original Sifre text must have actually read, "From where do we know-to the sayer-- "Blessed be the Name..."

[4] A response incorporating praise of His eternity.

[5] The verse then would end, ("That happened at) the House of God." In Rabbinic literature "Maqom" serves as a divine name.

great..."(Ex. 14:31) which is why, *"Praise the greatness* of our God." We may dismiss as irrelevant that the servitude had been decreed much earlier (in Gen. 15:13) to last four hundred years. Even originally, the decree was specifically enacted for the purpose of having His name sanctified

Piska 307

His work is perfect:
Here "pe'ulato" is explained as "craft". The point is that everything he designed for his creatures was entirely complete[1]. No creature lacks any essential and useful limb. We may dismiss as irrelevant what at first glance seems obvious. That is, man would be better off if he could fly in the air. This is not so. If one could fly then others like him could fly also. This would result in direct flights of one group to suddenly attack another. No nation would be secure on its native soil. The fact is that such a capability would have been a defect.

Alternatively, "pe'ulato" is explained as "reward and punishment". Indeed Scripture has the usage, *"How great is your goodness which.... You craft as reward (pa'alta),"* (Ps. 31:20). This explanation suits what is said at the conclusion-- "He sits in judgment over every one".

For He declared the world worthy when He created it: This means that there would never be a world with an entirely evil population but some would be righteous and do what is upright in His eyes.

Deals uprightly: This refers to the fact that He does not judge anyone in accord with the evil deeds that he is going to commit in the future but in accord with his deeds at the time of judgment. This is as Scripture states, *"For God heard the voice of the lad according to where he was at present,"* (Gen. 21:17)[2].

Why did the...deserve: In other words, why were they fitting for such; or more plainly, what did they do to deserve this.

The trustee: For one deposits his soul each night with Him and although he owes Him a number of debts God returns his soul in the morning.

Philosophus opposed: It appears that "philosophus" is a term of lordship. (That philosophus actually denotes a sage is not relevant to the passage. Here it clearly connotes lordship and power. This is so since a governor who is appointed over a province must be sagacious to provide leadership for the citizens of the province.)[3].

----

[1] If God would have intended man to fly He would have given him wings.

[2] This follows the Rabbinic understanding of the verse in b Rosh Hashannah 16b.

[3] Why would our author begin by saying the term means an official; then backtrack to explain that it properly means a "philosopher" but cannot that mean that here; then go on to explain that it does refer to a governor since he has to be wise? The comment is very awkward. No less curious is his reference to "polipos" in the next comment as if this was the original term. "Polpos" is also found in piska 322 where our author suggests it may be the original behind the current "polomos" and after that he read "polpos" instead of the known variant "ploni". "Polpos" is a rare word and may have been pushed out of the majority of Sifre traditions (oral and written) since it was unknown but survived in that of our author. It makes more sense in the contexts than "philosopher" (piska 307) or "Mr. anybody." (piska 322). It seems likely that the original indeed read "plipos", i.e. *praepositus*, provost. With metathesis this becomes "plisof" or "prisof" (i.e. a military officer) which is mentioned in the *Aruch* s.v."bls". The glossator may have actually even had "PLPS" before him (note the reading in J) but not have distiguished between PWLPWS (attested by the Berlin Manuscript) and PYLWSWPWS (the majority reading). He added the erronious marginal comment (soon to fall into the text) to reconcile the author's comment with the known sense of "philosopher". It appears that an early scribe changed

He said, "My lord, do not let your mind gloat...": The point is that Polipos told the king he should take pride that he was granted so much power so as to burn the Torah.

For from the time: The point is that the Torah is not subject to burning. Rather the letters flew up in the air and returned to the heavens for originally they had been given from the heavens.

So also may your judgment be: That you be burnt like them-- for he had spoken insolently to him.

You have given me good news: By your saying that I should be like them I infer that this also is in regards to the World to Come.

Have I not said we should note the justification of the innocent: Which happens when the righteous are benefited and the wicked suffer. Here we see everything accords with justice and true judgment.

But even should we note the opposite: In which case it appears to people as if there is no truth and justice. To avoid drawing such conclusions Scripture states, "For all His ways are justice."

Piska 308

Israel became corrupt through all the negative commandments that are in the Torah: Here Corrupted him is explained to mean Israel corrupted itself in regard to every act which Scripture stated as a negative commandment.

And why use such an expression: This refers to what was said above. Even though they are corrupt, and they do not act properly, and they are blemished, they are nevertheless termed "children".

Twisted people: This is a form of "twist".

He repairs it by fire: At the outset with the fire of Torah. This is why it refers to ['mw (his mother)[1] for Scripture refers to "(the Torah) of your mother." (Prov. 1:8)".]

He chisels it with an adze: This refers to painful tribulations.

He throws it into the fire: This refers to Hell.

Piska 309

Reviles (tshwb): Showing anger, as in the expression "two dogs scowling (tshb) at each other" (Sanhed. 105a). The Aramaic rendering of "And her rival wife provoked anger" is "And she made her angry (tshb)." (1Sam. 1:6)

A councilman: This is the title of an official, the centurion is above him and the councillor is above him.

Shimon the son of Halafta says in his name: This refers to the above statement of Rabbi Judah.

One of three which were called possessions: In the baraita of "The Sages taught in the style of the Mishnah" [five][2] are enumerated. And the supplementary

---

"plisof" or "plipos" to "philosophus" to match the common Sifre reading.

[1] Our texts read 'wmn, craftsman. It seems one mistook 'mw, his mother, for 'wmn. All witnesses agree on the reading here and I suspect that the section I have marked is a corruption. The orginal I restore as-This is why it refers to 'wmn (craftsman), for Scripture (calls the Torah), '"wmn" (see Gen. R. 1:1). Our author distinguishes between the fire mentioned here and the fire mentioned two comments down.

[2] It seems to me that the word "hamishah" (five) was inadvertently dropped because it almost duplicates "mishnah" and so was overlooked.

two others are "Abraham" and "heaven and earth". And it would seem that there is no discrepancy. "Abraham" was included and "heaven and earth" was included. "Abraham" is here included in "Israel" who are his children and "heaven and earth" are here included in Torah, as Scripture says, *"Were it not for my covenant that is to be studied day and night, I would not have set the Laws of heaven and earth, "* (Jr. 33:25).[1]"

The till which contains everything: The furrow which contains everything.

[Scribes:] It would seem that the scribe is superior to the sage for he is able on his own, to cite texts, to expound them, and to confirm their meanings

Kwin kwin: Apertures and apertures. Or else, we should read here "firmly and firmly", meaning each is firmly situated and appropriately arranged in respect to the others-- and this interpretation is the more substantial.

He nourished you: He fed you.

Chambers and chambers: The intestines rest one upon the other and should one slip out of place a person would immediately die. This is a kind of warning-- See how you are dependent upon Him and so must always pray for mercy.

Piska 310

Yet shall not thy teacher be removed any more (Is. 30:20): The sense of "be removed" is "to be hidden"; "thy teacher" denotes a guide[2].

Piska 311

Cast them like bags: That is, like water pouches.

Merited to receive painful tribulations: From here we see that painful tribulations[3] are not meant as personal punishment since it says, "he merited" about them. Receiving tribulations showed his merit. Now you may question this on the grounds that the Rabbis in b Shabbat (55a) said that there can be no painful tribulation without sin. The truth is that this is also the case here. What they meant by saying that painful tribulations do not come upon a person except on account of sin is this: If he is not perfect, then the pain is for his sin; whereas if he is perfect, then it is for the sin of the generation (which, as a result, will not be destroyed).

They gradually began to manifest themselves: This refers to time when the punishments began to come. Now you may question this on the grounds that the merit of Abraham did not protect Sodom and Gommorah. But it can be answered. It is a fact that one of the painful tribulations was the war of the four kings (including the kings of Sodom and Gommorah). They specifically came against Abraham; for they said, "Let us begin by capturing Lot and finish by capturing Abraham"[4]. And it can be further answered. For when Abraham entered the Land the decree against

----

[1] See b Sanh. 32a for the Rabbinic understanding of this verse.

[2] While these comments seem somewhat obvious they are not. David Kimhi took "removed" as "gathered", and "thy teacher" as "thy rainfall". The verse implied blessing--that rain would no longer have to be stored as there would be ample supplies without storage. See his *Sepher HaShorashim*, s.v. YRH.

[3] Ms Oxford adds "of love".

[4] His merit did not extend to them as they were at one stage the ones to be protected against.

them had already been promulgated; resulting in the fact that they were not really members of one of the seven nations of Canaan for indeed they were brimstone and salt. Now once he had come into the Land his merit could only protect citizen-nations of the Land of Israel.

He specified the boundary of the Nations: So that they should not enter the Land of Israel. Now you may question this since He did indeed give the Land to the Hittites and the Amorites and the Canaanites. But it can be answered. It was known to Him that they would accumulate guilt until their measure was complete at which time they would be deserving to suffer extinction. Those who did not deserve to suffer extinction were driven far from the Land.

When the Most High gave the nations their inheritance....The fearer's of sin and the decent amongst them:The point refers to Greece and Media and all founding groups of nations who were sectioned in the days of Shem the son of Noah. When they divided up the world they were fearer's of sin and decent; however, regarding the seven nations which took the Land of Israel it is to be noted that not even the first generations were righteous[1].

There are sixty royalties (Song of Songs 6:8): That is, nations which have crowned monarchs.

And eighty concubines (Song of Songs 6:8): That is, eighty families which do not have kings. And I wanted to determine their reckoning.1) I have found in the Torah section of (the descendants of) Noah in connection with the verse *These are the generations of the sons of Noah* (Gen. 10:1) that it enumerates 57 nations. Now it is not useful to simply accept the count of 70 that indicates the justified sum of which the text states *From these there separated the groups of the nations,*(Gen 10:5). The 57 result when you remove from these 70 the duplication of those who were first counted and followed by their children who were again counted. The first son in such cases must not be counted. For example *The sons of Japhet are Gomer and Magog,* (Gen. 10:2)). *And the Children of Gomer are Ashkenaz...* (Gen 10:3). When a number is assigned to Gomer it is improper to count Ashkenaz and so on throughout the genealogies. If you tally in this way you get the result that there are only 57 nations, plus Amon, Moab and Esau for a grand sum of sixty.

2) Now the children of Hagar[2] total 14 families and the children of Ishmael are 12 princes for a sum of 26. The chieftains of the Horites who dwell in the land together with the chieftains of Edom come to less than 40. We then add on the Imites and the Philistine leaders and the dukes of Midian. The final total reaches eighty. All of these are to be considered as sub-groups within the seventy nations.

The nations merited to take two portions: Everything they took is only considered here to be two thirds of the world. In reality the Land of Israel is but one tenth of the area of the seventy nations (not 1/3). It has been related by the Rabbis that as a consequence of their recitation of their hymn at the sea in which they utilized the feminine form of "song" they received a one-tenth property inheritance as does a female. However, it would appear that since the nations descended through the dregs of Abraham and Isaac that the property of Esau and Ishmael are called two portions. Perhaps on this account all the nations are indicated here by these names-- for all of them adapted to these two religions, Edomite-Christianity

----

[1] Thus it was destined for Israel even then.

[2] According to the Rabbis, Gen. R. 61:4, Keturah was Hagar and the reference is really to the sons of Keturah.

and Ishmaelite-Islam[1].

Piska 312

Just as this (rope[2]-domain)[3] is threefold: It would appear that the reference here applies to the successive terms of identification of Israel who is called "treasured possession" (Ps. 135:4), "domain" (Deut. 14:2), "allotment" (Ps. 16:5,6[4]) It could not be thought to apply to Manasseh for what relevance is there in finding tripled identifications of Manasseh.

*A brother,'*ah, *is born for adversity*[5], (Prov. 17:17): Since his merit protected his generation against adversity. And a further sense is provided by the verse "*We have 'ahot*," (Cant. 8:8), meaning that he linked ('iha) the world to the Holy One, blessed be He, by teaching them the ways of God and so Scripture refers to him as *'ah.*

Two are better than one, (Eccl. 4:9): Scripture tells us who followed in the footsteps of Abraham, "*And Isaac dwelt and dug (the wells of water which were dug in the days of Abraham his father),*" (Gen. 26:18).

And the threefold cord, (Eccl. 4:12): Scripture tells us who followed in the footsteps of Isaac, "*And Jacob dwelt in the Land where his father had commuted,*" (Gen. 37:1). He commuted converts like his father.

Piska 313

He found him in a desert land: That the reference is to Abraham is shown by Scripture, "*And you found his heart...*" (Neh. 9:8).

In a place of unrest: No one had publicly recognized the One King, may His name be blessed and sanctified, in order to have His divine authority accepted. This acceptance is expressed by the notion that He would come into His palaces.

He gave him wisdom (ybwnnhw): This complex form is from the root "wisdom"(binah).

He ascertained for him (ymtsahw): This complex form is from a root meaning "to supply needs."

These are the Four Kingdoms: Indicated by Scripture's 1) *desert,* 2) *waste,* 3) *howling,* 4) *wilderness.*(Deut. 32:10)

Piska 315

Dan one, Judah one, Asher one: The order of verses here is not in sequence. Here is the order of verses as written in Ezekiel (48) *For these are his sides east and west; Dan one. And by the border of Dan, from the east side unto the west side; Asher one. And by the border of Asher, from the east side even unto the west side; Naphtali one. And by the border of Naphtali, from the east side unto the west side, Manasseh*

---

[1] The author accepting that Islam was a popular religion in the days of the Tannaim.

[2] HBL means both rope and domain.

[3] "Domain" is absent in J. and was added between the lines in O. See F. 352.

[4] Only Ps. 16:6 is cited in Sifre but is clear that the point needs both goral of vs. 5 as well as hbl of vs. 6.

[5] Adversity "tsarah" is spelled in O as "sarah"-- the brother of Sarah being Abraham and this doubtless is the point of the Sifre: tsarah = sarah.

one. And by the border of Manasseh ,from the east side unto the west side; Reuben one. And by the border of Reuben, from the east side unto the west side; Judah one.-
Rashi wrote in his commentary to Ezekiel: In the Sifre, parashat ha'azinu, we learn, " Why does Scripture state,*"Judah one; Dan one; Asher one*?--It is to tell us that in the future Israel will have its length from east to west measure by 25,000 reeds, which sum amounts to 75 miles."

Now from what source did they derive this measurement? From the dedicated portion which was equal to one of these portions as is explained in the narrative (Ez. 45:1). It measured 25,000 reeds which comes to 150,000 cubits for a reed contains 6 cubits (so Ez. 41:8). There are 2000 cubits in each mile as we learned in M Yoma (6:4), "Yet there are 10 booths from Jerusalem to Tsuk[1] ." Thus it is that 150,000 of them is equal to 75 miles. End quote of Rashi.

It does seem that the main point of exegesis in the midrash centers about the word *"one"*. Since we hear that the middle, central portions were all separate territories of what necessity was there to write such about Dan and Asher whose portions are at the head extremity or Judah who is at the end extremity. That we have these extraneous statements signifies that we are to find some deeper sense in them (hence they are singled out here for interpretation). Here is the sense of Rashi's comment, "Now from what source did they derive this measurement? From the dedicated portion which was equal to one of these portions."-- It was equal to one of these portions in length only. It is impossible to think that it could have been equal both in length and width for Scripture literally states, *"from the seaside unto the frontside."* Thus, everything that exists from the seaside, which is the west, to the frontside, which is the east, is the width of the tribal portions. Yet the measurements of the dedicated portion are stated as 25[000 reeds] in length by 10[000] in width.

Piska 316
Which are light to eat: That is, they do not constipate the stomach and this is learned from the word *"produce"*[2].
Sachne: And Gush Halab are place names.
Hardened figs: They were dried. The mention of honey refers to date honey.
Arguments *a fortiori*, the arguments by analogy, and comparisons: This text is accurate, *"butter"* and *"milk"* is explained as "light to heavy,"[3] *"with [fat of] lambs and rams of the breed of Bashan ,"* is explained as "analogy,"[4] *"and goats,"* is explained as "comparisons". We should not include the reading *"and refutations"*.

Piska 317
He made him ride ...this refers to the (gentile) world: The entire verse is exegeted in terms of the gentiles of Esau[5] as a fitting recipient of the actions "He

----

[1] BT mentions the common understanding of the Mishnah was that the distances between the middle booths were exactly 1 mile and the escorts could not go more than the 2000 cubit Sabbath limit. Thus the booths must have been set at 2000 cubits to allow for maximum escort. See Rashi to b Yoma 67a.

[2] "Tenuvah" from a root meaning "to flow".

[3] The visual images do so.

[4] The parallel structure of the verse suggests these terms.

[5] For the midrashist Esau is Rome, for the commentator it signifies later Rome with no distinction from its former character, that is Christendom,

made him ride" and "He made him suck". That is why it cites the verse *"The boar out of the woods doth ravage it,"* (Ps. 80:4). The meaning is--*"He will drive over him"*-- i.e. over Esau--*"upon the high places of the earth"*. The point is that the subject is Israel for it is written of them, *"And you shall trample on his high places,"* (Deut. 33:29). In like fashion you can interpret the entire verse.

And he shall devour the produce of the fields --this refers to the Four Kingdoms: For Edom is the Four Kingdoms which came after Alexander, king of Greece. Thus it is written,*"His kingdom shall be broken and shall be divided toward the four winds of heaven"* (Dan. 11:4); and indeed Edom did come to power after Greece.

These are the vine arrays that are in the Land of Israel[1]: In accord with the verse *"A land flowing with milk and honey,"* (Lev. 20:24).

Hypytqin and hegemonim: These are types of officials.

Kali-riqin: Types of elegant garments; and so is the poqiron except that the former goes above and the latter goes beneath and the trigon is worn between them. Now it is further possible to state that all of these are kinds of officials[2]. The trigon is located at a distance between the kali-riqin and the poqiron which is why it says here "who interprets between both of them." That is, they speak by gestures and he understands both of them so he can relay the words of the one to the other.

And split off: The term is used in Scripture, *"And he split me in pieces."* (Lam. 3:11)

A vat: A large wooden vessel.

Piska 318

From a sated state they were fit: That is, they were misfits who rebelled. The present reading belongs in the text.

And so you will find in regards to the "Days of the Messiah": This presents a problem for where do we find they are going to rebel in the future, in the "Days of the Messiah"? The answer is that the term "rebel" does not refer to an act of Israel but to an act of the nations of the world. This accords with what it goes on to say about three generations.[3]

And all the earth was of one language (Gen. 11:1): "Language (safa)," "One ('ahat)", is explained as "sated state (sova)," and "tranquility". This accords with the exegesis of," *And they pastured in the swamp ('aho),"* (Gen. 41:18). Namely, when

----

[1] Reading here "'atsion," rather than the common reading of "matsikim" (conductores who took the proper ties confiscated by Rome). According to Rashi b Babba Batra 12a the array describes a row of twelve vines.

[2] The readings here are somewhat different from our present texts. the commenator knows that poqiron and trigon are clothing terms and so he suggests that kaliriqin is also and he determines the positions because he knows the reading that the trigon is situated between them. On the other hand kaliriqin is a known term of an official and so he suggests that alternatively all three terms are terms for officials and believes this best suits the reading that the trigon interprets between the other two.

[3] See two comments below.

there is a state of satedness (pasturing) in the world there is tranquility ('ahva)[1] in the world.

The end parts of the yoke: These are the straps of the yoke.

These are the three generations that precede the "Days of the Messiah": That is, The three generations of which the gentiles will control which immediately precede the "Messianic Era." On account of their wealth they will rebel excessively and take pride in their false gods and idols.

Do not read, "...and he despised" but "And he despised...": Understand "despise (nbl)" from the Biblical root, cause to wither (nbl), as in "the flower is withered," (Is. 40:7,8). The sense then is that, if such an image could be imagined, "He will cause His power to wither so that He is incapable of saving."

Things pertaining to male organs[2]: For she made an abominable image like a male organ so that she could have sexual relations with an idol.

A Jewish image: One made by a Jew.

Piska 319

About the merit of your ancestors: Scripture's *"who gave you birth"* is exegeted from a root (hll, profane[3]) so as to mean, "those who profaned themselves to bring him into the world". In other words it means "his father and his mother."

The God who gave birth for you: That is He created the world for you. This is derived from Scripture's language, ["gave birth to me." (Prov. 8:26)[4]].

Who experienced pain: This is derived from Scripture's , "Pangs, as of a woman in travail," (Jer. 4:31).[5]

Who caused His name to be associated with you: As it is written, *"And you shall be to me a private property,"* (Ex. 19:5).

Lowly: That is to say that everyone else will rule over you.

The voice of The Lord is upon the waters, (Ps. 29:3 ff.): The verse applies a sense of elevation concerning those who study Torah as it states,*"on"*, but when they become low-- it states,*"He strips off"* meaning he uncovers their heads[6] (removing his authority and protection).

----

[1] Thus 'ahat means the tranquility that comes as a result of bounty. See Targum Onkelos to Gen. 41:18.

[2] He reads "zkrut" whereas we have "zarut" (foreigness).

[3] The comments here and following center around derivations of the root hll as it occurs in Deut. 32:18.

[4] The mss are lacking the prooftext.

[5] This appears in our texts as a proof text suggesting either that "who experienced pain"should be stricken from the text so that the verse is said to act as a prooftext for "God who gave you birth" or that the prooftext was absent from the author's reading.

[6] An expression connoting open disobedience. God thus shows who they are by this action in the very way that the High Priest uncovers the head of an unfaithful wife. Ex. R. 15:1 claims the righteous covered their heads when the servitude to Egypt began. They uncovered their heads when redemption was announced. Servitude was over.

Piska 320
From Moses there descended scorners[1]: Scripture writes about this, "The son of Gershom, the son of M[N]SH," (Judges 18:30)[2]

A perverse...upsets: Two upsets are indicated. When they turn for the worse, the divine rod of punishment turns upon them.

They are rebellious: Perverted.[3]

But "**by a lvi nation**": It would seem that this is the same root as vnlvh, "and were joined to" (Is. 14:1). The sense is of a composite people; one from Amon, one from Moab, one from every nation and kingdom.

Four Kingdoms: I explained above that it refers to those who came after Alexander. So it states in b Yev. 63a[4] -- Evil comes to the world specifically for the sake of Israel.

Piska 321
Plagued: Swollen. This is the correct reading. *"Plagued by hunger,"*(Deut. 32:24), is rendered into the Aramaic version as "swollen by hunger."

That all who are possessed by a demon do froth: " Froth" here is like the Biblical expression, *"And he expelled his froth upon his beard* (1Sam. 21:14)." The sense is that he expels spit from his mouth.

Raise an ulcer: "Ulcer" is related to a Talmudic word connoting a scab on a wound as in "One who developed an ulcer on his flesh may leave it alone and die or cut it off and live." (Gen. R. 46, b Av. Zarah 10b)[5].

Bring in the foot: Do not go outside.

Scatter: Escape to another place where there is no hunger.

The chambers of his heart beat within him and he dies: This is related to the expression " his heart (mind) troubles (beats) him" (b Nidah 3a). The sense is that even if he did flee he has not escaped. Indeed he takes to heart some of the troubles that pain him and he dies.

This adds to these: We have "young man and maiden" who are killed and others added to them. On account of the double "also" which function as conjunctions we know even more things happened. There is more to add and indeed these things are specifically written[6] at the end of the verse-- *"The suckling with the gray haired man."* And likewise Sifre cites the verse *"For also the man..."* (Jer. 6:11),

---

[1] A very strange reading here of "mmsh baim lw" compared to the mss of Sifre "mmh shnaim lw".

[2] Moses is called MSH in Hebrew and wicked Menasseh is called MNSH. The N in his name was suspended, it was claimed (b Babba Batra 109b) to show he was descended from MSH, Moses.

[3] "Potin" means "lacking understanding". Our texts of Sifre vary here but "potin" is not found. Perhaps his text read "poranim" as ours do. His comment appears to read in the mss "It is in error - t'wt." I have translated as if it said "perverted-- m'wt".

[4] Our texts here have poranut, punishment.

[5] Text in A. Z 10 b ,Gen. R. 46 and see Aruch¦nima

[6] Even if they were not written we would know that there were more tragedies.

as an illustration that we shouldn't impute more to the "also's" than are found at the end of the verse[1].

You have caused: Here the twin terms "also" mean-- You are certainly the cause for the killing of the general population but even more than them[2], the young men and the maidens who had never experienced sin.

Suckling: This is the correct reading. It means they enjoyed Torah study as if they had never had a previous taste of it before, like a virgin who enjoys her first sexual experience.

Bound in fetters: Tied in fetters-- they are chains.

Piska 322

Hand them over: That is, deliver them into the hands of the enemy.

They flatter (khs): They agreed that they were greater than them. This usage accords with the verse, *"And your enemies shall flatter you,* (Psalm 66:3).

In the war (polomos): And if one reads "polpos" here it refers to the commander who is appointed over the soldiers.[3]

Decarion: A warrior's title.

Before he reached him: Before the decarion reached the Jew.

A snake came out and enwrapped him: Enwrapped himself around the heel of the Jew. This demonstrated that he was being killed by Heaven. and not by the strength of the Decarion. For this reason the text states, "He said to him," meaning the Jew to the Decarion.

Say to Polpos[4]: This is the correct reading. In other words, "to your chief."

Piska 323

If they would have reflected upon what Jacob their father had told them: This presents a problem for where do we find that he told them these things? The answer is that these things are derived from the verse, *"And this is the thing which their father told them and he blessed them. (And he commanded...),"* (Gen. 49:28).

"And this is the thing"-- accounts for "the acceptance of the yoke of the kingdom of Heaven". The principle is that "And this" specifically refers to Torah[5]. The performance of its commandments constitutes the acceptance of the yoke of kingship.

"Which their father told them"-- the point is (in the next verse, although missing in detail) he gave them his testaments. This accounts for "and

----

[1] Just as we have two types of people in the verse so we have two others at the end showing that the set of who is to be added is complete.

[2] Not "also" but "yea" and as such they are not terms which call for something to be added to the text.

[3] The Oxford manuscript reads "polpos" while both B and J read "polomos". Considering that he is providing an alternative to "polomos" this reading has to be discarded. Two comments further it seems that "polpos" is the majority reading and is correct. The problem requires further study.

[4] O reads polmos but both B (Plpos) and J (polpos) agree closely, see polomos two comments above. The explanation here of PLPS as an official accords with what he says two comments above and at the end of piska 307. It is a term of authority.

[5] See above "And Scripture further states..." Our Sifre texts at that point cite the common tradition to this effect and our author sees it all as redundant.

reconcile each other with the fear of Heaven".

"And he blessed them"--accounts for "and deal with each other charitably". This passage, immediately after the word "blessed", refers to charitable behavior (of proper burial).

Consider it bought[1]: It was a heavy article which could not be carried away without great difficulty. Thus it happened that the buyer did not carry it away immediately.

Like the impure into the hands of the pure: As if you were impure and the nations of the world were pure so you shall be delivered into their hands.

Immediately: Quickly and without difficulty.[2]

Specifically the holy seed: That is, yet they made themselves into the planting[3] of Sodom.

Their bitterness[4] is dispersed amongst them: It refers to their punishment and agrees with the Aramaic rendering, "Their punishments...are their bitterness," (Deut. 32:32).

Piska 324

As a sima: A store.

(And mhwsr:[5]) A hoard, related to " store" ('otsar).

It might be thought that it would become weak, so Scripture stated, "strong wine": It refers to its reaching a pale state so that would no longer be wine-like but water-like.

Of marrow (mwh): From a semantic view the reference is to blobs which dissolve (nmh) as if there is nothing there. The midrash equates this with pqitm; i.e. olive pits, which are refuse.

If you would say they do: Namely, that their deeds would yield more results; the effect would be that they would destroy the world.

Piska 325

This is the correct reading--"Vengeance is mine and I will recompense it," is not written here but rather,"And recompense": Had it said "And I will recompense it", the sense would be "to mete out their punishment" and nothing else. But now that it is in fact written, "And recompense," the sense of the verse is "Vengeance is mine" i.e. to mete out their punishment and also "recompense" i.e.[to mete out the punishments for those deeds of theirs which were done also by their ancestors.][6]

----

[1] A rather intriguing reading for the problematic 'eved qiri' in our texts.

[2] This belongs after "Consider it bought".

[3] It appears that he read "seed" whereas we have planting in our Sifre texts proper.

[4] O and J read mktn as do our sifre texts, but this must be considered a later emendation for our author's mrtn which is the only reading to explain his use of the Targumic kmrrn."Disperse" r efers to payment.

[5] This bracketted section is absent in our texts but apparently belongs. The reading "as a sima" appears in J and also in O but here a second hand has erased and written over "as a sima" so that the text reads "kmus wmhwsr --A hoard, related to store ('otsr)"; instead of what is given here.

[6] The bracketed section does not appear in the mss, but something like it clearly belongs here.

["For the day of their calamity is at hand.":] The point is that their tribulations will not be suffered consecutively, how much more so, we[1], of whom Scripture states, *"And after many days shall they be punished,* (Is. 24:22).

Piska 326

[Remorse (thwt):] This is as the usage in the expression "When he is sorry about (btwha) his earlier sins."[2]

When he sees that all walk before him: When he sees that they return in penitence on account of their tribulations. It explains[3] the sense of the verse -- When he sees that the message of the punishing hand has gotten through to them.

Hand: He explains this to mean a peruta coin[4].

[Like Moses:] Of whom Scripture writes-- *"And his hands were steadfast until the sun set,"* (Ex. 17:12).

Like Aaron: Of whom Scripture writes-- *"Take the fire-pans,"* (Num. 17:11); " *And Aaron took as Moses had commanded,"* (Num. 17:12).

Like Phineas: Of whom Scripture states:" *And he took the shield in his hand,"* (Num. 25:7).

Piska 327

Israel will say to the Nations of the World: That is, in the Messianic Era.

Piska 328

Aspanonit: The wages for his troops.

Donativa: A meal for kings.

Salania: Tax.

Let them help yourselves (vy'zrwkm): The sense of this is (that it refers to officials)-- Let them help you and themselves.

Let them help you: That is, "Let Him give help for your needs," And so it refers to God[5].

Piska 330

Hpqti: A term denoting an official.

Enters into the province: That is, a royal province. If an officer entered it with his army, plundering and looting it; it could happen that the king could not punish him. For example, if he fled back to his own country no one could exact retribution from him.

If he can exact retribution from the officer: That is, while the officer is alive.

----

[1] "They" is the euphemism in the text.

[2] See b Kid. 40a and Num. R. 10:1

[3] His use of pst here is to read the verse midrashically, not to give a literal rendition.

[4] Perhaps he means it is something which is commonly grasped in the hand.

[5] This passage is somewhat corrupt but able to be restored by its wording in the comments of Soliman Ohana. We see that mš(y'zrw) is to be read as mš' = mšm'and so mšh is to be read as mš' vy('zr), vy corrupting to h in the sphardic hand- style.

Piska 331
This is one....And this is two: That is, two judges or else two times.

Piska 332
Make others drunk: This refers to the birds who naturally feed off carcasses and dogs which naturally consume blood.

Retributions (pr'wt): He explains this as if it were a form of "pharaoh".

Piska 333
It is atonement for them: This is exegeted in accordance with Scripture's *"They have spilled their blood* [around Jerusalem]," (Ps. 79:3).

They remove: This is a passive usage-- they are removed from them.

They bear: The usage here is like that of *"He shall bear her sin,"* (Num. 30:16).

All who live in the Land of Israel etc.: The Land of Israel is called holy and holy refers to the holy place[1].

And recites the Shma liturgy in the mornings and the evenings: This follows the ruling of the sage who ruled in tractate Menahot 99b-- he thereby fulfills the commandment of *"And you shall speak of them day and night,"* (Josh.1:8). The Shma liturgy is based upon sanctifying His name and committing oneself to His unity and to the yoke of His kingship.

And speak in the holy language: This completes the three holinesses[2]; the holiness of the Land, the holiness of His name, and the holiness of His language. Or else, the point is that the whole world was created, at its inception, within the Land of Israel so that it is referred to as the navel of the world.[3] This is as it is written, *"From Zion it became finished in beauty,"* (Ps. 50:2). Now the world was created by the holy language. Therefore one should speak in the holy language in the Land of Israel.

It refers to the present: *"For I shall call upon the name of the Lord."*[4]

It refers to the past: *"Let it drop like the rain,"* which refers to the giving of the Torah.

It refers to the Future Era: *"For the Lord will judge his nation."*

It refers to this world: The essence of the entire Song.

It refers to Coming World: *"O nations, rejoice over his people."*

Piska 334
It is impossible to say "And he came etc.": It would seem that we are referring to what was said prior to the Song. There Scripture states, *"And Moses went...and he spoke to the Children of Israel..."*(Deut. 31:1), signifying that he was then with Israel. Since that was the case it might seem that it was unnecessary for Scripture to state, *"And he came"*. Rather the point is to teach you that his time[5]

----

[1] Namely, the Temple site.

[2] That is, these things partake of the divine realm and give people access to the divine.

[3] See "Midrash adonai behochma yisad aretz," in A. Jellinek, *Bet Ha-Midrasch*, pt.5, p.63, and BT Yoma 54b.

[4] The need for salvation.

[5] And not that Moses came.

had already come. "Came" here is an expression such as in "When the sun came," (Genesis 28:11) which has the sense of setting.

Diatikos: This word expresses an appointed time to depart from the world.

And authority was given: I.e. The power of rule was delivered to Joshua.

But yet it has already stated: That is to say, also at that point he was properly named Joshua.

Piska 335

Like mountains: An important law and major tenet can depend upon a single scriptural word or a single exegetical tradition.

Offer them strong thanks: Encourage them by telling them how much they will be rewarded.

Would not be all the same: Read it as a rhetorical question.[1]

Piska 336

And by this word (Deut. 32:47): Which refers to the Torah.[2]

Honoring of father and of mother: The rewards in this world and the next are derived from the Scripture which states, "*And it shall be good for you,*" (Deut. 5:16) which refers to this world, while "*And you shall prolong your days,*" (ibid.), refers to the Coming World. Likewise is the derivation of sending away the mother bird (since Deut. 22:7 contains the same expressions.)

Piska 338

Mt. Nebo: This is explained as if its root were nbwah, prophecy.

Piska 340

This [light] word: "*And you shall speak to the rock,*" (Num. 20:8).

----

[1] I.e. "Would it not be all the same!"

[2] Thus the "length of days" mentioned in the verse refers to the reward of Torah study in the Future World.

Part Three

SIFRE HA'AZINU WITH COMMENTARY
(Hebrew)

Part Three

ס פ ר י   ה א ז י נ ו

נוסח דפוס ראשון (ש״ר)
עם פירוש חכם גדול
על פי כתבי יד שלא נדפסו עד הנה

אקספורד= כ״י 425 (Mich. 376) בספריה באדליאן באוקספורד
סמנריה= כ״י בוסקי #5 (REEL 56) בJTS ניו יורק (מקורם כ״י שׂון 598/2#)
ברית אברהם= פירוש אברהם בן גדליה על ילקוט שמעוני, ליוורנו, ח״י.

Part Three
SIFRE HA'AZINU WITH COMMENTARY (Hebrew)

ס פ ר י

פ י ר ו ש

פרשת האזינו השמים שו

היה רבי מאיר אומר בשהיו ישראל
צבאים היו מעירים בעצמם שנאמר
ויאמר יהושע ע' העם עדים אתם בכם.
קילקלו בעצמם שנאמר סבבוני בכחש
אפרים ובמרמה בית ישראל. העיד בהם
שבט יהודה ובנימן שנאמר ועתה יושבי
ירושלם ואיש יהודה שפטו נא ביני ובין
כרמי . מה לעשורת עוד לכרמי . קילקלו
שבט יהודה שנאמר בגדה יהודה. העיד
בהם ארץ הנביאים שנאמר ויער יהוה
בישראל וביהודה . ביד נביאים כל חוזה.
קילקלו בנביאים שנאמר ויהיו מלעיבים
כמלאכי אלהים ומתעתעים בנביאיו . העיד
בהם ארץ השמים שנאמר העידותי בכם

(פסקא שו)
הם היו מעירים בעצמם. כלומר
היו מעירים על הקרוש ברוך הוא
שהוא חי וקים ויכול ועושה עמהם
נסים בכל עת ובכל שעה:
העיד בהם. התרה בהם. פירוש
מתרה עליהם שראויים לבא עליהם
צרות:
העיד בהם הנביאים. שיחזרו
בתשובה:
העיד בהם השמים. משום דכחיב
רך העדים (דברים יז.ז.), לומר
שימנעו מליחן סל ומסר והוא הדין
שהעיד בהם הארץ אלא משום רבעי
למימר קלקלו בשמים כלומר שקללו
על ידי צבא השמים לעובדם, וקימא
לן כאם שנפרעין מן העובד כך
נפרעין מן הנעבר (בראשית רבה
צו.א). והיינו טעמא רכולהו:

היום ארץ השמים וארץ הארץ . קלקלו
בשמים שנאמר האינך רואה מה חם
עושים שנאמר הבנים מלקטים עצים
והאבות סבערים את האש וחנשים לשות
בצק לעשורר כונים למלברת השמים.
העיד בהם ארץ הארץ שנאמר שמעי ארץ
חנה אני מביא רעה . קילקלו בארץ
שנאמר מכבחתם כנלים על חלמי שדי.
העיד בהם ארץ הדרכים שנאמר כל
ראש דרך נגורת בבית רמתך . שמע
ארץ הנוים . עמד עד דרכים קלקלו
דרכים. העיד בהם הנגורת קלקלו מנגורת
העיד בהם ארץ הנוים . קילקלו בנוים
שנאמר ויתערבו בנוים וילמדו מעשיהם
העיד בהם ארץ הדרים שנאמר שמע
הרים את ריב יהוה. קלקלו בהרים שנאמר
על ראשי הדרים יזבחו . העיד בהם ארץ
תבוסם שנאמר ירע שור קנוד וחמור
אבס בעליו . קלקלו בבהמה שנאמר
ויסירו את כבודם מבחנית שור אוכל
חסיד בשמים ירעה מוע'דיה . ותזר וסיס
ונער. קלקל בחוה שנאמר ואשוב וארא
והנה תבנית רמש ובהמה שקץ . העיד
בהם את הרנים שנאמר או שיח לארץ
ותורך ויספר כי דני חים . קלקל בדנים
שנאמר ותעשה אדם כרני חים . העיד
בהם את תנבלה שנאמר לך ל נמלה על
ראה דרכיה וחכם אשר אין לה קצין .
חכין בקיץ לחמה . רבי שמעון בן אמר
אסר עלוב היה אדם זה שצריך ללמו
סן תנבלה אילו למד תעשה עלוב היה לא
שצריך ללמו סרדכיה ולא למר . עזורה
נבסת ישראל שתאמר לפני הקרוש ברוך
הוא רבונו של עולם הרי עדי קיסים
שנאמר העירותי בכם את השמים ואת
הארץ אסר לה הרי אגו סעבירן . שנאמר

ויטירו את כבודם (תהלים
קו, כ). אדרב דדרשי לה על מעשה
הענל נם נאמר על עולי ירדבעם
ואתכי:

עלוב הוא אדם שצריך ללמור סן
הנבלה. כלומר אדם יש לו דעה
כננר כל הבריווח וסן הרין שכל
הבריות ילמרו ממנו ואם הוא צריך
ללמור סן הנבלה עלוב הוא. וכל
שכן אם היה לו ללמור ולא למד:
הרי עדי קיימין. כלומר, ואני
סתכי'ויה ופתירהה מהם:

כי חגי כבוד וזהו אחר מחקוני
הסופרים: עין ספרי כמדבר צד:

6 עין מלכים א יב, כח ונם שם
מז. ל א (ורד'ק ורש'י):

הריני סעבירם שנאמר כל נוא ונשא .
אומרת לפניו רבונו של עלם הרי שמי
קיים אומר לה הריני סעבירו שנאמר
קרא לך שם חרש . אומרת לפניו
רבונו של עולם הרי שמך קרוי על שם
תבעלים. אסר לה הריני סעבירו שנאמר
וחסירוחי את שמות תבעלים ספיה .
ואומרת לפניו רבונו של עלם אף על
פי כן בן בני בית מזבירים אותו אומר
לה ולא יזברו עד בשמם . שוב למתר
עתירה שתאמר לפניו רבונו של עלם
כבר כתבת לאסר הן ישלח איש את
אשתו והלכה מאתו וחיתה לאיש אחר.
אוסר לה כלום הבתבתי לך לא איש
הלא כבר נאמר כי ל אנכי ולא איש .
כי נרושים אתם לי בית ישרא' . והלא
כבר נאמר כה אסר יהוה יתוה איזה ספר
כריותרת אמכם אשר שלחתיו אי, סי
מנושי אשר סכרתי אחבם לו. דבר אחר
האזנו השמים ססל למלך ססור ארץ

[פירוג. אומן.
זהיינו שמים
וארץ:]

בנו לפירנגג להוירת יושב ומשסרו . אסר
אותו הבן כסבור אבא שהועיל כלום
שמסרני לפירוג. עכשיו חריני משסרו כרי
שיאכל וישתרה וישן ואלך אני אעשה
רצוני וצרכי . אסר לו אכיו אף אני ל לא
סמרתיך לפירוגג כרי שלא יחיר סזיקך.
כך אסר להם משה לישרא' שמא אתם
סבורים לברות מעל כנפי השבינה או
לוז מעל הארץ. ולא עד ולא שהשמים
נותבים שנאמר ינלו שמים עונו וסני
שאף הארץ סורעת שנאמר ואמר וארץ
מתקוססתא לו . עתורה מכר ישרא'
שתעמיד ליים לפני הסקום . ואוסרת
לפני רבונו של עולם. איני יודעת סי
קילקל בסי וסי שינרה בסי אם ישרא'
קילקלו לפני הסקום ואם הסקום שינרה
בהם בישרא' כשתאוא אוסר וינורו שמים
צדק . הוי ישרא' קילקלו לפני הסקום
ואין הסקום שינרה בהם בישרא' שנאמר

כי אני יהוה לא שניתי · דבר אחר
האזינו השמים היה רבי יהודה אומר
משל למלך שהיו לו אפוטרופוסים
במדינה והשלים להם את שלו ומסר
להם את בנו ואמר להם · כל זמן
שבני עושין לי רצוני היו מעדנים
ומעדנים אותו ומפנקים אותו ומאכילים
אותו ומשקים אותו · וכשאין בני עושין
רצוני ל וטעמו סטלי כלום כן בזמן
שישראל עושים רצונו של מקום סרה
נאמר בהם יפתח יהוה לך את אוצרו
הטוב את השמים לתת מטר ארצך
בעתו · וכשאין ישראל עושים רצונו של
מקום סרה נאמר בהם וחרה אף יהוה
בכם ועצר את השמים ולא יהיה
מטר והאדמה לא תתן את יבולה ·
דבר אחר האזינו השמים · משל למלך
שיצא בנו לתרבות רעה התחיל לקבל
עליו באחיו · התחיל לקבל עליו באוהביו ·
התחיל לקבל עליו בשכניו · התחיל
לקבל עליו בקרוביו · לא זו האב ההוא
מלהיות קובל והולך עד שאמר לשמים
למי אקבול עליו חוץ מאילו לכך נאמר
האזינו השמים · דבר אחר האזינו השמים
אילו שאין דין של צדיקים ולא
שמרחיבים על העולם שתם מתוב
שבזכורת ששיראל עושים רצונו של מקום
סרה נאמר בהם יפתח יהוה לך את
אוצרו הטוב את השמים ואין לשון
פתיחה אלא לשן הרווחה שנאמר ויפתח
את רחמה ואילו אין דין של רשעים
ולא שרוחקים את העולם שתם בתוכו ·
שבשעה שאין עושם רצונו של מקום.
סרה נאמר בהם ועצר השמים · ואין
לשון עצירה אלא לשן רוחק שנאמר
כי עצר עצר יהוה בעד כל רחם ·
דבר אחר האזינו השמים ואנכ ברד ·
אמר לו הקדש ברוך למשה אמור להם
לישראל הכתכלתי בשמים ובארץ שבראתי
לשמשכם שמא שינו את מידתם או
שבא נלגד חמר אינו עולם. אלא מן
המזרח ומאיר לכל העולם כולו ולא
כענין שנאמר וחית חשמש ובא חשמש ·
ולא עוד ל שמא לעשות לי רצוני
שנאמר והוא כחתן יצא מחותו ויש
כנגדו לרוץ אורח · וחשמע הארץ אמרי
פי · הסתכלו בארץ שבראתי לשמשכם
שמא שינתרו את מירתם שמא זרעתם

קובל. צועק ומתרעם:
מרויחין. מגדילין:
ועצר. שנעצרין ונעשים
קשים:

ולא צמחה שמא זרעתה חיטים
העלית שעורים או שמא פרה אינה
רשה ואינה חורשת היום · או שמא
חמור זר אינו טוען ואינו הולך · וכי
לענין הים הוא אומר האותי לא תיראו
נאם יהוה אם מפני לא תחילו אשר
שמתי חול גבול לים · שמשערה שנזרתי
על הים שמא שינה את מידותיו
ואומר אעלה ואצוף את העולם לא
כענין שנאמר ואשבור עליו חוקי ואומר
עד פה תבוא ולא תוסיף ולא עוד
אלא שמצטער ואין יכול מה לעשות
בענין שנאמר יהמו גליו ולא יכלו והרי
דברים קל וחומר · ומה שלא נעשו לא
לשכר ולא להפסד אם זוכים אין מקבלים
שכר ואם חוטאים אין מקבלים פורענות
ואין חסים על בניהם ועל בנותיהם לא
שינו את מידתם אתם שאם זכיתם אתם
מקבלים שכר ואם חטאתם אתם מקבלים
פורענות ואתם חסים על בניכם ובנותיכם
על אחת כמה וכמה שאתם צריכים
שלא תשנו את סרוחיכם · דבר אחר
האזינו השמים · היה רבי בנאה אומר
בזמן שאדם מתחייבים אין פושטים בו יד ·
אלא עדים שנאמר יד העדים תהיה בו
בראשונה להמיתו ואחר כך כל העם
שמשתמשים ובאים שנאמר ויד כל העם
באחרונה בזמן שאין ישראל עושים רצונו
של מקום סה נאמר בהם וחרה אף
יהוה בכם ועצר השמים ואחר פורענות
משתחשרת ובאה שנאמר ואבדתי בהם ·
ובזמן שישראל עושים רצונו של מקום מה
נאמר בהם והיה ביום ההוא נאם יהוה
אענה את השמים והארץ תענה ·
וזרעתיה לי בארץ · דבר אחר האזינו
השמים וארנבה היה רבי יהושע בן חנניה
אומר בשעה שאמר משה האזינו השמים
היו השמים ושני השמים רומסים ובשעה
שאמר וחשמע הארץ אמרי פי היתה
הארץ וכל אשר עליה רומסים · ואם
תמיה אתה על הדבר צא וראה מן
נאמר ביהושע ויאמר לעיני ישראל שמש
בנבעון רום ירח בעמק אילון · וידום
השמש וירח עמד · ולא היה ביום ההוא
נמצינו לסירים שהצריקים שולטים בכל
העולם כולו · דבר אחר האזינו השמים
לפי שהיה משה קרוב לשמים לפיכך אמר
האזינו השמים ולפי שהיה רחוק מן הארץ

דומין. שוחקין ·

לפיכך אסר ותשמע הארץ אמרי פי. מא
ישעיה וסמך לדבר ואמר שמע שמים
והאזיני ארץ . שמע שמים שהיח רחוק
מן השמים והאזיני ארץ שחיה קרוב
לארץ. דבר אחר לפי שהיו שמים מרובים
פתח בהם בלשון מרובה ולפי שהיתה
ארץ מועטה פתח בה בלשון מועט.
ותשמע הארץ אמרי פי . בא ישעיה
וסמך לדבר . ואמר שמע שמים והאזיני
ארץ . ליתן ארץ הרוובה בסרובים ואת
המעוטה למעוטים וחכמים אומרים
אין הדבר כן לא שהעדים מעידים אם
נמצאו דבריהם סכוונים כאחד עדותם
קיימת . ואם לאו אין עדותם קיימת,
כך אילו אמר משה האזינו השמים
ושותק היו שמים אוסרים לא שמענו
לא בהאזנה . ותשמע הארץ . חיתה
הארץ אוסרת לא שמעתי לא בשמיעה
בא ישעיה וסמך לדבר שמעו שמים
והאזיני ארץ ליתן האזנה ושמיעה
לשמים והאזנה ושטיעה לארץ . דבר
אחר האזינו השמים על שם שניתנה
תורה מן השמים שנאמר אתם ראיתם
כי מן השמים דברתי עמכם . ותשמע
הארץ אמרי פי . שעלירז עמד ישראל
ואמרו כל אשר דבר יהוה נעשה ונשמע.
דבר אחר האזינו השמים שלא עשו
מצוורת שניתנו להם מן חשמים עיבור
שנים . וקביעורת חדשים . שנאמר והיו
לאותרת ולמעדים וליטים ושנים .
ותשמע הארץ. שלא עשו נצוות שניתנו
להם בארץ לקט שכחה ופיאה תרומות
ומעשרות שמיטים ויובלורת . דבר אחר
האזינו השמים שלא עשו כל מצוות
שניתנו להם מן השמים ולא עשו כל
מצוות שניתנו להם בארץ . משרה חזיק

בלשון מרובה. והאזינו:
שהיו השמים מרובין. כדאמרינן
במגינה (יב:): שבעה רקיעים ואמ״ג
דאמרינן כמדרש שבעה ארצות
(ויקרא רבה כס.ס, פרר״א יח.
שר״ם צב), נראה רשמים הן זה
למעלה מזה אבל הארצות אינן זו
למעלה מזה אלא כולן אחת
והמקומות נרעוד זה סזה:

וחכמים אומרים אין הדבר כן.
נראה לי דלא פליגי רבנן בהא
רשמים מרובין אלא על מה דאמרו
דעל כן שינה ישעיה הלשון כדי
לסתור לדבר על זא פליני:
אלא. לכוין דברי העדים:

על שהתורה ניתנה מן השמים. לא
בא אלא שלא לפרש דבור לשמים
ואמירה לארץ:
יעבור שנים. חלוי כרייאת הירח
שהיא כשמים:

בישראל שני עדים שהם קיימים לעולם
ולעולמי עולמים אמר להם אני בשר
ודם למחר אני מרד אם ירצו לוסר לא
קבלנו את התורה סי בא וכבחישם
לפיכך העיד עליהם שני עדים שהם
קיימים לעולם ולעלמי עולמים . והמקים
העיד בהם ארץ השירח שנאמר למען
תהיה לי השירה הזאת לעד לבני
ישראל אסר שירה תעיד בהם למסן אני
למעלה ומנין שהמקום קרוי עד מסהר
שנ:אמר וקרבתי לכב למשפט והייתי עד
מסהר . ואומר ואנכי חוורע ועד . ואוסר
יהיה יהוה אחכים בנם לעד . יערף
כמטר לקחי . אין לקחי אלא דברי תורה
שנאמר כי לקח טוב נתחי לכם . ואוסר
קחו מוסרי ול כסף ואין מוסר לא דברי
תורה שנאמר שמע בני מוסר אביך,
ואוסר שמע מוסר וחכמה ואוסר החזק
במוסר. ול תרף ואוסר קחו עצכם דברים
ושובו ל יהורה ואוסר ואין דברים לא דברי
תורה שנאמר ארת חרברים האלח דבר
יהורה ל כל קהלכם. כמטר. מרד מטר,
חיים לעולם אף דברי תורה חיים
לעולם , אי מרד מטר מקצרץ עולם
שמחים וסקצרת עולם עצינים בו מי
שבטור ונתא סלא יין ונתו וגורנו לפני
מצירים לו אף דברי תורה כן חלמוד
לוסר חזי כטל אסרחם . מרה טל כל כך
חעולם כולו שמחים בו אף דברי תורה
כל חעולם כולו שמחים בו . בשעירים עלי
רשא . סרה שעירים 'הללו יורדים על
עשבים ומעלים אותם ומגדלים אותם כך
דברי תורה מעלים לוטריחם ומגדלים
אותם חלמור לוסר סלסליה ותרוססך.
ורכרבים עלי עשב . סרה רביבים חללו
יורדים על עשבים ומערנים אותם וספנקים

ואומר קחו מוסרי (משלי ח.י.)
לא גרסינן ואוסר דאינו אלא
ייפוי דרשא דברוב מקום רבחיב
קיחה סיירי כמורה ולא שייך כאן
מאי ואוסר:

מה שעירים הללו יורדין על
עשבים ומגדלין. השתא דריש
שעררים-- מטר, ושמא לפי
שירורה בסערה ובני רביבים
אור מערינים לפי שירורד) בנחת:
הוי כונס דברי חורה כללים. והא
דריש פרסתיב בראש על רשא כלל
סיני רשאים והרר עלי עשב
רמשמע כל עשב ועשב רהיינו פרט:

אוחן וכן דברי תורה מעניים אותם
ומפנקים אותם . וכן הוא אומר כי לוית
חן הם לראשך . ואמר חתן לראשך לויח
חן . דבר אחר חיה רבי יהודה אומר
לעולם הוי כונס דברי תורה כללים
ומוציאם כללים שנאמר יערף כמטר לקחי .
ואין יערף אלא לשון כנעני . משל איך
אדם אומר לחבירו פרוט לי סלע זו ולא
ערוף לי סלע זו כך הוי כונס דברי תורה
כללים ופורט ומוציאם כטיפים הללו של
טל ולא כטיפין הללו של מטר נחלורה
אלא כטיפים הללו של טל שהם קטנים.
בשעירים עלי רשא . מה שעירים הללו
יורדים על עשבים ומפשפשים בהם כדי
שלא יחליעורה כך הוי מפשפש בדברי
תורה. כרי שלא תשכחם . כך אמר ליה
רבי יעקב ברבי חנינא לרבי בוא ונפשפש
בהלכות בשביל שלא יעלו חלורה .
וכרביבים עלי עשב . מה רביבים הללו
יורדים על עשבים ומנקים אותם ומשפפשים
אותם ומפטמים אותם כך הוי מפטם
בדברי תורה ושונה ומשלש ומרבע.
דבר אחר יערף רבי טיעזר בנו של רבי
יוסי הנלילי אומר אין יערף אלא לשן
הריגה שנאמר וערפו שם ארת הענגלה
בנחל. מה ענלה מכפרת על שפיכת
דמים כך דברי תורה מכפרים על
שפיכורת דמים. בשעירים עלי רשא . מה
שעירים הללו באים על חטאורת וככפרים
כך דברי תורה מכפרים על עוונורת.
דבר אחר יערף כמטר . חכמים אומרים
אמר להם משרה לישראל שמא. אתם
יורעים כמרה צער נצטערתי על החורה
וכמרה עסל עמלתי ברח וסרה יניערה
יניעת בה בעניך שנאמר ויהי שם עם
יהוה ארבעים יום וארבעים לילה. ונכנסתי
לבין המלאכים ונכנסתי לבין החיות
ונכנסתי לבין השרפים שאחר מהם יכול
לשרוף כל העלם כולו שנאמר
שרפים עומרים מטעל לו . נתחי נפשי
עליה רמי נתחי עליה כשם שלמרתי אותה
בצער כך תהיו אתם למירים אותה בצער.
או כדרך שאתם למירים אותה בצער כך
תהיו מלמרים אותה בצער חלומר לומר
חזל כטר אמרתי . תהיו רואים אותורת
בצור אחר משלש וארבע בסלע. בשעירים
עלי רשא . כאדם שהולך ללמוד תורה
תחילה נתחילה נופלת עליו כשעיר.

לשון כנעני . פירוש שלשון כנען
רוצה לומר פרוט, רוצה לומר
שירקדק על כל הדיבור ודבור ועל
כל אות ואות.
מה שעירים הללו...ומפשפשים.
השתא דריש ליה לשון רוח בתרגומו
כרוחי סמרא:
כאין על החצאות. כנגד שעיר
הרגלים ושל ראש חדש ושל יום
הכפורים, השתא לשון שעיר עזים
בנחל. מה ענלה מכפרת:
כאין חפירים. דריש רביבים
לשון חלבים תרגום חלב (תרבא)
(ויקרא ג.ג.)
כך תהיו מלמרין אותה בצער.
כלומר שלא תאמרו דברי תורה עד
שיצער השואל. חלמוד לומר
ו(כולי:
נופלת עליו כשעיר. היינו שר
שאים מתמחר ממנן, כך בתאתם סטן
ומחזירין אותו לבית הספר על כרחו
ומחירא מן הרצוע:

ואין שעיר אלא שד שנאמר ושעירים
ירקדו שם . דבר אחר יעדוף כמטר לקחי
חיה רבי בנאה אומר אם עשירת דברי
תורה לשמם דברי תורה חיים הם
למוצאיהם ולמכל בשרו טרפא הם . ולא
עשירת דברי תורה לשמם דברי תורה
סמיום אותן שנאמר יערף כמטר לקחי.
ואין עריפה אלא הריגה שנאמר וערפו
ארת חענלה בנחיל . ואוסר כי רבים
חללים הפילה ועצמים הרוגים. דבר אחר
יערף כמטר לקחי . רבי דוסתאי ברבי
יהודה אוסר אם דברי תורה כנסת כדרך
שכונסים מטר לבור לסוף שאתה מנול .
ומשקה אתרים שנאמר ונגלים מתוך
באר יפוצו מעיינותיך חוצה. דבר אחר
יערף כמטר לקחי . רבי יהודה אומר
לעולם הוי אדם כונס דברי תורה כללים
שאם כונם פרטים מייגעים אותו ואין יודע
מה לעשורת . משל למלך שהלך לקסרי
וצריך לו מאת זה או סאותים זו הוצארה
נוטלים פרט מייגעים אותו ואין יודע מה
לעשורת אבל אם מצרפם סלעים אותו
סלעים פורט ומוציא בכל מקום שירצח,
וכן מי שהלך לשוק וצריך מאה סנה או
שני רבוא אם מצרפם סלעים
מייגעים אותו ואין יודע מה לעשורת אבל
אם מצרפם ועשה אותם סלעים ועשה
אותם דיניךי זהב פורט ומוציא בכל מקום
שירצח . בשעירים עלי רשא ורביבים.
כארם שחולך ללמור תורה בתחזילה איני
יודע מה לעשורת עד ששונה שני סדרים
או שני ספרים ואחר כך נמשכרן אחריו
כרביבים . לכן נאמר וכרביבים עלי עשב.
דבר אחר יערף כמטר . מה מטר
זה יורד על האאלנות ונותן בהם מטעמים
לכל אחר ואחד לפי מח שחם כנגן ,
לפי מח שהם בירה . לפי מח שהם
בחאיננה כך דברי תורה כולם אחר ,
ובם מקרא ומשנה הלכורת ואנדורה.
בשעירים עלי רשא . מה שעירים הללו
יורדים על עשבים ומעלים אותם . ויש
בם ירוקים ויש בהם ארומים ויש בהם
שחורים כך דברי תורה יש בהם רבנים
יש נהם כשרים יש בהם חכמים ויש בהם
צדיקים ויש בהם חסידים . דבר אחר
יערף כמטר . מה הטסר הזה אי אתה

אין עריפה אלא לשון
הריגה...וכן הוא אומר כי רבים
חללים הפילה (משלי ז.כו).
רבי ואליעזר בנו של רבי | יוסי
הנלילי נמי דריש לעיל עריפה
לשון הריגה, מכל מקום איכא
בנייהו טובא דלרבי ואליעזר בנו
של רבן יוסי הנלילי הוי לשבח
ולכלוסר לשמה שמתכפרת בעולה
ערופה; ורדי בנאה הרי לגנאי
ולשון הוראה שמתרנא בהם שאם לא
יעסקו לשמה יערפה אותם וכן
מציני שהעונש שלא לשמה; מה דמחיב
כי רבים שהעונש לשמה. מה דמחיב
אליס הוא רחוק רחוק רבית
לקדרי. שם מקום שהוא רחוק רבית
נותן מטעמים לכל אתר ואאד. הכי
גרסינן, ורביש לשון מחוק
חרנגומו יבסם (שמות סז.כה):

ג כן הוא לשון הספרי אבל חסר
בעדים של הפירוש:
ד כנראה שדריש לא גרס יורד אלא
יורה וכנראה שהיה לפניו פסוק
ראיה, ויורה ה' עץ...ויסתקו
המים וכו׳ (שמות סו.כה):

רואהו עד שבא וכן הוא אומר ויהי עד
נר ועד נר והשמים התקררו בעמים.
כן תלמידי חכמים אי אתה יודע מאין
עד שישונה משנה הלכות ואגדות או
עד שיתחבר פרנס על הציבור. דבר
אחר יערף כמטר לא כמטר הזה שבא
מן הדרום שכולו לשדפון. כולו לירקון
כולו לקללה אלא כמטר הזה שבא
מן המערב שכולו לברכה. היה רבי
סימאי אומר מנין אתה אומר כשם
שהעיד משה לישראל שמים וארץ כך
העיד להם ארבע רוחות השמים
שנאמר יערף כמטר לקחי זה רוח
מערבית שהוא ערופו של עולם שכולו
לברכה. תזל כטל אמרתי. זה רוח
צפונית שעושה את הרקיע נקיה
כזהב. כשעירים עלי דשא. זה רוח
שמשחיר את הרקיע כשעיר. וכרביבים
עלי עשב. זה רוח דרומית שמארגת
את הרקיע כרביב. דבר אחר יערף כמטר
היה רבי סימאי אומר לא נאמר ארבע
רוחות הללו אלא כנגד ארבע רוחות
השמים צפונית בימות החמה יפה
ובימות הגשמים קשה. דרומית בימות
החמה קשה ובימות הגשמים יפה.
מזרחית לעולם יפה. מערבית לעולם
קשה. צפונית יפה לחיטים. בשעה
שכניסים שליש. וקשה לזיתים בשעה
שחונטין. וכן היה רבי סימאי אומר כל
הבריות שנבראו מן השמים נפשם
וגופם מן השמים. וכל בריות שנבראו
מן הארץ נפשם וגופם מן הארץ. לפיכך
עשר אדם תורה ועשה רצון אביו
שבשמים הרי הוא כבריות של מעלן.
שנאמר אני אמרתי אלהים אתם ובני
עליון כולכם. לא עשה תורה ולא
רצון אביו שבשמים שנאמר אכן
כאדם תמותון. וכן היה רבי סימאי
אומר אין כל פרשה שאין בה תחיית
המתים אלא שאין בנו כח לדרוש
שנאמר יקרא אל השמים מעל ולו הארץ
לדון עמו. יקרא אל השמים מעל זה
נשמה. ולו הארץ לדון עמו. מי דין
עמו. ומנין שאין סדבר אלא תחיית
המתים שנאמר מארבע רוחות באי
הרוח. כי שם יהוה אמרא. נמצינו
לסירים שלא הזכיר משה שמו של
מקום אלא לאחר עשרים ואחד דבר.

סמי למד מלאכי השרת שאין מלאכי
השרת מזכירים את השם אלא לאחר
שלש קדושות שנאמר וקרא זה אל זה
ואמר קדוש קדוש קדוש יהוה צבאות.
אמר משה בן שאהיה. כפתוח משבערה
למלאכי השרת. והרי דברים קל וחומר
ומה משה שהוא חכם חכמים גדול'
שבנדולים לא הזכיר שמו של מקום
אלא לאחר עשרים ואחד דבר המזכיר
שמו של מקום בחנם על אחת כמה
וכמה. רבי שמעון בן יוחי אומר מנין
שלא יאמר אדם ליהוה עלה ליהוה
מנחה ליהוה שלמים. אלא עלה
ליהוה מנחה ליהוה שלמים ליהוה
תלמוד לומר קרבן ליהוה. והרי דברים
קל וחומר ומה אילו שהם מוקדשים
לשמים אסר המקום ל יחל שמי עליהם
עד שקרבנו המקרש שמו של מקום
בחינם. ובמקום ביחיד על אחת כמה
וכמה. דבר אחר כי שם יהוה אקרא
רבי יוסי אומר מנין לעומרים בכרך
הכנסת ואומר ברכו את יהוה המבורך
שעונים אחריהם ברוך יהוה המבורך
לעולם ועד תלמוד לומר כי שם יהוה
אקרא חבו גודל לאלהינו , אמר לו רבי
נחוראי השמים דרך ארץ היא
שהגוים בסלחמר ונגבורים נצחים.
זמנין שאין מזמנים אלא כשלשה תלמוד
לומר כי שם יהוה אקרא , ומנין
שעונים אחר המברך תלמוד לומר חבו
גודל לאלהינו . ומנין שאומר ברכו את שם
ענים אחריו ברוך שם כבוד מלכותו
לעולם ועד תלמוד לומר כי שם יהוה
אקרא. ומנין לאומר יהא שמיה רבא
מברך שעונים אחריו לעולמי ולעולמי
עלמים תלמוד לומר חבו גודל לאלהינו.
וסנין אתה אומר שלא ירד אבותינו
למצרים אלא כדי שיעשרה נ סים
ונבורות בשביל לקדש את שמו הגדול
בעולם שנאמר ויהי בימים הרבים

יצולייריך. קרי לשליח צבור;
ונבבורים לעוניך ברוך, שהם
אומרים שבח שלם:
ומניין לאומר...ברוך שם.
מהבר גדול לייך. ווליף אקרא
מריקרא: כחיב הבא כי שם ה'
אקרא וכתיב ויקרא יעקב שם
המקום (בראשית בח.יסי).
הכי גרסינן:. ומניין שלא ורדו
למצרים אלא שיעשה להם נסים
ונפלאות לקרש שמו בעולם שנאמר
כי שם ה' אקרא. פירוש, משה
אמרו על ה' אקרא, כתיב
ויראת מן העבורה רדזער (שמות כ.כג-ו)
היינו כי שם ה' אקרא, (שמון
יד.לא) והיינו הבר גדול
נגודה גורל' ארבע מאות שנה לא
נגזרה מחתלה אלא לקרש שמו:

וזכן היא עצם בירסתו וכן גירסת
מדרש חכמים ופירוש הרבר בגירסת
הרהבה כדפוס הראשון; ומניין
לאומר ברוך שעוניים אחריו ברוך
ה מקום -- היינו שם ה':

שבא מן המערב. לשון עורף דורש
יערוף רהיינו אחרי שהוא מערב:
מארגת את הרקיע כרביב. גרסינן:
בימות החמה קשה. אוי הוא לשון
לשדפון ולירקון הרלעיל:
מערבית לעולם קשה. קשיא רהא
לעיל כולה לברכה, ושמא י"ל הא
רנאותא ניתא הוא הא ראחיא רדיא
רכי האי גוונא משני על רוח
דרומית פרק לא יחפור (נבא בתרא
כה:):

שם הוא מרב. זאת הוא לאחר
שנתעלה. אומר נביא ה' עד שהם בני
אבל וכן הוא אומר ויהי עד נר ועד נר
והשמים התקרר:

ומניין שאינו מזבר אלא בתחיית
המתים. אקרא רדעורף קאי רמיכ
ביה ארבע רוחות:

אלא ן אחר] כ"א רבר. כך חיבות
יש מן האזינו עד השם:

§ הנך החמה הוא מעלה בפנים העולם
המתים. וששן רמה החמה הוא מאחור:
‡ בכה"י יש מתא וחקנתי לפי גרסת
הנבלני:

ההם . וישמע אלהים את נאקתם .
ואומר כי שם יהוה אקרא. ומנין שלא
הביא הקב"ה פורענות עשר מכות
על פרעה ועל מצרים אלא על שלא
קירשו את שמו הגדול בעולם. בתחלת
הענין הוא אומר מי יהוה אשר אשמע
בקולו . ובסוף אמר יהוה הצדיק אני ועמי
הרשעים . מנין שלא עשרה הקב"ה
נסים ונבורות לאבותינו על הים ועל
הירדן ועל נחלי ארנון אלא בשביל
לקרש שמו בעולם שנאמר ולזי בשמע כל
המלכים אשר בעבר הירדן ימה . וכן
רחב אמרת לשלוחי יהושע כי שמענו
את אשר הוביש יהוה את מי ים סוף
ספנינפים תלמוד לומר כי שם יהוה אקרא
ומנין . שלא ירד דניל לגב אריות. ולא
כרי שיעשרה לו הקב"ה נסים ונבורות
בשביל לקרש שמו בעולם שנאמר כי שם
יהוה אקרא . ואומר מן קרם שים מטע
די בכל שולטן מלכותי ליהון זיעים
ורחילים מן קרם אלהא די דניל . ומנין
אתה אומר שלא ירדו חנניה מישל
ועזריה לכבשן האש אלא כרי שיעשרה להם
נסים ונבורות בשביל לקרש שמו בעולם
שנאמר אתיא ותמהיא דיעבד עם אלהא
עילאה שפר קרמי להחויא . אתוהי כמה
רבריבן ותמהוהי כמה תקיפין. ומנין שאין
מלאכי השרת מכירים שמו של מעלה
עד שמכירים שמו ישר אל שלמטה שנאמר
שמע ישראל יהוה אלהינו יהוה אחד . ואומף
ברן יחד כל כוכבי בקר והרד יריע נל.
בני אלהים . כוכבי בקר . אילו ישראל
שמשולים לכוכבים שנאמר והרבה ארבה
את זרע כנכבי חשמים , בני אלהים.
אילו מלאכי השרד . וכן הוא אומף
ויבוא בני האלהים .

סליק פיסקא

הצור תמים פעלו . הצייר שהוא צר שז
העולם תחילה וצר בו את האדם
שנאמר וייצר יהוה אלהים את האדם.
תמים פעל . פעולתו שלימרה על כל
באי העולם ואין לרהרהר אחר מידוחיו.
אפילו שנרה של כלום ואין אחד מהם
שיסתכל ויאמר אילו היו לי שלשה עינים
אילו היו לי שלשה ידים אילו היו לי
שלשרה רגלים אילו הייתי מהלך על
ראשי אילו היו פני הפוכים לאחורי .
כמרה היה נארה. תלמוד לומר כי כל
דרכיו משפט. יושב עם כל אחד ואחד.
בדין ונוחן לו מה שראוי לו . אל אמונה.
שהאמין בעולם ובראו . ואין עול . שלא
באו בני אדם לחיות רשעים אלא להיות
צריקים . וכן הוא אומר אשר עשרה
האלהים את האדם ישר והסרה בקש
חשבונורה רבים . צדיק וישר הוא שהוא
מתנהג בישרורה עם כל באי העולם .
רבר אחר הצור חתקיף . תמים פעלו .
פעולתו שלימרה על כל באי העולם
ואין לרהרהר אחר סידוחיו אפילו עינר.
של כלום ואין אחר מהם שיסתכל
ויאמר מרה ראו אנשי דור המבול
שנשטפו במים . ומרה ראו אנשי סנדל
שנתפזרו מסוף העולם ועד סופו . ומרה
ראו אנשי סדום ועמורה להשתטף באש
ונפרירה . ומרה ראה אהרן ליטול
הכהונה . ומרה ראה דוד ליטול ארץ
המלכות . ומרה ראה קורח ועדחו
שתבלעם הארץ . תלמוד לומר כי כל
דרכיו משפט . יושב עם כל אחד ואחד
ונוחן לו ארה הראוי לו . אל אמונה. בעל
פיקרון . ואין עול . נוברה ארה שלו
באחרונרה . שלא כמידרה מידרה בשר
ודם . סידרה בשר ודם מפקיד אצל
חבירו מאתים וים בידו סנד . בשהוא
בא ליטול את שלו אומר לו הוצא
מנרה שיש לי בידיך . והילך ארה השאר.
אבל. מי שאמר והירה עולם .אינו כן
אלא ל אמונה ואין על נוברה ארה שלו
באחרונה. צדיק וישר הוא. כענין שנאמר
כי צדיק יהוה וצדקורה אהב.ן דבר אחר
הצור התקוף חמים פעלו . פעולתו של
באי העולם שלימרה לפניו מחן שכרם
של צדיקים ומאחר פורעונחם של
רשעים . אילו לא נטלו כלום משלהם
בעולם הזרה ולו לא נטלו כלום משלהם

(פיסקא שז)

פעולתו שלימה . דרשו לשון
מלאכה, כלומר מה שפעל בכריוחו
הכל היה שלם ואין בריה חסרה
תחלה אבר ואח"ג דללאורה שמטע
שם היה אדם פורח באויר היה לו
סוב יוחר ; זה אינו, רמבו שהיה
הוא פורח כך היו פרוחיהו בני אדם
שכבוחו והיו בכאין אלו על אלו
בסיסם אחד ולא היה מרוחה לשם
אומה במקומה, נמצא שהיה
גריעותא[א]... ,יאס, דרלש לה
לשון אבר ועונג רבחיב מה רב
טרבך אשר פעלח (תהלים לא,כ.)
רקאמר מסיים יושב בדין עם כל
אחר:
שהאמין בעולם ובראו. כלומר שלא
יהוו כולם רשעים אלא מקצחם יהוו
צדיקים ויעשו הישר בעיניו :
מתנהג בישרורה. היינו שאינו רן
את הארם לפי מעשיו רעים שמחיר
לעסוו אלא לפי מעשיו של אוחרה
שעה רכחיב כי שמע אלהים גו'
(בראשית כא.יז)' מה ראו. כמו למה היו רואים
לכן, כמו מה. עשו:
בעל הפקרון. שארם מפקיר נשמתו
בכל לילה [ו]אר"פ שארם מחייב...
הםה חיובין מחזירה בכשר:

ן שין בראשית סו .יג'
ן אולי צל תהיה .
ן פר' אי נסי .
ן עין ראם חשנה סו ע' ב :
מ בסנהרריה, ובכריח אברהם נמצא
"מחייב":

בעולם הזה . שנאמר הלא הוא כמוס
עמדי חתום באוצרותי . אימתי אילו
נוטלים לומר כשהוא ,ישב ברוך . כי כל
דרכיו משפט לומר כשהוא יושב בין בדין
עם כל אחד ואחד ונותן לו ארח תראוי
לו . אל אמונה כשם שמשלם לצדיק
נמור שכר מצוה שעשה בעולם הזה
לעולם הבא . כך משלם לרשע נמור שכר
מצוה קלה שעשה בעולם הזה . וכשם
שנפרע מרשע נמור מעבירה שעשה
בעולם הזה לעולם הבא . כך נפרע מצדיק
נמור על עבירה שעשה בעולם הזה . ואין
עול . כאשר נפטר מן העולם באים
כל מעשיו ונפרטים לפניו ואומר לו כך
עשירת ביום פלוני ואי אתה מאמין
בדברים הללו והוא אומר הן והן והוא
אומר לו חתום שנאמר ביד כל אדם
יחתום . צדיק וישר הוא . והוא מצדיק
את הדין ואומר יפה דנוני . וכן הוא
אומר למע תצדק בדברך תזכה בשפטיך .
דבר אחר ,כשתתפס את רבי חנינא בן
תרדיון נגזרה עליו גזרה לשרוף ספרו
אמרו לו גזירה נגזרה עליך לשרוף ספרד
קרא מקרא הזה הצור תמים פעלו
אמרו לאשתו נגזרת על בעלך גזירה
לשרוף ספרו עליו ועליך קראת
המקרא הזה אל אמונה ואין עול . אמרו
לבתו נגזרה גזירה על אביך לשרוף ספרו
בכרת עליו אמר בוכר . עליו ומסתבתבדרך
עליו הזה אומר אוי לי וזה אומר אוי לי
אבל אין זה הוי זה לא שיצא ליצלב
וכן הוא אומר אוי לנפשם כי נמלו להם
רעה . דור עקש ופתלתול . אמר להם
משה לישראל אתם עקמנים פתלתולים
אתם אין אתם הולכים לאור . משל
לאחר שהיה בידו סקל מעוקל וליחלן
לאומן לתקנו מתקנו באור . ואם לאו
מכוונו בסמינילרו ואם לאו מפסלו בטצר
ומשליכו לאור : וכן הוא אומר ונחתך
חזה רעתך . על ששרפת את התורה

בני אנשים בתערים חורשי משחירת . דבר
אחר דוד עקש ופתלתול . אמר להם
סטה לישרא בסדרת שסרדהם בני
סדרכם לכם . וכן הוא אוסר עם נבר
תתבר ועם עקש תתפתל . חליותר
תנצלו זארn . משל לאחד שהיה עומד
וצוהב כנגד בליוסטוס בשוק אמרו לו
השוסעים שוטה שבעולם כנגד בלאוסטוס
אתה עומד וצוהב אם רצה לתהבוך
לקרע ארם בסוחך . ולחבשך בבית
האיסורים אדם יכול לו . אם חית קטרן
שנרול היסנו על אחרן נסח וכסח .
אם היה הפחקם נרול משניהם על
אחרן כמה וכמה . דבר אחר חליותר
תנצלו זארn . משל לאחר שהיה עומד
וצוחב כנגד אביו אמר לו שוטה שבעולם
כנגד מי אחה יושב וצוחב כנגד אביך
שנע כמה כמה עמל בך וכסה יניעה
ינע בך אם לא כיברתו לשעבר צריך
אתה לכבדו עכשיו שלא יהיה כותב כל
נכסיו לאחרים. כך אסר להם משה לישרא
אי אתם זכורים נסים ונבורות שעשה
לכם הסקום במצרים הזכרו כסה טובה
שעתיר ליחן לכם לעולם הבא עם נבל.
לשעבר . ולא חכם. לעתיר לבוא . כיוצא
בן אתה אוסר ישרא לא ירע לשעבר לא
התבונן, ישרא לא ירע לשעבר . ועם לא
התבונן לעתיר . מי נרם להם לישרא
שיהיו סנוולים וסטוסשפשים שלא חוו בנים
ברבר תורה . וכן הוא אוסר חלא נע
יתרם בם . יסותו ולא בחכמה . הלא
הוא אביך קנך . רבי שמעון בן חלפתא
אוסר משטו שאם חיה חלש למעלה ונבור
למטה מי נוצח סטא ארק יכול לו.
וכל שכן שנינור לסעלה וחלש לסטה .
וכן הוא אוסר L חבריל ארק מיך ולבך
L יסהר להוציא דבר לפני הלוחים כי
לוחים בשמים ואתה על הארץ . דבר
אחר הלא הוא אביך קנך . אמר להם

מטה לישרא חביבים אתם לי קנינים
אתם לי ואי אתם ירושה לי . משל לאחד
שהורישו אביו עשר שרורו ועסר וקנה
שרה אחר משלו ואותה היה אותב מכל
שרורה שהורישו אביו . וכן מי שתורישו
אביו עשר פלטוריות ועסר וקנה פלטורה
אחר משלו ואותה היה אותב מכל
פלטורה שהנתחילו אביו כך אסר לחם משה
לישרא חביבים אתם לי קנינים אתם לי
ואי אתם ירושה לי . קנך זה אחר משלשה
שנקראו קנין למקום ואלו הם תורה וישרא
ובירת הסקרש . תורה נקראת קנין למקום
שנאסר יהוה קנני ראשית דרכו . ישרא
נקראו קנין למקום שנאסר אביך קנך .
בירת הסקרש נקרא קנין למקום שנאסר
חר זה קנתה יסינו . הוא עשך ויכוננך
היה רבי מאיר אוסר כרסא רכולא בית
כהניו סתרכו. נביאי סתרכו. סופריו סתרכו,
וכן הוא אוסר ססנו פנה ססנו יתר . רבי
יהודה אוסר עשאו טיך כוך . רבי שסעון
בן יהודה אוסר הושיבן על בסיסך .
הלעינך בירת שבערת עססים ונתן לך
סה שנשבע לך והרוישך סה שהבטחתיך .
רבי דוסתאי בן יהודה אוסר עשאו כנונים
בנונים סכסנים שאם תעלה אחר סהם על
נב חבירתה אין אתה יכול לעסור,

סליק פיסקא

זכור יסורת עולם. הזהרו סה שעשיתי
בדורות הראשונים סה שעשיתי באנשי
דור הסבול סה שעשיתי באנשי דור
הפלנה. סה שעשיתי באנשי סרם ועסורה
בינו שנות דור ודור . אין לך דור שאין
בו סאנשי דור הסבול . ואין לך דור שאין
בו סאנשי דור הפלנה. וכאנשי סרם. אא
שנדון כל אחר ואחר לפי מעשיו . שאל
אביך וינדך . אילו נביאים כענין שנאסר
ואישע רואת והוא מצעק אבי אבי . זקניך
ויאסרו לך . אילו זקנים כענין שנאסר
אספרה לי שבעים איש מזקני ישרא.
דבר ארק , זכור יסורת עולם. אסר להם
כל זסן שהסקום ססיא יסורים עליכם

אחר משלשה שנקראו קנין.
בכריתא ושנו חכמים בלשונה המשנה
[וחסתן] חשיב והשבים תחירים על
אלו הם אברהם ושסים וארץ, ונראה
דאברהם בכלל, שסים וארץ בכלל,
[ואברהם] בכלל ישראל שהם בניו
היו, ושסים וארץ בכלל המזרה
רכחיב אם לא בריתי יומם
ולילה חקות שסים וארץ לא
שסתי, (ויחסיהו לג.כה): וכן
ברסא רכולא ביה. חריסה שהבל
בה:
[סתברים.] נראה ספוסר יותר
מתחכם שהוא יורע לספור ולדרוש
ולתת טעם מעצמו:
בויך בויך. חלונות חלונות, אי
נסי נרסיני כנין כנין: פירוש,
כן נרסיני כנין על חברו, ועיקר:
הלעימך. האכילך:
כנונים כנונים. בני סעים יושבין
זה על גב זה ואם אחה מהן מחלק
סקוסה סיד יסות והוא כסו החראה,
ראה שאותה בירו ואחה צריך לו
תסיר לבקש רחסים:

יש לגרוס כאן כסו באקספורד
ובסנצריה- "ונראה דאברהם בכלל
שסים וארץ בכלל, [ואברהם] בכלל
ישראל..." ומפני הרוסות רלב
הסופר "אברהם": וראיה שאברהם
השני סקורו היא שכל הסקוM בין
בכרית אברהם מפני הרוסות בין
אברהם לאברהם הסופי:
עין סנהדרין לב.:

(פסקא שט)
צוהב. כועס כסו שני כלבים
צהובין זה בזה (סנהררין קה.).
תרנום ובעמטה צרחה וסהבכא לה
(שסואל א א.ו):
בליוכוסי. שם שרה וקטרון נרול
ססנו והפיסקס נרול ססנו:
שסעון בן חלפתא אוסר משטו.
אתבי יהודה ראייירי לעיל קאי:

בבכלי לפנינו. משל לאני כלבים
שהיו עסד והוו צהובין זה לזה:
לפנינו בערי הספרי
"בולינוס":

(פסקא שי)
לא יכנף עוד מוריך
(ישעיהו ל.כ). לשון כנף--
סתכסם; מוריך-- לשון טורה
רודי.

(פסקא שיא)
הצים מכזיים. כלומר כנורות.
זכה לקבל ייסורין. מבאן
שיסורין אינן בעבור עונצ מרצאאת
זה שבכות היה לו קבלה היסורין?
ואם תאמר הבא פרק במה בהמה (שבת
נה.) אמרו אין ייסורין בלא עון,
אין הכי נמי שד"ל אין ייסורין
באין על אדם זולת על עון-- אם
אינו אדם שלם בעון שלו, ואם הוא
אדם שלם בעון הרור?
--החחיל מתשמסין. היינו
כשמתחילין לבא. ואם תאמר הא לא
הגיד זכונו של אברהם ע"ה על
סרום ועמורה, וי"ל משום דאאמר
מן הייסורין סלחמת הארבעה
מלכים; שלא כאו אלא בעבורו
שאמרו נחחיל כלום ונסורין
באברהם; ועוד יש לומר שבשעה שבא
לארץ כבר נגזרהר, לא היו סד'
עמפין וין אין ייסורין בלא עוון
משבא לארץ אלא על בני ארץ ושאל
ראאתי גמירה ומלא הם.
פירש מחוזמ על אומות. שלא
יכנסו לארץ, ואם תאמר הרי נתן
הארץ לחמי ואמורי ונכנעך, יש
לומר שאותם היה גלוי לפניג
שיתחייבו ויתמלא סאם וירהוך
חוטבים בליויה מכל אותם שראיגו
שלא נחחייבך כלויה הרחיקו
תהאר.

הזכרו כמה טובות ונחמות עתיד ליתן
לכם לעולם הבא . ביט שנורך דור
ודור . זרע דורו של משיח שיש בו שלש
דורות שנאמר יראוך עם שמש ולפני
ירח דור דורים . שו אבין וינגד . למהר
עתידים ישרל להיות רואים ושומעים
כשומעים ספי הקורו שנאמר ואזנך
תשמענה. דבר מאחריך לאמר. ואוסר לא
יכנע עוד מוריך זקניך ויאסרו לך סרח
שהראיתו לזקנים בהר כענין שנאמר ואל
משה אמר עלה ש יהורה אתה ואהרן
נדב ואביהוא ושבעים מזקני ישראל.

בהנחיל עליון גוים...ירא
חמא וכשרין שבהן. פירוש, יון
ומרי ונכל ראשי אומות שנחלקו
ביסי שם בן נח ובנשחלקו את
העולם ירא חמא וכשרים היו אבל
שבע אומות שנסלו ארץ ישראל
אפילו ראשי דורות לא היו
צדיקים:
שים ותה מלכות (שיר השירים
ו.ה.) היינו אומות שיש להן בחר
מלכות:
רשמונגרס פלגשים (שיר
השירים ו.ח). שמונים ספפחות
אין להם מלך; ורציחו לפמרו על
סיניכם ומצאחי כפרשת בני נח
גבי אלה תולדרת בני נח
(בראשית י.א) חשיבי ג"ז אומות
ואף על פי כי לפי החחבון יש שם
שבעים.--והיינו רבחיב מאלה
נפררו איר הגרים, (בראשית
י.ה), כשהסיר מהם אחם שכנבו
הרי הוא אומר ששים המה מלכות
ושמונים פילנשים . ששים ושמונים הרי
מאה וארבעים. ואבוחינו לא ירדו
במצרים אלא בשבעים נפש . דבר אחר
יצב נבולות עמים . יצב נבול עמים אין
כתב כאן אלא יצב נבולות עמים זכ
אומרת לימוזל שני חלקים במספר בני

צפון כולם וכל צידונים . שמרה סרי
בכל וארום סלכיה וכל נסיכיה ואם
תאמר מי נוטל עושרם וכבודם של אילו
חוי אומר יצב נבולות עמים . דבר אחר
בהנחיל עליון נוים . כשהנחיל המקום סן
האומות יראי חטא וכשרים שבהן.
בחפריר בני אדם זרע לוט . ויפררו איש
מעל אחיו . יצב נבולות עמים . רבי
שיער בנו של רבי יוסי הנלילי אומר
הרי הוא אומר ששים המה מלכות
ושמונים פילנשים . (בראשית
ו.ה) אם
חנבה לגרסר אין ראוי למנות
אסכנז ובן בנגלה . חמצא שאין בהם
אלא חמשים ושבעה עספוּר ועמון
ומואב ועשו הרי שמים; וכני
הגרים ל"ז משפחות וכני ישמאאל
שנים עשר ובאלילי אדום יש
קרוב לם'. ואיפס ומרי פלישמים
הני קורא לכל האומות האא חלקים
נחוברים" לשמעיא וכולם
נחמרו אומה?

כי חלק יהוה עמו . משל למלך
שהיה לו שדה ונתגרה לעריסים התחיל
העריסים ונונבים אותה נטלה
ונתנה לבניהם הת מזאילו לחיות רעים יותר
סן הראשונים נולר לו בן אסר להם צאו
מתוך שלי אי איפשר שתהיו בתוכה תנו
לי חלקי שאהיה מכירו . כן כשבא
אברהם אבינו לעולם יצא ממנו פסולת
ישמעאל ובני קטורה , בא אבינו יצחק
לעולם יצא ממנו פסולת עשו כל אופי
אדום חזרו להיות רעים יותר מן הראשונים
כשבא יעקב לא יצא ממנו פסולת
אלא נולדו כל בניו כשרים כמותו שנאמר
ויעקב איש תם יושב אהלים . מהיכן
חמקום מכיר ארת חלקי סיעקב שנאמר
כי יעקב בחר לו יה ישרל . ואומר כי
חלק יהודה עסו יעקב חבל נחלתו .
וערין חלי ברלא חלי . אין אנו יודעים
אם חמקום בחר לו ישרל לסנולת . ואם
ישראל בחרו להקדוש ברוך הוא תל"מד

x ולא בסו הרר"ק שפירש הספוק
במהבך שהיה ספסיק מסר ולא יהיה
צורך לאסוף (כנף) מסרך (מוריך).
עין ספר השרשים ערך י ר ה:
ז על בני סרום ועמורה.

ב כן בבל המדיה:
aa ה' באוספורוד:
bb הוא היא קרורה לפי חז"ל.
עין בראשית רבה סא.ד:
cc במהדורה פינקלסטיין נמצא
"נמסכים:"

יבוננהו . בעשרת הדברות . סלסר שהיה
הדיבר יוצא ספי חקדוש ברוך הוא והיו
ישראל מסתכלים בו ויורעים כמה סדרשים
יש בו וכמה הלכות יש בו וכמה קלים
וחסורים יש בו וכמה גזירות שוות יש
בו . יצרנהו כאישון עינו . הולכים שנים
עשר סיל וחוזרים שנים עשר סיל על
כל ריבור וריבור ולא היו נרחעים לא
סקיל הקולור ולא סקול' חלפירים .
דבר אחר יסצאהו בארץ סרבר ובתוהו .
הכל סצוי וסמתוקן . וסמוסף להם בסרבר
באר עולה להם . סן עולה לחם . שליו
מצוי להם . ענני כבוד סקיפורת להם .
ובחתהו ילל ישיסון בסקום הצרות בסקום
חניסות . בסקום ליסטורה בסקום הטנופת .
יסובבנהו . ברנלים . שלשרה מן הצפח .
שלשרה מן הדרום . שלשרה מן הסזרח .
שלשרה מן המערב . יבוננהו בשתי מתנות .
סלסר שכשהיה אחר סן האוסרוא פורש
ירו לקבל סן לא היה בירו עולה כלום .
לסאורה מים סן הבאר . לא חיו עולים
בירו כלום . יצרנהו כאישון עינו . כענין
שנאמר קוסרה יהודה ויפוצו אויבך וינוסו
משנאיך . יסצאהו בארץ סרבר . כענין
שנאמר חנרה אנכי ספתירה והלכנחירה
הסברברה . ובחתהו ילל ישיסון . אלו
ארבע סלכיורת כענין שנאמר חסוליך
בסרבר חנרול והנורא נחש שרף ועקרב .
יסובבנהו בזקנים . יבוננהו בנביאים .
יצרנהו כאישון עינו . משסרתם סן המזיקים שלא
יזיקוהו כענין שנאמר כי הנוגע בכם נונע
בבברת עינו .

סליק פיסקא

שיד בנשר יעיר קינו . סרה נשר זרה אין
נכנס לקינו סיר ער שטורא סצרף ארה
בניו בכנפיו בין אילן לחבירו בין סוכה
לחבירתה כדי שיעירה בניו ויהיה בנו

לוסר ובן בחר יהורה לחין . וסנין שאף
יעקב בחר לו הקרוש ברוך הוא . שנאמר
לא כאלה חלק יעקב כי יוצר הכל הוא
וישראל שבט נחלתו יהורה . צבאורה שמו .
יעקב הבל נהלתו . אין הבל אלא נורל
שנאמר הבלים נפלו לי בנעיסים . ואוסר
ויפלו הבלי מנשה עשרה . סהבל בני
יהורה נחלת בני שסען סרה הבל זה
יהורה כך היה יעקב שלישי לאבות
וקיבל שכר כולם . כשנולר אברהם סרו
אוסר ואת לצרה יולד . כשנולר יצחק
סרו אוסר טובים השנים סן האחר .
כשנולר יעקב סרו אוסר והתוט הסשולש
לא בסהרה ינתק.

סליק פיסקא

שי ג יסצאהו בארץ סרבר . זרה אברהם
אבינו סשל למלך שיצא הוא וחיילוחיו
לסרבר חניחוחו חיילוחיו בסקום הצרורת
ובסקום הניסורה ובסקום ליסטורה והלב
להם . נחסברה לו ניבור אחר אסר לו
של כלום חיך שאיני סניחך על שחינבנא
לפלטוריים שלך וחושן על מיסתך כענין
שנאמר ויאסר ליו אני יהורה אשר
הוצאתיך סאור כשרים . יסובבנהו כענין
שנאמר ויאסר יהורה ל אברם לך לך .
יבוננהו . ער שלא בא אבינו אברהם
לעולם כביכול לא היה הקרוש ברוך
הוא סלך אלא על השמים בלבר שנאמר
יהורה ולהי השסים אשר לקחני . אבל
סשבא אבינו אברהם לעולם חסליכו
על השסים ועל הארץ . כענין שנאמר
ואשביעך ביהורה ולהי השסים ולהי הארץ .
יצרנהו כאשׁון עינו . ובחתהו ילל ישיסון .
סאבינו אברהם נלגל' עינו היה נוחן לו
ולא נלגל' עינו בלבר נוחן לו ולא לא אף
נפשו הוא נוחן לו שחזכינה עליו סן הבל
אשר אהבת ארה יצחק . והלא בירוע
שהוא בנו יחורו ולא זו נפש שנקראת
יהורה שנאמר הצילה מהרב נפשי סיי
סרבר . דבר אחר יסצאהו בארץ כענין
בסרבר סצאתי ישראל . ובתהתו ילל ישיסון .
בסקום הצרורת בסקום חניסורה . בסקום
ליסטורה, יסובבנהו . לפני הר סיני . כענין
שנאמר והנבלרה ארה העם סביב לאסר .

(מסקא שיב)
מה (תכל) וו משולם. נראה
רקא ארקרייה סנוללה(תהלים
קלה.ה), רתכל'ל (דברים יד.ב) דלינם
לפימר רקאי אסנשה רמה עניו
שילוש אצל סנה:
את לצרה*** יולד (משלי
יז.יז), לפי שהגיץ זכוחו אבני
רורור, ועור רכחיב אחות לנו
(שיר ח.ח) שאיתה את העולם
להקב"ה ולרוסם דרכי המקום ולהכי
קרי ליה את:
סרכים השנים סן האחר (קהלת
ד.ס), רכחיב ורשב' רצחק
רחסזור.... (בראשית כו.יח),
רהתוט הסשלש (קהלת ד.יב),
רכחיב רעקב בארץ (בראשית לז.א)
שהיה סגויר גיורוים'** סביו:

(מסקא שיג)
יסצאהו בארץ סרבר . רכחיב
רמצאת את לבבו (נחמיה ט.ח).
בסקום הסרבוא. שלא היה שום בריה
סכיר יחור סלכוחו רחברך וקרוש
שהו ררכים להסליכו והיינו ער
שהגיע לסלסרין:
יבוננהו. סלשון בינה.
יסצאהו. לשון סיפוק צורך:
אלו ארבע סלכיורת. מרבר.
רחבהה, רלל, רשיסם: (דברים
לב.י)

dd כנראה שאין לנרום הבל.
באקספוורר נחלה בין העיסיו
ובאמבריה חסר. אבל כן הוא
בנוסח ערי הספרי.
** באקספוורר הסוגר כחב לפרה
בסקום לצדה וכזה פירש עצם בוונה
של הספרי אבל אין ספק שרבינו לא
כחב בכה בפירושו. פירושו לרברי
הספרי רחוק ואינו סבובס על
החילוף צרה-שרה:
ה ובם יש נוסח גרים:

(מסקא שטו)

דן אחד יהורה אחד אשר אחר ולא ששתי רוחות · כענין שנאמר
אחד. אין זה סרר הפסוקים אלא
הכי כתיב קראי ביחזקאל (פרק
מח) ורוד לך פאן קדים הים
דן אחד, ועל גבול דן פאתה
קדים עד פאת ים אשר אחד,
ועל גבול אשר (ם)פאת
קדמה ועד פאת ים נפתלי יהוה
אחד, ועל גבול נפתלי מפאת
קדמה עד פאת ים מנשה אחד,
ועל גבול מנשה מפאת קדמה
עד פאת ים אפרים אחד, ועל
גבול אפרים מפאת קדים ועד
פאת ים ראובן אחד, ועל
גבול ראובן מפאת קדים עד
פאת ים יהודה אחד:

ונכתב רש"י ז"ל בפירוש
יחזקאל:
בספרי במשיה האוזינו שנינו מד״ל
יהורה מאר דן אחר אשר אחד מלמד
שעתירין ישראל ליפול ארוך מן
הצפון למדרב דרומב עשרים וחמשה
אלפים קנים שיעורן חמשה ושבעים
מיל, מהיכן למרו השיעור הזה, מן
התרומה שהיא באחד מן החלקים
הללו כמו שמפורש בענין ביחזקאל
מה.א) והוא רוחב עשרים וחמשה
אלף קנים מאה וחמשים אלף אמה
שהקנה שש אמות (כך ביחזקאל
מא.ח) וכל אלפים אמה מיל כמו
שקינינו בסס׳ יומא (משנה ו.ד.
בכל יו ') אבל עשר סוכות
מירושלים ועד צוק; הרי מאה
וחמשים אלף עולים לערב מיל, עד
כאן לשרי רש״י דל,
ונראה לעריק הנרצאה הוא מאחד
והנראל וכתוב באמצעים למה
הוצרך לבתוב דן ואשר שהם
ראשונים לבשיל זהוא אחר דן,
אלא, אינו אלא לדרשא; למה
שפירש, מהיכן למרו השיעור הזה
מן התרומה שהוא באחד מן החלקים
הללו... ר״ל הוא באורך באחד מן
החלקים הללו ברוחב ראלו באורך
וברוחב א׳ אשר רוב כתיב מפאת
ים ועד קרים משמע כל מה שיש
מפאת ים דהיינו מערב ועד פאת
קרים דהיינו מזרח והתרומה בתוך
זה חמשה ועשרים אורך בעשרה
רוחביי:

כח לקכלו · כך כשנגלרה חסקום ליד
חורה לישראל לא נגלרה עליהם מרוה
אחר ולא ששתי רוחות · כענין שנאמר
ויאסר יהוה מסיני בא וזרח משעיר למ.
מהן · ואיו היא רוח רביעירת וזרח מדזון
יבוא · יפרוש כנפיו יקחהו · כענין שנאמר
ובמדבר אשר ראירת אשר נשאך יהוה
אלהיך · ישאהו על אברתו · כענין שנאמר
ואשא אחכם על כנפי נשרים · דבר
אחר כנשר יעיר קינו · זה לעתיד לבוא
כענין שנאמר קול דודי הנה זה בא ·

יפרוש כנפיו · כענין שנאמר אומר לצפון
חני · ישאהו על אברתו · חביאי בניך
בחוצן · יהוה ברד ינחנו · אמר להם
המקום לישראל ברך שישבחם יחורים
בעולם הזה ולא נהגחם מן האמומורת
כלום · כך אני אחר מן האומורת ונתנה אכם
לבוא ואין אחר מן האומות נותנה אכם
כלום · ואין עמו ל נבר · שלא תחא
רשורת לאחר מן האמומות לבוא ולשלוש
בכם כענין שנאמר ואני יוצא והנה שר
יון בא · ושר סלבורת פרס עמד לנגרי,
אבל אניד לך ארת הרשום בכתב אמת
דבר אחר יהוה ברד ינחנו · עתיד הקרוש
ברוך הוא להשים אחכם נוחלים סאסף
צפון ועד סופו · וכן הוא אומר מפארת
צפון ועד פארם · דן אחר · יהודה
אחר · אשר אחר · ועד גבול ים ספארת
קרים ועד פאת ים יהורה אחר על גבול
יהורה ספארת קרים ועד פארת ים מנשה
אחר · נפתלי אחר · מה חלסוד לומר
יהורה אחר אשר אחר דן אחר · שעדידים
ישראל אורך מן מזמורח למערב עד רוחב
עשרים וחמשרת לפים קנים שיעורם
חמשה ושבעים מיל · ואין עמו ל נבר ·
שלא יחו יכם בני אדם שעוברים עבודת
זרה · וכן הוא אומר לבן מארת יכופר

בני אדם שעוסקים בפרנטטיא של כלום.
כענין שנאמר יהי פיסרא כר בארץ שיהו
חטם מוציאים נלוסקאורת כסלא פיסרר
יד · ירעש כלבנן פריו · שירו חטם שפורט
זה כבו ונשורד סולחן בארן וארה בא
ונוטר הימנה · סלא פיסר זו של יד
כרי פרנסתך · ירכיבהו על בסחי ארץ. שמ״ז
זו ארץ ישראל שהיא גבוהה סכ״ל
הארצות כענין שנאמר עלה בארץ וירשנו
אותה · ויעל ויתורו ארת הארץ ויעלו
בנגב · ויאבל תנובות שדי · אילו פירורת
ארץ ישרו שקלים לאכיל מפירורת של
כל הארצורת. ויניקהו רבש סטלע · כגון
סכני וחפוניחויה · מעשה שאמר רבי יהודה
לבנו בסיכני צא והבא לי קציעורת מן
החבירת, אמר לו אבא של רבש. השקיע שמ"ז
ירך לחוכה וארת מעלה קציעורת מתוכה ·
ושם מחלמיש צור · אילו זיתים של נוש
חלב · מעשה שאמר רבי יוסי לבנו בצפורי
ומצא ארת העלייה שצפה ברבש | חמאת
בקר וחלב צאן · זה היה ביםי שלמה,
שנאמר עשרה בקר מריאים ועשרים בקר
רעי ומאה צאן · עם חלב כרים ואילים
בני ומאה צאן · הם היו בימי עשרין
השבטים שנאמר אוכלים כרים מצאן
ועלים מחוך מרבק · עם חלב כליורת
חיטה · זה היה בימי שלמה שנאמר ויחי
להם שלמה ליום אחר וגו' · ודם ע״ב
תשתה חסר · זה היה בימי עשרה
השבטים שנאמר השוחים במזרקי יין, זה
כירת המקדש שנבנה בכל חעלם שנאמר
וקסרת ועליהו · ואוסו והלכו עמים רבים
ואסרו לכו ונעלה אכל הר יהות · ויאבל
תנובורת שדי · אילו סלי ביכורים · ויניקהו
רבש סטלע · אילו נסכי שמן · חמאת
בקר וחלב צאן עם חלב כרים ואילים בני
בשן ועחורים · זו חטאורת עזלה ושלטים
ואשם ותורה וקדשים קלים · עם חלב
כליורת חיטה · אילו סלתורת · ודם ענב
תשתה חמר · אילו נסכי יין · דבר אחר
ירביכהו על במתי ארץ. זו תורה שנאמר
יהוה קנני ראשירת דרכו. ויאבך תנובורת
שדי · זו סקרא · ויניקהו רבש מסלע · זו
משנה. ושם מחלמיש צור · זה תכמוד ·
חמארת בקר וחלב צאן עם חלב כרים
ואילים בני בשן ועחורים · אילו קלים

שקלין לאכול. פירוש, ואין
מכברין על האטסומבא ומחנורבת
ילוד:
סכני. וגוש חלב, שם מקוטות הם:
קציעורת תאנים. יבשים; והאי רבש
רוצה לומר רבש תאנים:

באקסטורד ובקסטנבריא "לשמ":
הלשון אינה ברוקב כמו עון יעקב · דבר אחר יהוה ברד ינחנו
במסורה:
עתיר אני להושיך אחכם בנהרד רוח
בעולם · ואין עמו ל נבר · שלא יהו יכם

(פסקא שיז)
ק־ו ונ־ץ והקמנה. גרסינן.
חמאה וחלב רועש ק־ו עם כרים
ואילים בני בשן ורו־ש נ־ש.
ועתודרים רועש הקטה ולא גרסינן
וחטרונות:
ירמינבהו זה העולם. דרוש כולדה
ק ר א   ב ע ש ו .
רבינבהו... רינביקרו, מרמיוחי
קרא רברסמנה חזדר מיער
רברכיבהו... לעשו, על במרחי
ארץ הרינו ישראל רכמיב ביה
ראתה על במרחימר הדרוך
(דבריט לב.כמ) וכן בל הפסוק:
ויאבל. חנובת שדי אלו ארבע
מלכיות. לפי שעדרום ארבע מלכיות
שהיו אחר אלבסנדרוס מלך יוון
רכחיב חשבר מלכבוחה וחחיק
לארבע רוחות השמים (רניאל
יא.ד) וארוס היו אחר יוון
אלו אנין רבאדן ישראל. כחיב
ארץ זבת חלב ודבש (ויקרא
כ.כד)
הפיסקוין והנמנוגין. מיני שרדה:
בלי־רקין. בגריוס חשובין וכן
מירטון אלא שהאחר למעלהי והאחד
למטה, וטרינגין לובשיים באמצעי
עוד רי לומר שהם כלם מיניי שרדה
והמרינגון עומר כין בלי־רקין
למיירנו והיינו דקאמר שבנינין
מכין שניהם; פירוש, שמדברים
כדמו וזה מכין אח שניהם ומוריע
רברי זה לזה:

וחמורים ונזרות שווח וחשובות. עם
חלב כליורח חיטה . אילו חלבורת שחם
נופה של חורם . ורם ענב חשתח חסר.
אילו הנזורת שמושבורח לב ארם כיין .
דבר אחר ירכינבהו על במדי ארץ . זה
העולם הזה שנאמר יברסמנה חזיר מיער .
ויאבל חנובת שדי . אילו ארבע מלכיות.
וינחקו רבש מסלע. אילו מציקים שהחחיק
בה בארץ ישראל והם קשים לחוציא מהם
פרוטה כצור , לסחר הרי ישראל יורשים
את נכסיהם והם עריבים להם כרבש
ושטן . דבר אחר חמאת בקר אילו אילו
חפיטקים והנמונים שלהם . עם חלב כליות
אילו כלים ריקים שלהם . ואילים . אילו
בני פוקרים שלהם . בני בשן . אילו
קיטרינים שסטכינין מבין שיניהם . ועתורים
אילו סנקנירקוס שלהם . עם חלב כליורח
חיטה . אילו מטרוניות שלהם . ורם ענב
תשתת חסר אילו ישראל שלסמר יורשים
את נכסיהם ועריבים להם כשטן ורבש.
רבר אחר כליורח חיטה עחידרה כל חיטה
וחיטה להיורח כשתי כליורח של שור
גדול משקל ארבעת עשר ליטרים
בציפורי . ואל תחמה ברבר הסארבל
בראשי לפתורה . מעשה ושקלו ראש לפח
שלשים ליטרים של ציפורי . ומעשה
שקינן שועל בראש חלפרח . ועוד מעשה
בשיחים בקלח של חררל שחיו בו שלשה
כורים ונשתה אחר מהם . וסיככו בו סכח
יוצרים וחטבו ומצאו בו חשעה קבין
חררל . אסר רבי שמען בן חלפתא
מעשה בקלח של כרוב שהיה בתוך שלנו
והייתי עולה יורד בו כעולה ויורד במלם.
רבר אחר ורם ענב תשתח חסר שלא

ונפח. לשון רישפחני (איכה
ג.יא):

⸸ ח' בכה־י:

רתיו יניעים לא לדרוך ולא לכצור אלא
ארם סביא בעגלה וזוקפה בזיח . וסמחפק
וחלך כשותה מן הפיטום:

פלוס. קנקן של עץ גדול:

סליק פיסקא

שיח

וישמן ישורון ויבעט . לפי שבעם ״סורדים

(פסקא שיח)
מתוך ארבע הן ראויין. פירוש.
נם סורדין. גרסינן:

וכן אחה מוצא באנשי דור הטבול שלא
סרדו לפני הסקום אלא מחוך מאכל
ומשתח ומחוך שלוה . מה נאמר כהם
בתיהם שלום מפחר . כולה כריוחא באלה
הדברים וכן מציגו באנשי סדום שלא
סרדו לפני הסקום אלא מחוך מאכל
ומחוך משקה ומחוך שלוה . וכן הוא אוסר
חי אני נאםיהוה אם עשחה סדום אחוחך .
וכן באנשי סנרל שלא מרדו לפני הסקום
לא מחוך מאכל ומחוך משקרח ומחוך
שלוה . לכן הוא אוסר ויהי כל הארץ
שפח אחרת כולרה בריוחא . וכן אחה
מוצא באנשי דור המבול שלא סרדו
לפני הקרוש ברוך הוא לא מחוך מאכל
ומשתח שנאמר וישב העם לאכול
ושחרה . סרה נאסר בהם סרו סחר סן
הורך. אסר לו הקרוש ברוך הוא לסשרה
אמור להם לישרא כשאחם נבנסים
לארץ אין אחם עחידים לסרור לא
מחוך אכילה ושחיירה שנאמר כי אביאנ
ו האדמרה אשר נשבעחי לאבוחיכם
זברח חלב ורבש ואכל ושבע ורשן ופנרה
ו לחים אחרים . אמר לחם משרה
לישרא כשאחם נבנסים לארץ אי אחם
עחירים לסרור לא מחוך אכילה ושחיירה
ומחוך שלורה. שנאסר מן חאכל ושבעת.
ובקרך וצאנך ירבין סרה נאסר בחם ורם
לבנך ושנאחר ארץ יהוה וחיך. וכן אחה
מוצא בבניו ובכנוחיו של איוב שלא
כאחרה לחם פורענורה לא מחוך אכילה
ושחיירה ומחוך שלורה שנאסר עד בדבר
זרה בא ויאמר בניך ובנוחך אוכלים
ושוחים יין וחגרח רוח נחולרה נאה .
וכן אחרה מוצא בעשרה חשבטים שלא

וכן אחה מוצא ליפוח המשיח.
חיפא. היכן מצינו שליפוח המשיח
עחירין לפרוד. ויש לומר דלא קאי
אישראל אלא אאומוח העולם:
והיינו דקאפר שלשה דרורוח:
ריהה כל הארץ שפה אחח
(בראשיח יא.א). ודיש שובע ושלוה
בדרדריץ ורחענגה באחר (בראשיח
מא.יח). בזפן שטובע בעולם אהוה
ושלום בעולם:
שלפנין. הם רצועוח העול:
אלן שלשה דרורוח שלפני יפוח
המשיח. רוצה לוטר שלשה דרורוח של
גוים רסמוכין לפשיח שחהיך עושה
ישראל יוחר פראי ויחנאו בחלילים
ופסילים:
אל תקרי ריגבל אלא ריגבל.
פלשון נבל צדיק (ישעיהו מ.ז.
ח); פירוח בכינול הבחיש חוקפו
שלא יוכל להושיע:
דברים של זכרונם. שעשה מפצלת
כעין זכרוה להיוח נכבלח לעבודה
זוה:
צלם יהורי. שנטאו יהורי:

נלו לא פחוך אכילה ושחיוה ומחוך
שלוה. שנאפר השוכבים על פטח שן
השוחים במורקי יין לכן עחה נלו בראש
נלים. וכן אחה פוצא ביפוח המשיח
שאין עחירים לפרוד לא פחוך אכילה
ושחיוה ושלוח סרה נאפר בחם וישפן
שורוך וינבט. פשל לאדם אחד שחיוה
לו עגל והיה פפשפשו ופגרדו ופאכילו
כרשינים בשביל שיהיה חורשים
בו כשהנדיל חענל נחן בעליו עלו עליו
וקירטע ושיבר אח העול ופסק אח
הסחינייניס. וכן הוא אופר סוטות עץ
שברה. שמנח ביסי ירבעם. עביר
ביסי אחאב. כסירה הכל ביסי יהוא
דבר אחר שמנח עביר כסיר. שפנה
ביסי אחז. עביר ביסי פנשה. כסיר
הכל ביסי חזקיה. דבר אחר שמנר
עביר כסיר. כארם ששטן טבפנים
ועשה כלים סמחוני. וכן הוא אופר
כי כסה פניו בחלבו ויעש פיפה עלי
כסל. דבר אחר שמנר עביר כסיר.
אילו שלשה דרורה שלפני יפוח המשיח
שנאפר וחפלא ארצו כסף והב. וחפלא
ארצו סוליים. ויטוש אוה עשרו. נטשר
שמים ויוסד ארץ. כי יהם רעית עשה
עפי. אסר להם הקרוש כרוך הוא בסרה
שסרוחהם כי פרדתי לנם עבוחי ארן
ביחי. נטשתי אח נחלתי. ויטש פשכן
שילה. כי נטשר עסך בירח יעקב. דבר
אחר ויטוש אוה עשרו. שנאפר ויביאני
ל החצר הפניטיח והגה כפחח ושער
בעשרים וחפשה איש אוחריהם אל
היכל יהוה. רבי הסחאי ברבי יהודה
אוסר ל חקרי ויגבל לא ויגבל צור
ישועתו. כענין שנאפר ל חנאץ למען
שסך ול חנבל נסא כבוד. יקנאוח
בזרים. שחלבו חעשו דברים של זרוה
וגם הוא אוסר וגם אם אסא וסירה
סנבירה אשר עשחה ספלצחה לאשירה.
בחעובוה יכעיסוהו. זר סשכב זבור ?. וכן
חוא אוסר וארח זר לא חשכב משכני:

jj באקספוורד ובסאנדריה יש "ירות"
וכבהי"ד על הספר "זרות" ונראה
שרבינו גרס זכרות:

אשה חועבה היא : אוסך ונם קרש
היה בארץ . יכהו לשרים . אילו הם
שעוברים לחסה וללגנרה לכוכבים
ולפזלוח ורברים שחם צורך העולם
וחניירה לעולם לא היה הגאה כפולה
לא הם עבברים לרבר שאן סטינים
לחם ולא פריעים לחם . לשרים . סרה
דרכו של שיר נכנס לאדם וכופה אוחו .
אחיום לא ירעון . שאין אומות העולם
סכירים אוחם . חרשים סקרוב באו .
שכל זמן שהיה אחר סך האומוח רואה
אוחו אסר צלם יהורי הוא . וכן הוא
אוסר כאשר סצאוה ירי לפסלכת האליל .
סלסד שירושלם ושוסרין פפסקורת רפוס
לכל באי העולם. לא שערום אבוחיום
שלא עסודה שערם אבוחיכם בפניהם .
דבר אחר לא שערום אבוחיכם ל חקרי
לא שערום אלא לא שעם אבוחיכם
אף על פי שמחבחים להם וסקטרים
להם ולא יראים סהם . וכן הוא אוסר
צור ילד חשי . אסר להם הקרוש כרוך
אוחי כאילו אני זכר ובקש ליל עשיחם
אילו היחרה חיים יושבין על הפשבר לא
היחרה פצטערח כענין שנאפר כי באו
בנים עד פשבר . ואילו היחרה חולה
וסכנירה לא היחה פצטערח כענין
שנאפר כי קול כחולה שמעחו צרה
כסבכירה . אילו היו שנים בסעירה לא
היחרה פצטערח כענין שנאפר וחרוצצו
הבנים בקרבה . אילו היור זכר שאין
דרכו ליל ובקש ליל לא צערו כפול .
וסכופל כענין שנאפר שאו נא וראו אם
יולר איש זכר . דבר אחר צור ילרך חשי .
שכחחם אוחי בזכוח אבוחיכם . וכן הוא
אוסר הביטו ל צור אברהם . אכינם ול שרה
חחוללנם , רבר אחר צור ילרך חשי . כל זמן שאני
טבקש להטיב אחכם אחם סחיים כח
של סעלה . עמדחם על חיים ואסרחם
זה אלי ואנוהו , חזרחם ואסרחם נחנה

(פיסקא שיז)
כוכחא אבוחיכם. רורש מחוללרך,
אוחם הפחחוללים להביאו לעולם
ההיינו אביו ואסו:

ראש ונשוברה סדנים . ובקשתי להטיב
אתכם חזרתם עמדתם על הר סיני
ואמרתם כל אשר דבר יהודה נעשה
ונשמע ובקשתי להטיב לכם חזרתם בכם
ואמרתם לעבוד ערז אלהי ישרה. תוי כל
זמן שאני מבקש להטיב לכם אתם
מרשיעים כוחו של מעלה . ותשלח אל
סתוליליך . רבי מאיר אומר אל שהתחיל
בך . אל שנצטער בך בענין שנאמר. חיל
כיולרה. רני מאיר אומר אל שעשאך מחילים
סחילים . דבר אחר ותשכח ל מתוללליך
אל שהתחיל שמו עליך סרך שלא תחיל
שמו . על כד אומם וסלבוח. וכן הוא
אומר אנכי יהודה אלוהיך . רבי נחמירה
אומר אל שעשאם חולים על כל באי
העולם בעשין שאו אתה עשרה על הטים
וכן הוא אומר קול יהודה על הטים
קול יהודה יחולל איילורה . דבר אחר
ותשכח אל סתוליליך . אל שמוחל לך
על כל עוונותיך .

סליק פיסקא
[שב]

וירא יהודה וינאץ . רבי יהודה אומד
מחה שהם נאים לו מנאצים לפניו .
רבי מאיר אומר מכעם בניו ובנותיו והרי
דברים קל וחומר ומה בזמן שמכעיסים
קרוים בנים. אילו לא היו מכעיסים על
אחרת כמרה וכמה . ויאמר אסתירה פני
מהם . אמר הקרוש ברוך הוא הריני
סלק שכינתי סריניכם . אראה סה
אחריהם. ארן סרה בספויתן . דבר אחר
הריני מוסרם ביד ארבע מלביורת שיהא
משעבדין אותם . כי דור תפהוכורת
הסה . דור הפוך דור התפול אין כתיב
כאן כי אם דור תחפוכורת . הפכפכנים
הם פורנים הם. בנים לא אמון בם.
בנים אתם שאין בכם אמונה . עקמתם
לפני הר סיני ואמרתם כל אשר דבר
יהודה נעשה ונשמע . אף אני אמרתי
לכם אנן אנם אלהים חמותן. הנכנסתי אתכם
אל ארץ אבותיכם ונתתי לכם ביר
הבחורה אמרתם לכם לא תחי גוליס
סמגרה לעולם . כיך שאמרתם אין לנו
חלק בדור . אף אני אמרתי לכם ושראל
נלה יולה סער אדמתו . רבי רוסתאי
בן יהודה אומר אל חקרי לא אמון בם
לא לא אמן בם שלא חיו רוצים
לעמוד אמן אחר הנביאים בשעה

שמברכים אותם . וכן הוא אומר למען
חקים את השבועה אשר נשבע יהודה
לאבותיכם לתרר לנו ארן זבת חלק
ורבש . ולא היה אחד מהם שפתם פיי
ועונה אמן עד שבא ירמירה וענה
אמן שנאמר ואען ואומר אמן יהוד . הם
קנואים בלא אל ביעסני בהבליהם יש
לך אדם עונר לצלם דבר הרואה אותו
אבל הם עובדים לבבואה ולא לכבואה
כלבד אלא להבל זרה שעליה סך
הקרירה בעניין שנאמר כעסני בהבליהם.
ואני אקנאים בלא עם . אל חקרי בלא
עם אלא בלוי עם אילו הבאים סבין
האומות וסלניורת וסוציאים אותם מתוך
בתיהם. דבר אחר אילו הבאים סברבריא
וטטוגט וטמורטגיא . שמהלכים ערומים
בשוק . בני נבל אבעיסם . אילו המינים
וכן הוא אומר , אמר נבל בלבו אין
אלהים. כי אם קרחה באפי. בשתמורענות
יוצארה סן העולם אין יוצאה לא באף.
סנין אף בתוך גיהנם שנאמר וחיקד על
שאול תחתי . ותאבל אש ויכבלר . זו
ארן ישראל . ותלהט מוסרי הרים. זו
ירושלם. בענין שנאמר ירושלם תרים סביב
לה ויתורה סביב לעמו . דבר אחר ותאבל
ארן ויבולרה זר העולם . ותלהט מוסרי
הרים אילו ארבע סלביורת יוצאות סבין
שני הרים. והדרים הרי נחשרה.

סליק פיסקא
[שכא]

אספרה עליסו רעורה . הריני מבנים
וסביא עליהם נל הפורענורת כולם
כאחרת . דבר אחר אסף עליסו רעורה
אין כתיב כאן אלא אספה שיתו כל
הפורעניורת כלורה . והם אינן כלים . וכן
הוא אומר חצי אכלה בם . חצי יכלו
אותם אין כתיב כאן , אלא חצי אכלה

אל שהול בך . פירוש, שברא העולם
בעבורך, מלשון וחוללתי (משלי
ח.כו)ף:
שנצטער. מלשון חיל כיולרה
(ירמיהו ר.לא):
שהול שמו. כדכתיב והריתם לי
לסגולה. (שמות יס.ה):
חולין. שהבל שולטני בך:
קול ה׳ על הטים (תהלים
כט.ג). בעוסקים בתורה בלשון
עילוי רכתיב על ; בשנעשה
חולין. ויהוסף, מגלה ראמם:

(פסקא שב)
מטאה נאים לו מנאצים. רכתיב
בהר בן גרשום בן מנשה
(שופטים יח.ל):
דור הפוך...(הפכפכנים). שתי
הבנים, בשהם מתהפחים להרע סרת
הרין מתהפם עליהם:
פותיןד הן. מעווה: הוא:
אלא בלו'ין עם . נראה שהוא
מלשון ורלוה (ישעיהו יד.א):
אחר מעמן ואחר מפואל וכן מכל
אומר וטלכות:
ארבע מלביות. פירשתי למעלה...
אוטם שהיו אחר אלכסנדרוס
באראריין בינמות (סנ.) ואין רטה
סה לעולם אלא במביל ישראל:

44 לפנינו בספרי כ"י כרלין:
"מסה שהם נאים לו מנאצים":
וו לפנינו במרי הספרי "פורגים":
ווו כנהר"י "טעות הוא׳.. וחקנם
לפי סברא:
וווו באקספורוד "בלו", בסמנדריה
"בלוין". ונוראה מפירושו ד"בלוי"
היה לפני רבינו:

(פסקא שמו)
מאזין. נפוחין, גרסינן; מזי
רעב חרגוספי נפיחי כפן (ודברים
ל:כד).
שכל מהמר בו מורד. מלשון
וקטב סרירי על זקנר (שמואל
א כו,יד) שירצין ספיו ריריו.
מעלה נופי. לשון חלורה כמכה
כמו מי שעלתה לו נימא על בשרו
וניחמה ויסוח או יקפענה ויחיה
(בראשית רבה פ' סו, עבורה זרה
י:ז):
כנס את הרגל. לא תבא לחוץ.
פזר. גלה לסקום אחר שאין בו
רעב:
וחרדי לבו נקפיו עליו ומס. כמו
לבו נוקפו (נדה נ:), שירוש ארי"ם
שברת אינני נפלס אלא מן הצע
שנ:מער נוחבו אל לבו ומס:
הא וימרא לאלו. הרי כחור
ובתולה שמסחים ייותרו עליהם,
ובעבור הגם-ים שהם ריבוים הוצרך
לפרש והיונו מה שסעורש כסוף
הספוק רונק עם איש שיבה
והיינו דמירחי רונמא-- רלא ריבה
כגם-ים אלא אם שהזכיר כסוף
הספוק-- כי נם איש:
אמם נרסתם. והאתם הגם-ים לא
מביש א שנרסתם להרוג הבינונים
אלא אפילו הבחורים שלי ואפילו
הבתולות שלא סעסו טעם חטא:

נם שיש חצי כלים והם אינן כלים.
דבר אחר חצי אכלה נם אילו חמי רעב
וכן הוא אוסר בשלחי את חצי הרעב
הרעים בהם . מי רעב ולחומי רשף
שיהיה ל?אומים ברעב וסשלכים בתוצות
וכן הוא אוסר והעם אשר הם נבאים
לכם . יהיו סושלכים בתוצות ירושלם
וקטב סרירי . לפי דרכנו אתרה לסר שכל
סי שהשיר בן סורד , ושן בתמורה . אל
תקרי ושן בחמורה לא ושן בהם . אשלח
בם . שיש סתחסמים וסתחורים על כל
עביריור . דבר אחר שיהא אחר מהם
סתחסם וסושך עצמו וסעלה נסי וסר
והולך נם . ובר אסר סעשרה חיר
שהרחלים נושכים וסמיחים . עם חמת
זוחלי עפר ; שיהיו סוזחלין בעפר . דבר
אחר אילו עשנים שאין שלטמון אלא
בעפר . מחוץ תשכל חרב . סיכן אסרו
בשעת סלחמר כנס אחד הרנל . בשעה
רעב פזר אחד הרנל . וכן הוא אוסר
אם יצאתי השדה והנה חללי חרב
ואם באתי העיר והנה תחלואי רעב .
ואוסר אשר בשרה בחרב יסורת . ואשר
בעיר רעב ודבר יאכלנו . וסתדרים איסר
היר רואה החרב שהיא באר לשוק
אם יכול לברות ולהסלט היסנר אז
חררי לבו נקפים עליו וסר והולך נד .
רבר אחר . סתוץ תשכל חרב על סה
שעשו בתוצורה שנאסר כי ספסר-ערץ
הוו אלהיך יהורה . וסתדרים איסר . על
סה שעשו בתרי חדרים . וכן הוא אוסר
אשר זקני בירת ישרא עשים בתושך
אוסר עזב יהוה ארץ הארץ ואין יהוד
רואה . נם בחור נם בתולה . הותרה
לאילו יונק עם איש שיכרה . וכן הוא
אוסר נם איש עם אשר ולנדו זקן עם
סלא יסים . דבר אחר אתם נרסתם
לי לשלוח יד בבחור וכן הוא אוסר ויען
יחתשע בן נן ספרות משה סבחורו . נם

בתולה סנין שיהיו מנוקים מן החטא
כבתולה זאת שלא טעמה טעם חטא.
יונק . שיהיו יונקים דברי תורה כינק
עד שיונק חלב סדרי אמו , עם איש
שיכרה . אל חקרי איש שיכרה לא איש
ישיכרה . סלמר שיהיו כולם ראוים לישב
בישיכרה . וכן הוא אומר הכל גבורים
עשי מלחמה וכי מה נבורה עושים
בני אדם ההולכים בנולה וזרה מלחמה
עשי"ם בני אדם הזקוקים בזיקים ונתונים
בשלשלאות לא הכל גבורים . גבורי
מלחמתה של תורה . וכן הוא אומר
ברכו יהוד מלאכיו נבורי כח עושי דבר
ולשמוע בקל דברו . עושי מלחמות שהיו
נושאים ונותנים במלחמתה של תורה
וכן הוא אומר על כן יאמר בספר
מלחמות יהוה ואומר התרש והמסגר
אלף הכל גבורים עשי מלחמה ויביאם
סלך בבל נולה בבלה . חורש אחד
סדבר והכל שותקן . והמסנר . הכל
עושבים לפניו ולסדרים היסנו . אחר שפותח
אין סנר , לקים סרה שנאמר ופתח ואין
סנר וסנר ואין פותח אסרתי אפאיהם
אסרתי באפי איד הם . אשביתה מאנוש
זכרם . לא יהו בעולם אבל סה אעשה
להם , לולי יהוה שהיה לנו יאמר נא
ישראל . לולי יהוה שהיה לנו בקום עלינו
אדם רע . דבר אחר לולא ויאמר
להשמידם לולא משה בחירו . לולי כעם
אויב אנור . סי גרם להם ליפרע מאילו
כעס של אומות שהיה כנוס לתוך
מעיהם . אנור . אין אנור אלא כנוס
שנאמר דברי אנור בן יקא . ואוסר ישי
מורה עליסו ירדו שאול חיים כי רעות
במנורם בקרבם פן ינכרו צריסו . בשער
צרתם של ישראל אוסח העולם סנב"ים
אותם ועושים אותם כאילו אין סכירים
אותם בעולם . וכן סצינו כשנכשו ישראל
לברוח כלפי צפון היו מסנירים אותם

מנוקין. גרסינן, פירוש, נהנין
שלו לא טעמו טעם הבתולה נהנית
בביא ראשונה:

זקוקין בזיקין. אסורין בזיקין
ורם כבלים:

מסגריך. פירוש, פוסרים אותם
מחוישין. מורים להם שהם גדולים
מהם״״ כמו ריכחשר אריכך לך
ניער בערב חלי אורותרא רדנים
(תהלים סג.ג):

(פסקא שכב)

טבחים של ישראל אומרים העולם
סבחשים להם ועשים אותם כאילו הם
אחת . ובן עשיו אמר ליעקב . אח אחי
יהי לך אשר לך . ובן חירם אמר לשלמה
סה העירם חאלה אשר נהרך לי אחי .
לא כמורח שאמרו אותם השוטים הלא
בחוקנו לקחנו לו קרנים . כי נו אוכר
עצורת הסה . רבי יהודה דורשם כלפי
ישראל . רבי נחמיה דורשם כלפי האמורה.
רבי יהודה דורשו כלפי ישראל . איבד
עיצה ולא תורה . שנאמר לי עצה
ותושחה ואין בהם חבונה . אין בהם אחר
סיכתבל ויאמר אמש אחר ממנו רודף
מן האמורה אלף ושנים ינוס רבבה .
אם לא כי צורם סכרם . רבי נחמיה
דורשו כלפי האמוהרו איכד האמות שבע
מצורו שנתתי להם . ואין בהם חבונה.
אין בהם אחר שיסתבל ויאמר עכשיו
אחד רודף ממנו אלף ושנים ינוס רבבה
לימורה המשיח . אחר מישראל רודף
ממנו אלף ושנים ינוס רבבה אם לא כי
צורם סכרם . ומעשה בפולמוס שביהודה
שרץ דיקרית אחד אחר . בן ישראל בסם
להורגו ולא חנינו עד שלא חנינו יצא
נחש וכרך לו על עקבו אמר לו בבקשה
ממך אמור לפולוני דבר אחד לא תחין
סורים לומר שאנו נטמרם ונמסרו ביתם.
אלא אם לא כי צורם סכרם וחוה
הסנירים לו חכמו ישבילו נערת אילו שכג
נטכלו ישראל בדברי תורה שניתנרה
להם לא שלשה נהם אחד ומלכות
וסה אמרח להם קבל עליכם על
מלכורת שמים . והרשיע נר ארך נר זה
בריארת שמים ותתנהגו נר ארך נר זה
כנליורת חסרים . איכה ירדוף אחר
אם אם לא עשויהם אר התורה היאך
אני עשרה הבטחתם היותם מבקשים
שיטא אחר. מכם רודף אף ושנים ינוס
רבבה עכשיו אחר מן האמורה רודף
אף ושנים ינוס רבבה אם לא כי
צורם סכרם וחוה הסנירים. אני סנגיר

(פסקא שכב)

אלו נחכלו בכה שאמר להם יעקב
אביהם. ואם תאמר היבן מציני
שאמר להם כך. יש לומר רבתיג
רזאת אשר דבר להם אברהם
ריברך אותם (בראשית מס.כח)
רזאת. היינו קבלו עול מלכות
שים ואין זאת אלא תורה ונכל
המצות יש קבלה עול מלכות. אשר
דבר להם אבריהם. רוצה לומר
וצרוחיו"" היינו והברינו זה אם
זה ביראת אלהים . ריברך אותם.
היינו והתגהגו זה עם זה בגמילות
חסרים רבני גמילות חסרים כתיב
ברכה:

∞ רק באקספורד, בסמבריה ונבדיס
אברהם יש "סמבר".

פפ באקספורד "פולפוס" ובעדים
האחרים פולופוס ועין מה שכתבתי
למעלה הערה . אבל גם עין רעיי
לע״ד ע: פלפוסא-- שר צבא
וערצ:

⸬⸬ באקספורד "על גבני החיל".

זז הקריאה הקשה "סלוני"- נמצא
ברוב ערי הסערי ובנראה שהיא
שבוש של "פולפוס (או פלפוס)"
כמו שעמד לפני רבינו לפי ערות
ברית אברהם וב'י בסמבריה.

אא באקספורד יש "סמבר".
בב באקספורד "רצורתניר":

אך אדם ואיה תורה . אשכלות פרורות
לטו . שהגרולים שבבם מרח פרוסר
נהם כנחש ואין אשכול* לא נחל*
שנאמר אין אשכול לאכול .

סליק פיסקא

הלא הוא כמוס עמדי. רבי מעזר בנו
של רבי יוסי הגלילי]אומר כום שהוד
נמוס ומטוכר יכול דיהרה תלמוד לומר
חסר , יכול שאין בו לא חצי תלמוד
לומר מלא מסך , יכול שאין חסר אפילו
טיפה אהרה תלמוד לומר ויגר מזה
מאותה טיפה שתו סמנרה אנשי דור
הטבול ואנשי דור הפלנה ואנשי]סדום
ו 60 מורה ופרעה וכל]חילו. סיסרא וכל
המונו נבוכנצר וכל חילו. סנחריב וכל
אנפיו. ומאותה טיפה עתידים לשתות
כל באי העולם עד סוף כל הדורות .
וכן הוא אומר ועשרה יהוד צבאות
לכל העמים בהר ההוא משתרה שמנים
משתה שטרים. שמנים סמוחים מוקקים.
יכול שמנים שיש בהם צורך תלמוד לומר
שמנים 6זוקקים . שמנים שאין כלום דבר
לא פקטים. וכן הוא אומר כוס זהב בכל
ביד יהוד . ואומר כוס אתורך תשתי
העמוקה ותרחבה תהיה לצחק וללענ
סרנה להביד. מה דרכו של זהב לאתר
שנשבר יש לו רפואה כך כשהפסוק
הפורעונרת מן האומות עתידרה לחזור
להם. כשהסנערה אצל ישראל מוא אומר
ושתית אותה ומצית ואת חרסיר
תנרמי . מה דרכו של חרס לאתר
שנשבר אין לו רפואה כך כשהפסוק
הפורעונרת מן ישרל לא עתירה לחזור
להם . חתום באוצרותי . מה אוצר גר
חתום ואין סנרל* פירות כך מעשיהם של
רשעים אין סנלים פירורת . אם אסררב
כן מאבים ארת העלם . וכן הוא אומר
אוי לרשע רע כי נמול* ירו יעשה לו ,
אבל מעשיהם של* צדיקים סנדלים פירות
ופרי פירורת וכן הוא אסר אסרו צדיק
כי טוב .כי פרי מעלליהם יאכלו, דבר אתר

(פסקא שבר)
כמו סימאי. אוצר:
]וזמחוסר.] גל מלשון אוצר:
יכול דיהה ח*ל חסר. פירוש
צלול ואינו כעין יין אלא כעין
טים:
מפוחים. שנמחו כאלו אינם היינו
פיקים כלוסר גרעיני זית היינו
פסולת:
אם אטרב כן. שמעשיהן יעשו
פירות נמצאו מאבדין את העולם:

ww באקספארדד הסופר המקורי כתב
כמו זה אבל נראה שביר אצרת נחקן
הנוסח להיות כמו ערי הספרי...
כמוס ומחוסר. גל מלשון אוצר:
בסמנריה הגוסח בריוק כמו המקורי
באקספורד בלי שום תקון ונראה
שזהו הנוסח הנכון:

סרח אוצר ערב חתום ואינו חסר כלום כך
צריקים לא נטלו כלום משלהם בעולם
הזה . וכנין שלא נטלו צדיקיסכלום משלהם
בעולם הזה שנאמר סרח. רב טובך אשר
צפנת ליראיך . וכנין שלא]נטלו רשעים
כלום משלהם בעולם הזה שנאמר אלא
הוא כמוס עמרי חתום באוצרותי . איתמי
שכד אילו ואילו נוטלים למסר כשחנוא נאולה
שנאמר לי נקם ושלם | לי נקם ושלם אני
בעצמי פורע מהם ואיני פורע מהם לא
על ירי סלאך ולא על ירי שליח כעניין
שנאמר ועתרה לכרה ואשלחך 6 פרעה .
ואומר ויצא סלאך יהוה וין במחנה אשור
לי נקם ואשלם אין כתיב. כא לא לי
נקם ושלם . משלם אני מעשים שעשו
אבותיהם לפני בעולם הזה . ואומר לא
אחשה כי אם שלמתי ושלמתי את חיקם.
ואומר ושלמתי ראשונה ושניה משנה
ענם וחטאתם. לערב חמט רגלם . כעניין
שנאמר תרמסנה רגל רגלי עני פעמי
דלים, כי קרוב יום ארם . אסר רבי יוסי
אם מי שנאמר בהם כי קרוב יום אידם
הרי פורענורת מסטעובדרת וכאורת מי
שנאמר בהם מרוב ימים יפקרו על אחת
כמה וכמה. וחש עתירות לטו . כשהסקום
מביא פורעניורת על* האומורת מרעיש
עליהם ארת העולם שנאמר יעופו כנשר
חש לאכול . ואומר האומרים ימהר
ויחישה מעשהו למען נראה ותקרב
ותבואה . כשהסקום מביא צד טוסרס לארבע
סלכיורת שיהיו מעונבדים בהם , וכן הוא
אומר 6 תירא כי אתך אני להושיעך.
כי ירין יהוה עמו . כשהסקום מביא
האומורת שמחה הוא לפניו שנאמר כי
יריק יהוה יהוד . וכשהסקום רן ארת
האומורת יהוה מהוורו לפניו שנאמר רן
כביטיל יש תהוורו לפניו שנאמר 6
עברי יתנחם.ואין נחמה לא תהות שנאמר
כי נחמתי כי עשיתים . ואומר נחמתי כי
המלכתי ארת שאול למלך . כי יראה כי
אזלרת יר , כשרואה הבל סהלכים לפניו
בשהכלה בטלה ,דבר אחר כשיתייאשו מן
הגאמלה כשהכלה פרוטה מן הכים שנאמר
ובכלתנפץ יר עם קורש תבלינה כל אלה.
רבר אחר כי יראה כי אזלרת יר כשהוא רואה
שאין בהם אדם שמבקש עליהם רחמים
כמשרת שנאמר ויאמר להשמירם · לולי
משה בחירו. דבר אחר כי יראה. כשהוא

(מסקא שבה)
הכי גרסינן:- לי נקם ואשלם לא
כתיב אלא ושלם. אי כתיב ואשלם
הוה משמע דשלום פורענותוהנני לי
השאא רכתיב רשלם משסל.- לי
נקם]היינו פורעניותהנני וגם
שלם]היינו]פורעניות מעשיהם
שעשו אבותיהם]:
כי קרוב רום ארם. כלוסר
שכן אוחם שנאסר נהם מרוב ימים
יפקרו,)ישעיהו כר.בב(.

שכו

)ותהוה.] כמו בחוהא על הראשונות
)קרושין מ(:
כשיראה הבל מהלכין לפניו]דן[.
כשיראה שיחזרו בתשובה פרוב
הם]יר המבה שמשמשם בהם:
כי נחמתי כי עשיתים . וורש לשון פרוסה:
)נמשה.] רכתיב ביה ויהי רדיר
אזלרת יד , כשרואה הבל סהלכים לפניו
בשהכלה בטלה . דבר אחר כשיתייאשו

ww חסר בכה"י ומלאתי על פי
סכרא:
xx נראה לי שצ"ל "חר:

סמהרון. רכתיב קח את המחתה רואה שאין בהם שטבקש עליהם באהרן
שנאמר, ויטר בין המתים ובין החיים
דבר אחר כי יראה. כשהוא רואה שאין
בהם אדם שמבקש עליהם כפינחס שנאמר
ויעמר פנחס ויפלל והתעצר המגפה. דבר
אחר כי יראה כי אין עזר שנאמר ואפס
עצור ועזוב. ואין עזר לישראל . ואמר א
להים . רבי יהודה דורשו כלפי ישראל .
ורבי נחמיה דורשו כלפי האומורת . רבי
יהודה אומר ישראל שאומרים להם לאומות
העולם היכן הפיטקים והנגמונים שלכם.

(פסקא שכז)
ישראל אומרים לאומות העולם.
פירוס. לימות המשיח:

אשר חלב זבחימו יאכלו שיהו נתונים

(פסקא שכח)
אפסכוניות. שכר לחיילותיו:
דינוסיבה. סעורת למלכים.
סלניה. סט:

להם אסטגיורה ועשים להם דונאטובי
וסעלים להם קלניא . יקומו ויערוכם

ורעודרוכם. מש׳ יעזרו אתכמ׳
ואת עצמם:

יקומו ויערו אהבכם אין כתיב כאן אלא
יקומו ויערוכם רבי נחמיה אומר טיטוס

דיעזרו אהכם. מש׳ יעזר לצדיכם
וכן קאי אטמים:״

בן אשתו של אספסיינוס נכנס לבית
קורדשי חקרשים ונידר ארת הפרכות בסייף
ואמר אם נוה הוא ינוא ויסמח . אשר
חלב זבחיסו יאכלו . אמר הללו משה
הטעם ואמר להם כנו לכם מזבח וחעלו
עליו עולורת ונבכו עליו נסכים בעינן
שנאמר ארת הכבש האחד תעשה בבקר.
יקומו ויערוכם יהי .עליכם סתרה . על

עין יהכן דורש ״וכם״.. ״גם עצמם
גם אהכם״:

הכל הוא מוחל על חילל חשם פורע
טיר ראו עתה כי אני אני הוא. זארת

שכם
בכהי״. ״ויעזרוכם מטיעזרו
אהכם ואת עצמם ויעזרו אהכם משה
עזר לצרכים ובן קאי אטמים.
בפירוש רבי ש. אורנבא.-- ״משמע
יעזור את עצמם.״ ונראה שדבריו
מבוססים על הירוש שלנו. והקנתי
משה .-- מש׳ י(עזר):

תשובה לאוסרים אין רשורת בשמים
האומר אין רשורת בשמס מטיכים אותו
ואוסר לו. ואין אלהים עסרי . או שמא
אין יכול לא להחיורת ולא להמיר.
לא להרע ולא .להטיב חלמור לומר אני
אמירת ואחייה״ ואוטר כה אמר יהוה מלך
ישראל וגואו יהות צבאורת אני ראשון ואני
אתרון וסבלעדי אין אלהים. דבר אחר אני

אמית ואחיה , זה שניגזן להם רסז לתחיית
המתים , אני אמירת ואחית , חמורת נפשי
סורת ישרים . יחי ראובן ואל ימורת ,
יחיינו סיומים , דבר אחר אני אמית ואחיה
שומע אני מירת באחר וחיים באחר
תלמוד לומר סחצתי ואני ארפא כדרך
סכה ורפואה באחר כך סיתה וחיים
באחר . ואין סירו מציל , אין אבורת
מצילים ארת הבנים לא אברהם מציל
ארת ישמעאל ולא יצחק מציל ארת
עשו . אין לי אלא אבורת שאן מצילים
ארת הבנים , אחים ארת אחים סנין
תלמוד לומר אח פדה לא יפדה איש .
לא יצחק מציל ארת ישמעאל ולא יעקב
מציל ארת עשו ואפילו נותנים לו כל
סמון שבעולם אין נותנים לו כפרו
שנאמר אח פדה לא יפדה איש ולא
יתן לאהים כופרו . ויקר פדיון נפשם והי
לעולם . יקרה היא נפש זו כשנארם
חוטא נרה זו אין לרה תשלומים . כי אשא
אל שמים ידי. כשבראו הקדוש ברוך הוא
לא ברא כי אם כסאמר. ולא בשבועה,
וסי גרם לו לישבע סתוסרי אסנרה הם
גרסו לו לישבע. שנאמר וישא ידו להם
להפיל אורתם במדבר ולהפיל זרעם
בגים . ואמרתי חי אנכי לעולם . שלא
בסירירת הקדוש ברוך הוא סירד בשר
ורם . מירד בשר ורם . הפיטקי 'נכנס
לתוך הפרכיא שלו אם יכול ליפרע
סכל אם לאו אין יכול ליפרע, וריןל
מי שאמר והיה העולם אינו כן , אם
אינו נפרע מן החיים נפרע מן המתים.
אם אינו נפרע בעולם הזה נפרע
בעולם הבא . אם שנותיו ברק חרבי
כשיפורעערה יוצאה סלפני קלה היא

יפסקא של)
והתקיף . לשון שרדה:
נכנס (לתורן) הפרכיא . פירוש
הפרכיא של מלך ; נכנס בה הפקסר
(ש׳) אחד עם חילו, ושללה וכזזה
ואין הסלך יכול ליפרע מסנו,
בגון שהלך לו אל ארצו, שוב אין
לו נקמה:
אינו נפרע מן החיים נפרע
בעולם הבא . פירוש
בחיי אפיקסי:

כבכב . ואף על פי כן ותאחז במשפט
(אשיב נקם לצרי, זה אחד, ולמשנאי אשלם. זה שנים)
ירי A אשיב נקם לצרים . איני נוחים
שנאמר וישטע שרי יתודרי וכניבם כי
בני הנולד בונים החיכל ונ' . ולמשנאי
אשלם . אילו הטינים . וכן הוא אמר
הלא משנאיך יהוה אשנא ומתקוטסיק
אתקוטט . תבליית שנארה שנאתים
לאויבים היו לי .

סליק פיסקא

שלב אשכיר חיצי סרם . וכי היאך אפשר
לחצים שישתכרו בדם . אלא הריני
משבר לאתרים טסרה שחיצי עושים .
וחרבי תאכל בשר . וכי היאך איפשר
לחרב שתאכל בשר אלא הריני מאכיר
אתרים טסרה שתרב עשרה כענין
שנאמר בן אדם אמור לצפור כל בנף
ולכל עוף השטים הקבצו ובאו תאספו
מסביב ל זבח אשר אני זובח . ואכלתם
חלב לשנגרה . ושתיחום רם לשכרון .
בשר נינורים תאכלו ורם נשיאי הארץ
תשתו ושבעתם על שולחני חלב ודם .
חרב ליהוה םלאה רם הורשנה מחלב .
לסרה כי זבח ליהוה בבצרה וטבח גרול
בארץ ארום . סרם חלל ושביה . מסת
שעשו בחללי עמי . וכן הוא אמר מי יתן
ראשי סים ועיני מקור רמעה ואבכה
יוסם ולילה את חללי ברת עמי.
ושביה . טמרה שעשו בשבווי עמי . וכן
הוא אומר והיו שובים לשוביהם . טראש
פרעות אויב . כשהסקום מביא פורענות
על האומות אין טביא עליהם שלהם
לא שלהם ושל אבותיהם מאברהם
ואילך . דבר אחר טראש פרעות אויב

פרעות. רוות לשון סרה: טרח ראו נל הטורעניות ליתלות בראשו
של פרעה מפני שפרעה הוא היה
תחילה שישיעבר ישראל. הרינו נוים עמו

זה אמר...וזה שנים. פירוש שני
ריינים אי נמי שני פעמים:

משבר אחרים. כלומר העופות
שורכן לאכול הגבלות והכלבים
שורכן לאכול את הרם:

למטר כשהסקום מביא נאולה לישרף
אומרת העולם סתרנגים לפניו ולא צ
תחולה להם ולא שכבר רגו מסקום כענין
שנאמר שמע עסם ירגזון . דבר אחר
הרינו נוים עמו שעתירים אוסורת העולם
להיות סקלסים לפני ישראל שנאמר הרינו
נוים עמו . ומנין שאף שטים וארץ שנאמר
רו שטים כי עשרה הריע תחתיות
ארץ . ומנין אף חרים ונבערה שנאמר
תהרים יפצתו לפניכם רינה וכל עצי
השרדה יסחאו כף . ומנין אף אבורד
ואיסמות שנאמר ירגו ושבר סלע וסראש
הרים יצחו . כי רם עבויו יקום ונקם
ישיב . שתי נקסורת נקם וכו' הרם ונקם
על החמס אומרת העולם ארץ ישראל מעלרה
עליהם כאילו רם נקי שפכו שנאמר
וקבצתי ארץ כל הנים והוררתים אל
עמק יהושפט ונשפטתי שם . מצרים
לשטרה תהיה וארום לסרבר שסמרר .
מחמס בני יהודרי אשר שפכו רם נקי
בארצם . באותרה שעה ויהוררד לעולם
תשב . ונקיתי רסם לא נקיתי . וכפר
ארמתו עסו . סנין אתרה אוסר שהרינתן
של ישראל ביד אוסורת העולם כפרה היא
להם לעולם הבא . שנאמר בזהור רסם כמוס
עהים באו נים נחלתן . שפכו רסם כמים
דבר אחר ארמתו עסו . סנין אתרה
אוסר שיריותם של רשעים בניהגם כפרה
היא להם לישראל בעולם הבא שנאמר
ונתתי כופרך מצרים כוש וסבא . מאשר
יקרתי בעיני נכברת ואני אהבתיך ואתן
ארום תחתיך . היה רבי מאיר אוסר כל
הוישב בארץ ישראל ארץ ישראל סכפרת
עליו שנאמר העם הוישב בה נשוא עון
ועך דבר תלי בדלא תלי . כי ארצם
בדלא תלי . ועריו אין אנו יורעים אם
פורקים עוונותיהם עליה ואם נושאים
עוונותיהם עליה כשהוא אוסר וכפר
ארמתו עסו הרי פורקים עוונותיהם עליה
ואין נושאים עוונותיהם עליה . וכן היה
רבי מאיר אוסר כל הר בארץ ישראל
וקורא קריה שמע שחרירי וערבירת
שלג ומרבר בלשון הקורש הרי הוא בן העולם

(פסקא שלג).
כפרה היא להם. משפכו רמם
תשב . (תהלים עט.ג) דריש:
פורקין. פירוש, פורקין מעליהם:
נושאין, כמו ישא את עונה
(במדבר ל.טז)
כל הרד בארץ ישראל וכו'. ארץ
ישראל היא קרויה קרש, מקום
הקרוש:
כמנא ראמר קריאת שמע שחרירת וערבירת
קיים מצות רהגרת בר רומם
ולילה (יהושע א.ח); וקריאת שמע
הוא קרושת שמו וקבלת יחוורו
ועול מלכותו:
ומרבר בלשון הקרש. לתשלים שלש
קרושות. קרושה הארץ וקרושת שמו
כולו נברא בארץ ישראל שהוא גם שהעולם
קריה מכורורת הארץ רתבוב מצרוך
מכלל ררפי (תהלים ב.ג)
והעולם נברא בלשון הקרש על כן
צריך לרבר בלשון הקרש בארץ
ישראל:

גמ כך כסמנריה. אכל באקסמנררי--
"קרויה קרוש מקום" בכברה
אברהם-- "קרויה מקום קרוש"
bbb עין בבלי יומא נו'; ובבית
המרש (יעללינק) חרד ה' ע' 63:

יש בה עכשיו . כי שם ה'
אקרא:
לשעבר . יערוף כמטר הריני
מזן תורה:
למחר לבא . כי ירדן ה' עמו:
בעולם הזה . כל השירה:
לעולם הבא . הרגינו גרים
עמו:

הבא . אמרת גדולה שירה שיש בה
עכשיו ויש בה לשעבר ויש בה לעתיד
לבא ויש בה לעולם הבא .

סליק שירתא

ויבא משה . נאמר כאן ויבא משה
ונאמר להלן וילך משה אי איפשר לומר
ויצא משה שכבר נאמר וילך משה . ואי
איפשר לומר ויל משה שכבר נאמר ויבוא
משה . אמור מעתה בא דיוקנים שלו
והרשות נתונה ביד אחר . וידבר משה
את כל דברי השירה הזאת באזני העם
סלוד שהיה משקיעם באזניהם . הוא
יהושע בן נון . ולמה אני צריך והלא כבר
נאמר ויקרא משה להושע בן נון ומה
תלמוד לומר הוא יהושע בן נון ללמוד
צרק של יהושע שומע אני שצפה דעתו
עליו משנתחמנה ברשות חלמוד לומר הוא
והושע בן נון . הושע בצרקו . אף על פי
שנתחמנה פרנס על 'הציבור הוא והשע
בצדקו . כיוצא בו אתה אומר יוסף היה
במצרים . וכי אין אנו יודעים שיוסף היה
במצרים אלא להודיע צדקו של יוסף .
יוסף היה רועה ארן צאן אביו ואף על
פי שנעשה מלך במצרים הרי הוא בצדקו
כיוצא בו אתה אומר ורוד הוא הקטן
וכי אין אנו יודעים שדוד הוא הקטן אלא
להודיע צרקו של דוד . ודוד היה רועה
ארן צאן אביו . ואף על פי שנעשה מלך
ויהם שיטו לבנבב . ויאמר אדם שיהיה
עיניו ולבו ואזניו מכוונים לדברי תורה .
וכן הוא אומר בן אדם ראה בעיניך ובאזניך
שמע ושים לבך על כל אשר אני דובר
איך . ושמטר לבך לכל מבוא הבית ולכל
מוצאי המקדש . והרי דברים קל וחומר
ומה בירת המקדש שנראה בעינים ונמדד
ביד צריך אדם שיהו עיניו ולבו ואזניו
סכוונים לדברי תורה שהם כהררים התלויים
בסערה על אחרת כמה וכמה , אשר
חצום . אמר להם צריך אני להתחזק לכם
טובה שתחקיסו את התורה אחריכם אף
אתם צריכים להתחזק טובה לבניכם שיקיימו
ארן התורה אחריכם . מעשה שבא רבינו
סלודקיא ונכנם רבי יוסי ברבי יהודה ורבי
יעזר בן יהודה וישבו לפניו אמר להם
קרבו לכם צריך אני לחתזק טובה לבניכם
שיתקימו ארן התורה אחריכם . אילו אין

(פסקא שלד)
אי אפשר לומר וירבא . נראה רה"ק
קורם השירה, רבתיב וירל
(רברים לא.א) . רעם ישראל היה,
אם כן לא היה צריך לומר וירבא
אלא [ל]אפרומינן שכבר בא זמנו
והוא לשון כי בא השמש (בראשית
כג.יא) והיינו לשון שקיעה.
ריימביום. לשון זמן וקץ להמטר
מן העולם.
ורהשוא כהונה. הממשלה ליהושוע
והרי כבר נאמר . פירוט, כמו
נמי הזך לקרותו יהושע:

מסדרין. הלמה גרולה וענין גרול
חלוי ברבור אחר או בדוא אחר:
החזיקו טובה. חזרו עליהם
ותריאים כמה שבר יהיה לכם:
לא היתה שוה. בחציה:

משה נדול דהא ואילו אחר וקיבלנו
תורתו ולא היתה תורתו שום על אחרת
כמה וכמה לכך נאמר אשר חצום שלו
כי לא דבר רק הוא מכם . אין לך דבר
ריקם בתורה . שאם תדרשנו שאין בו מחן
שכר בעולם הזה ותקרן קיימ לו לעולם
הבא . חרע שכן שהרי אמרו למה נכתב
ואחורי לוטן חמנע ותמנע היתה פלנבש
לפי שאמרה אין אני כרי שאהיה לו
לאשה אריה לו לפילנש וכל כך לסה
להוריע שבחו של אברהם אבינו שהיו
סלכ'ם ושולטונים מחאוים ליורבק בו והרי
דברים קל וחומר ומה עשו עשו שאות ביון
לא מצוה אחרת שכביר ארן אביו הוא
מלכים ושולטונים מחאוים ליורבק בו . על'
אחרן כמה וכמה שהיו רציף ליורבק
ביעקב הצדיק שקיים ארן כל התורה
כולה שנאמר ויעקב איש תם . וברבר הזה
האריכו ימיכם . זה אחר מן הדברים
שהעשה אותם אוכל' פירותיהם בעולם

(פסקא שלו)
ובדבר הזה (רברים לב.מז) .
היינו תורה
כבור אן ואם . ילוף לה מרבתיב
ריתב לך (רברים ה.טז) בעולם הזה,
ואם ארביון יסך (שם) לעולם הבא וכן בשלוח

חזת וארויכורת ימים לעולם הבא . ומפורש
בן בחלמוד תורה . וכיבור אב ואם סנין
חלמוד לוטר כבד ארן אביך ואך אסך והקן)
למען יאריכון יסך , בשילוח הקן סנין
חלמוד לוטר שלח תשלח ארן האם
וארן הבנים תקח לך למען ייטב לך
והארכבת ימים . בהבארך שלום מנן .
וכל בניך למודי יהוה ורב שלום בניך שלז ;
וידבר יהות % משה בעצם היום הזה ;

♢♢♢ בערי הגוטת "וטוב" (בטעות,
שהוא מלשון) בבלי ברבות כח ע' א
ברוטו על תהילים קכח.ב) . במקום
"ריטב" (לשון הפסוק) של בבור אב
ואם רברים ה.טז) "והארבת ימיך"
הקן, רברים כב.ז) במקום
"יאריכון יסיך" (רברים ה.טז)
וחקנתי לפי הבבלי קרוטין מ ע'
א:

בשלשה מקוטורת מקמטר נאמר בעצם היום
הזה , נאמר בנ׳ בעצם היום הזה.
לפי שהיו חוו אוטרים כך וכן אנו
סרנושום בו אין אנו מניחים אותו .
ולא עור ולא אנו נטליט כשיליה .
וקרדוטורת ומבקעים ארן התיבה אסף
המקוט החומי םמנינו לתוקבה בחצי היום

וכל מי שיש בו כח ליסחור יבוא
ויסחר . וסה ראה לוסר בסצרים
בעצם היום הוה לפי שהיו סצריים
אוסרים סכך וסכך אם אנו סרגישים
בהם אין אנו סניחים אותם ולא עד
לא נוטלים סיפים וחרבות ואנו חורגים
בהם . אסר הסקום הריני סוציאם
בחצי היום וכל מי שיש בו כח ליסחות
יבוא ויסחר . וסה ראה לוסר כאן
בעצם היום הוה לפי שהיו סצרים
סכך וסכך אם אנו סרגישים בו אין
אנו סניחים אותו וסה שהוציאנו ססצרים
וקרע לנו ארץ הים והוריד לנו ארץ
התורה והוריד לנו ארץ הסן והגיד לנו
ארץ השליו ועשה לנו' ניסים ונבורות
אין אנו סניחים אותו . אסר הסקום הריני
סכניס לסערה בחצי היום וכל סי שיש
בו כח יבוא ויסחר לכך נאסר בעצם
היום הוה לאסר | עלה ו' הר העברים
הזה עליה היא ל' ואינה ירידה .
הר העברים שהוא קרוי ארבע שסות הר
העברים הר נבו . הר ההר . ראש הפסנרה
ולסה קורים אותו הר נבו שנקברו בו
שלשה סתים . הללו שסתו לא סורי
עבירה זר סשה אהרן וסרים . אשר
בארץ סואב . אשר על פני יריחו . רבי
ליעזר אוסר באצבע הרה סראה סספטרן
לסשה והראהו את כל ארץ ישרו' עד
כאן תחוסו של אפרים עד כאן תחוסו
של סנשה . רבי יהושע אוסר סשה
בעצסו הוא ראה אוחה כיצד נחן כח
בעיניו של סשה וראה סססף העולם
ועד סופו וסה בהר אשר אתה עולה
שסה . אסר לפניו רבונו של עולם לסה
אני סרד לא טוב שיאסרו טוב סשה
סספראה סטוב סשה סשסועה . לא
טוב שיאסרו זה סשה שהוציאנו סססצרים
וקרע לנו ארץ הים והוריד לנו ארץ
התורה והוריד לנו ארץ הסן והגיד לנו
ארץ השליו ועשה לנו נסים ונבורות
סשיאסרו כך וכך עשה כך וכך אסר .
אסר לו כלך סשה נזירה היא סלפני
שורה בכל אדם שנאסר וזאת התורה
האדם כי יסות באהל . ואוסר זאת תורת
האדם יהודה להים . אסרו סלאכי השרת
לפני הקדוש ברוך הוא רבונו של עולם
לסה סרת אדם הראשון אסר להם שלא
עשה פיקורו והרי סשה עשרה עשרה פיקוריך

אסר להם נזירה היא סלפני שורה בכל
אדם שנאסר וזאת התורה אדם כי יסות
והאסף ל' עסך . אצל' אברהם יצחק ויעקב
אבותיך אצל' קהת ועסרם אבותיך אצל'
אהרן וסרים אחיך . כאשר סרת אהרן
אחיך . סיתה שחסדת ל' סתוכן חיסר
סשה סיתתו של אהרן בשעה שאסר לו
הסקום קח את אהרן ואת אלעזר בנו
והפשט אהרן את בנריו . הפשיטו בנרי
כתונה והלבישו לאלעזר וכן שני וכן
שלישי אסר לו הינכ' לסערה וננכנס ,
עלה לסיטרה ועלה . פשוט יריך ופשט ,
פשוט רנליך ופשט . קסוץ פיך וקסץ ,
עצום עיניך ועצם . באותה שעה אסר סשה
אשרי סי שסרת בסיתה זו לכך נאסר
כאשר סרת אהרן אחיך בשעה שאסר
לה. | על' אשר סלעסת כי . ואם נרסחם
לסעיל כי על אשר לא קירשחם אותי .
כאשר סריחם פי אתם נרסחם לסרוח
ארח פי אסר לו הקרוש ברוך הוא סשה
לא אסרחי לך סה זה ביך . השליכה'
ארצה והשלכתו סיך . וסה אוחתי
שביך לא עיכבתו דבר הקל' היה לך
לעכנו . וסנין שלא נפטרו סן העולם עד
שצררה לו שצררה ברוך הוא בכנפיו
שנאסר לכן לא תביאו את הקהל הוה
כי סנגד תראה את הארץ ושסה לא'
תבוא . נאסר כאן ושסה לא תבוא
ונאסר להלן ושסה לא תעבור . אי
איפשר לוסר ושסה לא תעבור . שהרי
כבר נאסר ושסה לא תבוא . ואי אפשר
לוסר ושסה לא תבוא שהרי כבר נאסר
ושסה תעבור וסה תלסוד לוסר
ושסה לא תבוא ושסה לא תעבור
אסר סשה לפני הקדוש ברוך הוא אם אם
איני נכנס בה סלך אכנס בה הריוט.
ואם איני נכנס בה חי אכנס בה סרת.
אסר לו הקדוש ברוך הוא ושסה לא
תבוא ושסה לא תעבור לא סלך ולא
הריוט ולא חי ולא סת.

סליק פיסקא . וסליק סידרא ,

רבנו [והקל] .ﬞﬞﬞ ורברתם אל
הסלע (בסדבר כ.ח):

שם

שסא

ﬞﬞﬞddd יש עוד נוסח בכ"י... רבנ
[הקל]:

(פסקא שלח)
הר גבר. דורש לשון נבואה:

שלח

שלס

פרשת האזינו השמים
(פסקא שו)

הם היו מעידים בעצמם. כלומר היו מעידים על הקדוש ברוך הוא שהוא חי וקים
ויכול ועושה עמהם נסים בכל עת ובכל שעה:

העיד בהם. התרה בהם, פירוש מתרה עליהם שראויים לבא עליהם צרות:
העיד בהם הנביאים. שיחזרו בתשובה:

העיד בהם השמים. משום דכתיב יד העדים (דברים יז.ז), לומר שימנעו מליתן
טל ומטר והוא הדין שהעיר בהם הארץ אלא משום רבעי למימר קלקלו בשמים כלומר
שקלקלו על ידי צבא השמים לעוברם, וקימא לן כשם שנפרעין מן העובד כך נפרעין
מן הנעבר (בראשית רבה צו.א) והיינו טעמא דכולהו:

וימירו את כבודם[a] (תהלים קו.כ). אע״ג דדרשי לה על מעשה העגל גם נאמר על
עגלי ירבעם ואחאב[b]:

עלוב הוא אדם שצריך ללמוד מן הנמלה. כלומר אדם יש לו דעה כנגד כל הבריות
ומן הדין שכל הבריות ילמדו ממנו ואם הוא צריך ללמוד מן הנמלה עלוב הוא, וכל
שכן אם היה לו ללמוד ולא למד:

הרי עדי קימין. כלומר, ואני מתביישת ומתיראה מהם:

פירדגג. אומן, והיינו שמים וארץ:

קובל. צועק ומתרעם:

מרויחין. מגרילין:

ועצר. שנעצרין ונעשים קטנים:

רומטין. שוחקין:

בלשון מרובה. האזינו:

שהיו השמים מרובין. כדאמרינן בחגיגה (יב:) שבעה רקיעים ואע״ג דאמרינן
במדרש שבעה ארצות (ויקרא רבה כט.ט, פרד״א יח, שו״ט צב), נראה דשמים הן זה
למעלה מזה אבל הארצות אינן זה למעלה מזה אלא כולן אחת והמקומות גרועין זה
מזה:

וחכמים אומרים אין הדבר כן. נראה לי דלא פליגי רבנן בהא דשמים מרובין אלא
על מה דאמרו דעל כן שינה ישעיה הלשון כדי לסמוך לדבר על הא פליגי:

אלא. לכוין דברי העדים:

על שהתורה ניתנה מן השמים. לא בא אלא שלא לפרש דבור לשמים ואמירה לארץ:

עבור שנים. חלוי בריאת הירח שהיא בשמים:

ואומר קחו מוסרי (משלי ח.י). לא גרסינן ואומר דאינו אלא יפוי דרשא
דברוב מקום דכתיב קיחה מיירי בתורה ולא שייך כאן מאי ואומר:

מה שעירים הללו יורדין על עשבים ומגדלין. השתא דריש שעירים-- מטר, ושמא
לפי שיורדת בסערה וגבי רביבים אומר מעדנים לפי שיורדין בנחת:

הוי כונס דברי תורה כללים. והא דריש מדכתיב בראש עלי דשא כל מיני דשאים
והדר עלי עשב דמשמע כל עשב ועשב דהיינו פרט:

----

[a] לשון כבוד וזהו אחד מתקוני הסופרים: עין ספרי במדבר צ״ד:

[b] עין מלכים א יב.כח וגם שם טז.לא (רד״ק ורש״י):

לשון כנעני. פירוש שלשון כנען רוצה לומר פרוט, רוצה לומר שידקרק על כל
דיבור ודבור ועל כל אות ואות:

מה שעירים הללו...ומפשפשים. השתא דריש ליה לשון רוח כתרגומו כרוחי מטרא:
באין על חמאות. כגון שעיר הרגלים ושל ראש חדש ושל יום הכפורים, השתא לשון
שעיר עזים (ויקרא ד.כג):

באין תמידים. דריש רביבים לשון חלבים תרגום חלב [תרבא] (ויקרא ג.ג):

כך חזיו מלמדין אותה בצער. כלומר שלא תאמרו דברי תורה עד שיצטער השואל,
תלמוד לומר [ו]כולי:

נופלת עליו כשעיר. היינו שר שארם מתפחד ממנו, כך כשארם קטן מוליכין אותו
לבית הספר על כרחו ומחירא מן הרצוע:

אין עריפה אלא לשון הריגה...וכן הוא אומר כי רבים חללים הפילה (משלי
ז.כו). רבי [אליעזר בנו של רבי] יוסי הגלילי נמי דריש לעיל עריפה לשון
הריגה, מכל מקום איבא בניהיו טובא דלרבי [אליעזר בנו של רבי] יוסי הגלילי
הוי לשבח ובלומר לשמה שמתכפרת בעגלה ערופה; ורבי כנאה הוי לגנאי ולשון
התראה שמתרה בהם שאם לא יעסקו לשמה יערוף אותם וכן מצינו שהעושה שלא לשמה
מת דכתיב כי רבים חללים הפילה:

לקסרי. שם מקום שהוא רחוק ובית איליס הוא רחוק מאד מאד:

נותן מטעמים לבל אחד ואחד. הכי גרסינן, דריש לשון מתוק^d כתרגומו יבסם
(שמות טז.כה):

שבא מן המערב. לשון עורף דורש יערוף דהיינו אחר שהוא מערב:
מאריגת את הרקיע כרביב. גרסינן:

בימות החמה קשה. אזי הוא לשון לשדפון ולירקון כדלעיל:

מערבית לעולם קשה. קשיא דהא לעיל כולה לברכה, ושמא י"ל הא ד[א]נתא^f ניחא
הוא הא דאחיא רזיא דבי האי גוונא משני על רוח דרומית פרק לא יחפור (בבא
בתרא כה:):

ומניין שאינו מדבר אלא בתחיית המתים. אקרא דיערוף קאי דכתיב ביה ארבע
רוחות:

אלא [אהרן כ"א דבר. כך תיבות יש מן האזינו עד השם:
גוליירין. קרי לשליח צבור; וגבורים לעניין ברוך, שהם אומרים שבח שלם:
ומניין לאומר...ברוך שם^g. מהבר גדול יליף, ויליף אקרא מריקרא; כתיב
הבא כי שם ה' אקרא וכתיב ויקרא יעקב שם המקום (בראשית כח.יטⁱ):

הכי גרסינן-- ומניין שלא ירדו למצרים אלא שיעשה להם נסים ונפלאות לקרש שמו
בעולם שנאמר כי שם ה' אקרא. ומניין, משה אמרו על [ה]שעבור דכתיב ריאנחר
בני ישראל מן העבודה ויזעקו (שמות ב.כג-ר) היינו כי שם ה' אקרא;
וירא ישראל את היד הגדולה (שמות יד.לא)-- והיינו הבו גדול לאלהינו,
ואף על פי שכבר נגזרה גזרהⁱ ארבע מאות שנה לא נגזרה מחחלה אלא לקרש שמו:

----
c כן הוא לשון הספרי אבל חסר בעדים של הפירוש:
d כנראה שרבינו לא גרס יורד אלא יורה ונראה שהיה לפניו פסוק ראיה. ויורהו
ה' עץ...וימתקו המים וכו' (שמות טו.כה):
e הנץ החמה הוא בפנים העולם ושקיעת החמה הוא באחור:
f בכה"י יש מתא ותקנתי לפי גרסת הבבלי:
g וכן היתה עצם גירסתו וכן גירסת מדרש חכמים ופירוש הדבר כגירסת הרחבה
בדפוס הראשון. ומניין לאומר ברוך שעונים אחריו ברוך שם...
h המקום -- היינו שם ה':
i עין בראשית טו.יג:

(פסקא שז)

פעולתו שלימה. דרשו לשון מלאכה, כלומר מה שפעל בבריותיו הכל היה שלם ואין
בריה חסרה תחלה אבר ואע״ג דלבאורה משמע שאם היה אדם פורח באויר היה לו טוב
יותר; זה אינו, דכמו שהיה הוא פורח כך היו פורחים בני אדם שכמותו והיו באין
אלו על אלו בטיסה אחת ולא היה[ו] מנוחה לשום אומה במקומה, נמצא שהיה
גריעותא[ן];-- ואם⁴, דריש לה לשון שכר ועונש דכתיב מה רב טובך אשר פעלת
(תהלים לט.כ) דקאמר מסיים יושב בדין עם כל אחד:

שהאמין בעולם ובראו. כלומר שלא יהיו כולם רשעים אלא מקצתם יהיו צדיקים
ויעשו הישר בעיניו:

מתנהג בישרות. היינו שאינו דן את האדם לפי מעשים רעים שעתיד לעשות אלא לפי
מעשיו של אותה שעה דכתיב כי שמע אלהים גו׳ (בראשית כא.יז)¹ :

מה ראו. כמו למה היו ראוים לכך, כמו מה עשו:

בעל הפקדון. שאדם מפקיד נשמתו בכל לילה]ו[אע״פ שאדם מתחייב^m כמה חיובין
מחזירה בבקר:

עמד פילוסופוס.^n נראה שהוא לשון שררה⁰ (ואע״ג דפילוסופוס^p הוא לשון חכם
בכאן הוא לשון שררה וממשלה לפי שהממונה על הפרכייא צריך להיות חכם להיות
מנהיג את בני המדינה):

אמר מרי.^q פירוש, פילופוס אמר למלך שלא יתגאה שניתן לו כל כך רשות לשרוף
התורה:

----

^j אולי צ״ל תהיה:
^k פי׳ אי נמי :
^l עין ראש השנה טז ע׳ ב:
^m בסמנריה, ובברית אברהם נמצא ״מחייב״:
^n כן הוא בכל עדי הפירוש. ונראה שלפני רבינו עמד נוסח אחר. בכ״י ברלין
ובנוסח הילקוט שמעוני שתקן אברהם בן גדליה הגרסא ״פולפוס״ וכן הוא בכ״י של
הסמנריה בפירוש עצמו--

עמד פליסופוס....ואע״ג

דפוליפוס הוא לשון חכם וכו׳. ודברי הפירוש קשה שאם לשון שררה הוא אין
צורך לכל ההמשך המסביר שאינו לשון שררה אלא לשון חכם. רע שבקטע הבא מיד וגם
למטה פסקא שכ״ב הגרסא הנראה כמקורי--״פליפוס ״ (לפי רוב העדים) . ואולי
רבינו ראה בו רק שם שרה והנשאר לא נבע מעטו. אם כן הדבר הוא כתב ״פליפוס״
כנראה פריפוס לשון praepositus, provost ובהפך אותיות ״פליסוף״, ״פרסוף״
כמו במדרש המובא בערוך ע׳ בלש ומובנו שר צבא. ואולי המחבר כתב גם כאן
״פלסוף״ או ״פליפוס״ ותלמיד אחר טעה ושינה את המלה להתאים ל״פילוסופוס״
הנמצא אצלו בספרו של הספרי וגם הוסיף פירוש לענין רבינו ללא צדק. מאד יתכן
שלא הבחין בין פלפוס ופילוסופוס וחשב שהיינו הך. לפי העדים בידינו הסופרים
תקן דבר המתחיל ״פלפוס״ לפילוסופוס:

⁰ בעל זרע אברהם על הספרי כתב שהוא ראה ״לשון שררה״ בגליון לילקוט
ומשחיקתו על השאר אולי יש מקום לשקול שבעל הגליון השתמש בפירושנו בלי
הדברים הנוספים. לכן שמתי אותם בסוגריים:

^p בסמנריה הגרסא ״פוליפוס״ ואולי כן כתב רבינו בדבר המתחיל והמוסיף לא
הבחין שלא כוון ל״פילוסוף״:

^q אמר מרי ״אל תזוח דעתך״:

שמשעה שיצאה. פירוש, לא שייך שריפה בתורה אלא האותיות פרחו באויר וחזרו
לשמים שמתחלה מן השמים ניתנו:

אף דינך. שחשרף כמותם בעבור שהטיח דברים כנגדו:

בשרתני. מאמרת כיוצא באלו משמע נמי לעולם הבא:

איני אומר לזכות את הזכאי. דהיינו צדיק וטוב לו רשע ורע לו שהכל הוא משפט
ודין אמת:

אלא אפילו להחליף. שנראה לבריות כאלו אינו אמת ומשפט והיינו׳ כי כל
דרכיו משפט:

(פסקא שח)

שיחתו ישראל בכל לאוין שבתורה. משחת לו דריש; פירוש, שחת לעצמו בכל דבר
שכתוב בו לאו:

וכל כך למה. אדלעיל קאי דקאמר אף על פי שמשחיתין ואין עושין ויש בהן מומין
קרויין בנים:

עמקנים. לשון עקום:

מתקנו באור. מתחלה באש של תורה והיינו אמר דכתיב [(תורת) אמך (משלי א.ח)[ᶜʰ
:[(

מפסלו במעצר. היינו יסורין:

משליכו לאור. היינו גהינם:

(פסקא שט)

צוהב. כועס כמו שני כלבים צהובין זה בזה (סנהדרין קה.ⁱ), תרגום רכעסתה
צרתה ומצהבא לה (שמואל א א.ו):

בליוקוסⁱ. שם שרה וקטרון גדול ממנו והפיטקס גדול ממנו:

שמעון בן חלפתא אומר משמו. ארבי יהודה דאיירי לעיל קאי:

אחר משלשה שנקראו קנין. בברייתא דשנו חכמים בלשון המשנה [חמשה] חשיב
והשנים יתירים על אלו הם אברהם ושמים וארץ, ונראה דאברהסⁱ בכלל, שמים וארץ
בכלל, [אברהם] בכלל ישראל שהם בניו היו, ושמים וארץ בכלל התורה דכתיב אם
לא בריתי יומם ולילה חוקת שמים וארץ לא שמתי, (ירמיהו לג.כה)ʷ:

כרבא דכולא ביה. חרישה שהכל בה:

[סופרים.] נראה שסופר יותר מהחכם שהוא יודע לספור ולדרוש ולתת טעם מעצמו:

בוין כוין. חלונות חלונות, אי נמי גרסינן כנין כנין; פירוש, כן עומד וסדור
על חברו, ועיקר:

ʳ באקספורד ״ואינו״:

ˢ נ״ל שהנוסח משובש וצ״ל ״והיינו אומן דכתיב אומן״. ופירושו מבוסס על
הענין בבראשית רבה א.א. קשה לו ענין האש בהתחלה וענין האש בסוף והבחין
ביניהם:

ᵗ בבבלי לפנינו. משל לשני כלבים שהיו בעדר והיו צהובין זה לזה:

ᵘ לפנינו בעדי הספרי ״בוליוטוס״:

ᵛ יש לגרוס כאן כמו באקספורד ובסמנריה-- ״ונראה דאברהם בכלל, שמים וארץ
בכלל, [אברהם] בכלל ישראל...״ ומפני הדומות דלג הסופר ״אברהם״: וראיה
שאברהם השני מקורי היא שכל הקטע ח׳ בברית אברהם מפני הדומות בין אברהם
לאברהם הסופי:

ʷ עין סנהדרין לב.:

הלעיטך. האכילך:

כנגים כנגים. בני מעים יושבין זה על גב זה ואם אחת מהן מחלפת מקומה מיד
ימות והוא כמו התראה, ראה שאתה בידו ואתה צריך לו תמיד לבקש רחמים:

(פסקא שי)

לא יכנף עוד מוריך (ישעיהו ל.כ). לשון כנף-- שמכסה; מוריך-- לשון
מורה דרך[x]:

(פסקא שיא)

הציפם כזיקים. כלומר כנגרות:

זכה לקבל ייסורין. מכאן שיסורין אינן בעבור עונש מדקאמר זכה שזכות היה לו
קבלת היסורין; ואם תאמר הכא פרק במה בהמה (שבת נה.) אמרו אין יסורין בלא
עון, אין הכי נמי שר״ל אין ייסורין באין על אדם זולת על עון-- אם אינו אדם
שלם בעון שלו, ואם הוא אדם שלם בעון הדור:

התחילו ממשמשין. היינו כשמתחילין לבא, ואם תאמר הא לא הגין זכותו של אברהם
ע״ה על סדום ועמורה, וי״ל משום דשאחר מן הייסורין מלחמת הארבעה מלכים; שלא
באו אלא בעבורו שאמרו נתחיל בלוט ונסיים באברהם; ועוד יש לומר שבשעה שבא
לארץ כבר נגזרה[y], לא היו מז׳ עממין ולא היתה זכותו מגינה משבא לארץ אלא על
בני ארץ וישראל דאכתי גפרית ומלח הם:

פירש תחומן של אומות. שלא יכנסו לארץ, ואם תאמר והרי נתן הארץ לחתי
ואמורי וכנעני, יש לומר שאותם היה גלוי לפניו שיתחייבו ויתמלא סאתם ויהיו
חייבים בלייה אבל אותם שראינו שלא נתחייבו בלייה הרחיקן מהארץ:

בהגחיל עליון גוים...ירא חטא וכשרין שבהן. פירוש, יון ומדי וכל
ראשי אומות שנחלקו בימי שם בן נח ו[נכש]חלקו את העולם יראי חטא וכשרים היו
אבל שבע אומות שנטלו ארץ ישראל אפילו ראשי דורות לא היו צדיקים:

שרים המה מלכות (שיר השירים ו.ח). היינו אומות שיש להן כתר מלכות:

ושמונים פלגשים (שיר השירים ו.ח). שמונים משפחות שאין להם[z] מלך;
ורציתי לעמוד על מינינם ומצאתי בפרשת בני[aa] נח גבי אלה תולדות בני נח
(בראשית י.א) חשיבי נ״ז אומות ואף על פי כי לפי החשבון יש שם שבעים--
והיינו דכתיב מאלה נפרדו איי הגוים, (בראשית י.ה), כשתסיר מהם אותם
שנמנו ראשונה ונמנו גם כן בניהם צריך שלא ימנו לו בן ראשון, כגון בני רפת
גומר ומגוג, ובני גומר אשכנז, (בראשית י.ג) אם תמנה לגומר אין ראוי
למנות אשכנז וכן כולם-- תמצא שאין בהם אלא חמשים ושבעה עממין ועמון ומואב
ועשו הרי שים; ובני הגר[bb] י״ד משפחות ובני ישמעאל שנים עשר נשיאים הרי כ״ו
ובאלוף החרי יושבי הארץ ובאלוף ארום יש קרוב למ׳, ואימים וסרני פלישתים
ונסיכי מרין יעלו לשמונים וכולם נחשבים[cc] לשבעים אומות:

----

x ולא כמו הרד״ק שפירש הפסוק במובן שיהיה מספיק מטר ולא יהיה צורך לאסוף
   (כנף) מטרך (מוריך). עין ספר השרשים ערך י ר ה:

y על בני סרום ועמורה:

z כן בכל העדים:

aa ח׳ באקספורד:

bb היא הגר היא קטורה לפי חז״ל. עין בראשית רבה סא.ד:

cc במהדורת פינקלשטיין נמצא ״נמשכים״:

זכו אומות ליטול שני גבולות. כלומר אינו חשוב כל מה שניטלו אלא כשני גבולות אבל ודאי ארץ ישראל אינו אלא אחד מעשרה משבעים אומות כראמרי׳ לפי שאמרו שירה בלשון נקבה נטלו עישור נכסים כנקבה (שה״ש רבה א.לז), מיהו מרמייתי מפסולת אברהם ויצחק משמע שקורא שני חלקים לגבול עשו וישמעאל, ושמא משום הכי קורא לכל האומות לשמם שכולם חזרו לאלו השתי רתוח של ארום וישמעאל:

(פסקא שיב)

מה (חבל) **dd זה משולש. נראה דקאי ארקרייה סגולה**(תהלים קלה.ר), **וחבלו** (דברים יד.ב), **גוררלו** (תהלים טז.ה-ו) דליכא למימר דקאי אמֱנשה דמה ענין שילוש אצל מנשה:

אֶת לַצֶרֱה ee יולד (משלי יז.יז). לפי שהגין זכותו אבני דורו, ועוד דכתיב **אחֹת לנו** (שיר ח.ח) שאיחה את העולם להקב״ה ולימרם דרכי המקום ולהכי קרי ליה אח:

טובים השנים מן האחד (קהלת ר.ט). דכתיב וישב יצחק ויחפור....: (בראשית כו.יח):

והֹחֹוֹט המשֹֹֹֹֹלֹשֹ (קהלת ר.יב). דכתיב וישב יעקב בארץ מגורי אביו (בראשית לז.א) שהיה מגייר גיורים ff כאביו:

(פסקא שיג)

ימצאהו בארץ מדבר. דכתיב ומצאת את לבבו (נחמיה ט.ח): במקום הצרות. שלא היה שום בריה מכיר יחוד מלכותו יתברך וקדוש שמו ברבים להמליכו והיינו עד שהגיע לפלטרין:

יברֹננהֹו. מלשון בינה:

ימצאהו. לשון סיפוק צורך: אלו ארבע מלכיות. מדבר, ובתהו, ילל, ישימֱן: (דברים לב.י)

----

dd כנראה שאין לגרוס חבל. באקספורר נתלה בין השיטין ובסמגריה חסר. אבל כן הוא בנוסח ערי הספרי:

ee באקספורר הסופר כתב לשרה במקום לצרה ובזה פירש עצם כוונה של הספרי אבל אין ספק שרבינו לא כתב ככה בפירושו. פירושו לדברי הספרי רחוק ואינו מבוסט על החילוף צרה=שרה:

ff וגם יש נוסח גרים:

(פסקא שטו)

דן אחד יהודה אחד אשר אחד. אין זה סדר הפסוקים אלא הכי כתיב קראי
ביחזקאל (פרק מח); והיו לו פאת קדים הים דן אחד, ועל גבול דן מפאת
קדים עד פאת ימה אשר אחד, ועל גבול אשר [מן]פאת&& קדמה ועד פאת
ימה נפתלי אחד, ועל גבול נפתלי מפאת קדמה עד פאת ימה מנשה אחד,
ועל גבול מנשה מפאת קדמה עד פאת ימה אפרים אחד, ועל גבול אפרים
מפאת קדים ועד פאת ימה ראובן אחד, ועל גבול ראובן מפאת קדים
עד פאת ימה יהודה אחד;

וכתב רש״י ז״ל בפירוש יחזקאל;

בספרי בפרשת האזינו שנינו מת״ל יהודה אחד דן אחד אשר אחד מלמד   שעתידין
ישראל ליסול אורך מן המזרח למערב כרוחב עשרים וחמשה אלפים קנים שיעורן חמשה
ושבעים מיל, מהיכן למדו השיעור הזה, מן התרומה שהיא כאחד מן החלקים הללו
כמו שמפורש בענין (יחזקאל מה.א) והוא רוחב עשרים וחמשה אלף קנים מאה וחמשים
אלף אמה שהקנה שש אמות (כך ביחזקאל מא.ח) וכל אלפים אמה מיל כמו ששנינו
במס׳ יומא (משנה ו.ד, בכלי סז.) אבל עשר סוכות מירושלים ועד צוק; הרי מאה
וחמשים אלף עולים לע״ה מיל, עד כאן לשון רש״י ז״ל;

ונראה דעיקר הדרשא הוא מאחד דהואיל וכתיב באמצעיים למה הוצרך לכתוב כדן
ואשר שהם ראשונים וביהודה שהוא אחרון, אלא, אינו אלא לדרשא;   למה שפירש,
מהיכן למדו השיעור הזה מן התרומה שהוא כאחד מן החלקים הללו-- ר״ל הוא באורך
כאחד מן החלקים הללו ברוחב דאלו באורך וברוחב אי אפשר דהא כתיב מפאת ים
ועד קדים משמע כל מה שיש מפאת ים דהיינו מערב ועד פאת קדים דהיינו מזרח
והתרומה כתיב בה חמשה ועשרים אורך בעשרה רוחבhh:

(פסקא שטז)

שקלין לאכול. פירוש, ואין מכבדין על האסטומכא ומתנובבות יליף:

סכני. וגוש חלב, שם מקומות הם:

קציעות תאנים. יבשים; והאי דבש רוצה לומר דבש תאנים:

(פיסקא שיז)

ק״ו וג״ש והקשות. גרסינן, חמאה וחלב דורש ק״ו עם כרים ואילים
בני בשן דריש ג״ש; ועתורדים דורש הקשה ולא גרסינן וחשובות:
ירכיבהו זה העולם. דריש כוליה קרא בעשו, ירכיבהו... ריניקהו, מרמיחתי
קרא יברסמנה חזיר מיער (תהלים פ.ר) ורוצה לומר ירכיבהו-- לעשו, על
במותי ארץ דהיינו ישראל דכתיב ביה ואתה על במותימו תדרוך (דברים
לג.כט) וכן כל הפסוק:
ויאכל תנובת שדי אלו ארבע מלכיות. לפי שארום ארבע מלכיות שהיו אחר
אלכסנדרוס מלך יון דכתיב תשבר מלכותו ותיחץ לארבע רוחות השמים
(דניאל יא.ד) וארום היו אחר יון:
אלו אצין דבארץ ישראל. כתיב ארץ זבת חלב ודבש (ויקרא כ.כד):
היפיסקין והגמונין. מיני שררה:
בלי-רקין. בגרים חשובין וכן פיקרון אלא שהאחד למעלהii והאחד למטה, וטריגון
לובשים באמצע; עוד יש לומר שהם כלם מיני שרה והטריגון עומר בין כלי-ריקין
----

hh הלשון אינה בדיוק כמו במסורה:
ii ח׳ בכה״י:

לפיקרון והיינו דקאמר שמבינין מבין שניהם; פירוש, שמדברים ברמז וזה מבין את
שניהם ומודיע דברי זה לזה:
ונפשח. לשון וישפחני (איכה ג.יא):
פסוס. קנקן של עץ גדול:

(פסקא שיח)
מתוך שובע הן ראויין. פירוש, הם מורדין, גרסינן:
וכן אנה מוצא לימות המשיח. תימא, היכן מצינו שלימות המשיח עתידין למרוד,
ויש לומר דלא קאי אישראל אלא אאומות העולם; והיינו דקאמר שלשה דורות:
ריהי כל הארץ שפה אחת (בראשית יא.א). דריש שובע ושלוה כדדריש ותרענה
באחר (בראשית מא.יח), בזמן ששובע בעולם אחוה ושלום בעולם:
סלמנין. הם רצועות העול:
אלו שלשה דורות שלפני ימות המשיח. רוצה לומר שלשה דורות של גוים רסמוכין
למשיח שמתוך עושרם ימרדו יותר מראי ויתגאו באלילים ופסילים:
אל תקרי רינבל אלא רינבל. מלשון נבל ציץ (ישעיהו מ.ז-ח); פירוש
כביכול הכחיש תוקפו שלא יוכל להושיע:
דברים של זכרות[u]. שעשתה מפצלת כעין זכרות להיות נבעלת לעבודה זרה:
צלם יהודי. שעשאו יהודי:

(פיסקא שיט)
בזכות אבותיכם. דורש מחולליך, אותם המתחוללים להביאו לעולם דהיינו אביו
ואמו:
אל שהחל בך. פירוש, שברא העולם בעבורך, מלשון [חוללתי (משלי ח.כו)]:
שנצטער. מלשון חיל כיולדה (ירמיהו ר.לא):
שהחל שמו. כדכתיב והייתם לי לסגולה (שמות יט.ה):
חולין. שהכל שולטין בך:
קול ה' על המים (תהלים כט.ג). בעוסקים בתורה בלשון עילוי דכתיב על;
כשנעשה חולין-- **ריחשוף,** מגלה ראשם:

(פסקא שכ)
ממשה באים לו מנאצים[kk]. דכתיב בהו בן גרשום בן מ[נ]שה (שופטים יח.ל):
דור הפוך... [הפכפכנים]. שתי הפכים, כשהם מתהפכים להרע מרת הדין מתהפכת
עליהם:
פותין[ll] הן. מעותת[mm] הוא:
אלא בלוי[מ] עם. נראה שהוא מלשון רנלרה (ישעיהו יד.א); אחד מעמון ואחד
ממואב וכן מכל אומה ומלכות:

[ii] באקספורד ובסמנריה יש "ידות" ובכה"י של הספרי "זרות" ונראה שרבינו גרס
זכרות:
[kk] לפנינו בספרי כ"י ברלין-- "מה שהם נאים לו מנאצים":
[ll] לפנינו בערי הספרי "פורנים":
[mm] בכה"י "טעות הוא"-- ותקנתי לפי סברא:
[nn] באקספורד "בלוי", בסמנריה "בלון". ונראה מפירושו ש"בלוי" היה לפני
רבינו:

ארבע מלכיות. פירשתי למעלה.-- אותם שהיו אחר אלכסנדרוס כדאמרינן ביבמות
(סג.) דאין רעה באה לעולם אלא בשביל ישראל:

(פסקא שבא)
מאזין. נפוחין, גרסינן; מזי רעב תרגומו נפיחי כפן (דברים לב.כד):
שבל שהשד בו מוריר. מלשון ויורד רירר על זקנו (שמואל א כא.יד) שיוצאין
מפיו רירין:
מעלה נומי. לשון חלודה במכה כמו מי שעלתה לו נימא על בשרו יניחנה וימות או
יקטענה ויחיה   (בראשית רבה פ׳ מו, עבודה זרה י׳):
כנס את הרגל. לא תצא לחוץ:
פזר. גלה למקום אחר שאין בו רעב:
חררי לבו נקפין עליו ומת. כמו לבו נוקפו (נדה ג.), פירוש אע״פ שברח אינו
נמלט אלא מן הצער שנצטער נותנו אל לבו ומת:
הא ויתרא לאלו. הרי בחור ובתולה שממתים ויותר עליהם, ובעבור הגמ־ים שהם
ריבונים הוצרך לפרש דהיינו מה שמפרש בסוף הפסוק ירנק עם איש שיבה והיינו
דמיחי דוגמא.-- דלא ריבה בגמ־ים אלא מה שהזכיר בסוף הפסוק.-- כי גם איש:
אתם גרמתם. והשתא הגמ־ים לא מבעיא שגרמתם להרוג הבינונים אלא אפילו
הבחורים שלי ואפילו הבתולות שלא טעמו טעם חטא:
מינוקין. גרסינן, פירוש, נהנין כאלו לא טעמו כמו הבתולה נהנית בביאה
ראשונה:
זקוקין בזיקין. אסורין בזיקין והם כבלים:

(פסקא שבב)
מסגירין. פירוש, מוסרים אותם ביד האויבים:
מכחישין. מורים להם שהם גרולים מהם[oo] כמו ויכחשו אויבך לך (תהלים
סג.ג:
בפולמוס. ואי גרסינן פולפוס[pp] הוא השר הגדול הממונה על בני החיל[qq]:
דרקריון. שם גבור:
עד שלא הגיעו. עד שלא ישיגנו הדרקריון לישראל:
יצא נחש וכרך לו. לישראל על עקבו להראות שמן השמים היו הורגין אותו ולא
בכח הדרקריון והיינו דקאמר אמר לו כלומר הישראלי לדרקריון:
אמר לפולפוס[rr]. גרסינן, כלומר לארון שלך:

(פסקא שבג)
אלו נסתכלו במה שאמר להם יעקב אביהם. ואם תאמר היכן מצינו שאמר להם כך, יש
לומר דכתיב וזאת אשר דבר להם אביהם ויברך אותם (בראשית מט.כח);
וזאת.-- היינו קבלו עול מלכות שמים דאין זאת אלא תורה ובכל המצות יש קבלת

[oo] רק באקספפורד, בסמנריה ובברית אברהם יש ״סמנו״:
[pp] באקספפורד ״פולפוס״ ״פולפוס״ ובעדים האחרים פולומוס ועין מה שכתבתי למעלה הערה [n]
אבל גם עין רש״י לע״ז: ב: פלמוטא.-- שר צבא וצע״ג:
[qq] באקספפורד ״על גבי החיל״:
[rr] הקריאה הקשה ״פלוני״ נמצא ברוב עדי הספרי וכנראה שהיא שבוש של ״פולפוס״
(או פלפוס)״ כמו שעמר לפני רבינו לפי עדות ברית אברהם וכ״י בסמנריה.
באקספפורד יש ״פולמוס״:

עול מלכות; **אשר דבר להם אביהם.**-- רוצה לומר וצויתיו[ss] היינו והכריעו זה
את זה ביראת שמים; **ויברך אותם.**-- היינו והתנהגו זה עם זה בגמילות חסדים
דגבי גמילות חסדים כתיב ברכה:

עביד קני. חפץ כבר שאי אפשר להוליכו אלא בקושי, נמצא הלוקח שאינו מוליכו
מיד:

בטמאים ביד טהורים. כאילו היתם טמאים וכאלו אומות העולם טהורים כך אתם
נמסרים בידם:

מיד. במהרה ולא בקושי:[tt]

אלא זרע קדש. פירוש, אבל הם עשו עצמן מטעה של סרום:

מרתן פרוטה בהם. היינו עונשין כתרגומו פרענותהון...כמררן להון (דברים
לב. לב)[uu]:

(פסקא שכר)

כמו סימאי[vv]**. אוצר:**

[ומחוסר.] גל מלשון אוצר:

יכול דיהה ח״ל חמר. פירוש צלול ואינו כעין יין אלא כעין מים:

ממוחים. שנמחו כאלו אינם היינו פקיטם כלומר גרעיני זית דהיינו פסולת:

אם אמרת כן. שמעשיהן יעשו פירות נמצאן מאבדין את העולם:

[ss]   באקספורד ״וצורכיו״:
[tt]   שייך למעלה אחרי עביד קני:
[uu]   במקראות גדולות הגרסה ״כמררותהון״:
[vv]   באקספורד הסופר המקורי כתב כמו זה אבל נראה שביד אחרת נתקן הנוסח
להיות כמו ערי הספרי-- כמוס ומחוסר. גל מלשון אוצר: בסמנריה הנוסח בדיוק
כמו המקורי באקספורד בלי שום תקון ונראה שזהו הנוסח הנכון:

(פסקא שכה)

הכי גרסינן-- לי נקם ואשלם לא כתיב אלא ושלם. אי כתיב ואשלם הוה משמע
תשלום פורענותהון, השתא דכתיב ושלם משמע-- לי נקם דהיינו פורענותהון וגם
שלם דהיינו [פורענות מעשיהם שעשו אבותיהם][ww]

כי קרוב יום אידם. כלומר אין הצרות ב(י)חר[xx] לחברתה כל שכן אותם שנאמר
בהם מרוב ימים יפקדו, (ישעיהו כד. כב).

(פסקא שכו)

[תהות.] כמו בתוהא על הראשונות (קדושין מ:):
כשיראה הכל מהלכין לפנין [yy]. כשיראה שיחזרו בתשובה מרוב צרות, ופשט הפסוק
כי יראה שהלכה בהם היד המכה שמשמשת בהם:
יד. דורש לשון פרוטה:
[כמשה.] דכתיב ביה ויהי ידיו אמונה עד בא השמש (שמות יז. יא):
באהרון. דכתיב קח את המחתה (במדבר יז. יא); **ויקח אהרון כאשר דבר משה**
(שמות יז. יב):
כפנחס. דכתיב ביה ויקח רומח בידו (במדבר כה. ז):

(פסקא שכז)

ישראל אומרים לאומות העולם. פירוש, פירוש, לימות המשיח:

(פסקא שכח)

אפסנונית. שכר לחיילותיו:
דינטיבה. סעודה למלכים:
סלניה. מס:
ויעזרוכם. מש׳ יעזרו אתכם[yy] ואת עצמם:
ויעזרו אתכם. מש׳ יעזר לצרכיכם וכן קאי אשמים:[zz]

[ww]   חסר בכה״י ומלאתי על פי סברא:
[xx]   נראה לי שצ״ל ״חר״:
[yy]   יתכן דורש ״וכם״-- ״גם עצמם גם אתכם״:

[zz]   בכה״י-- ״ויעזרוכם משיעזרו אתכם ואת עצמם ויעזרו אתכם משה עזר לצרכיכם
וכן קאי אשמים.״ בפירוש רבי ש. אוחנא-- ״משמע יעזרו את עצמם.״ ונראה שדבריו
מבוססים על הפירוש שלנו. ותקנתי משה -- מש׳ י (עזר):

(פסקא של)

הפקטי. לשון שררה:

נכנס ולתורן הפרכיא. פירוש, הפרכיא של מלך; נכנס בה הפקטי (שר) אחד עם
חילו, ושללה ובזזה ואין המלך יכול ליפרע ממנו, כגון שהלך לו אל ארצו, שוב
אין לו נקמה:

אם יכול ליפרע מאיפקטי. פירוש בחיי אפיקטי:

(פסקא שלא)

זה אחר...וזה שנים. פירוש שני דיינים אי נמי שני פעמים:

(פסקא שלב)

משבר אזרים. כלומר העופות שדרכן לאכול הנבלות והכלבים שדרכן לאכול את הדם:

פרעות. דורש לשון פרעה:

(פסקא שלג)

כפרה היא להם. משפכר דמם (תהלים עט.ג) דריש:

פורקין. פירוש, פורקין מעליהם:

נושאין. כמו ישא את עונה (במדבר ל.טז):

כל הדר בארץ ישראל וכו׳. ארץ ישראל היא קרויה קרש, מקום הקרוש[aaa]

וקורא קריאת שמע שחרית וערבית. כמאן דאמר במסכת מנחות (צט:) קיים מצות
והגית בר יומם ולילה (יהושע א.ח); וקריאת שמע הוא קדושת שמו וקבלת
ייחודו ועול מלכותו:

ומדבר בלשון הקרש. להשלים שלש קרושות.-- קרושת הארץ וקרושת שמו וקרושת
לשונו אי נמי שהעולם כולו נברא בארץ ישראל שהיא קרויה טבור[bbb] הארץ דכתיב
מצירון מכלל יופי (תהלים נ.ב), והעולם נברא בלשון הקרש על כן צריך לדבר
בלשון הקרש בארץ ישראל:

יש בה עשיו. כי שם ה׳ אקרא:

לשעבר. יערוף כמטר דהיינו מתן תורה:

לעתיד לבא. כי ידין ה׳ עמו:

בעולם הזה. כל השירה:

לעולם הבא. הרנינו גוים עמו:

[aaa] כך בסמנריה. אבל באקספורד-- ״קרויה קרוש מקום״; בברית אברהם-- ״קרויה
מקום קרוש״:

[bbb] עין בבלי יומא נד: ובבית המדרש (יעללינק) חדר ה׳ ע׳ 63:

(פסקא שלד)

אי אפשר לומר **ויבא**. נראה דה״פ קודם השירה, דכחיב **וילך משה**...**וידבר אל
בני ישראל** (דברים לא.א.); דעם ישראל היה, אם כן לא היה צריך לומר ויבא
אלא [ל]אשמועינן שכבר בא זמנו והוא לשון כי בא השמש (בראשית כח.יא)
והיינו לשון שקיעה:

דייתיכוס. לשון זמן וקץ להפטר מן העולם:

והרשות נתונה. הממשלה ליהושע:

והרי כבר נאמר. פירוש, בכאן נמי היה לקרותו יהושע:

(פסקא שלה)

כהדרין. הלכה גדולה וענין גדול תלוי בדבור אחד או בדרש אחד:

החזיקו טובה. חזרו עליהם ותודיעם כמה שכר יהיה לכם:

לא היתה שוה. בתמיה:

(פסקא שלו)

ובדבר הזה (דברים לב.מז). היינו תורה:

כבוד אב ואם. יליף לה מדכתיב **ריטב לך** ccc (דברים ה.טז) בעולם הזה,
יאריכון ימיך (שם) לעולם הבא וכן בשלוח [הקן]:

(פסקא שלח)

הר נבר. דורש לשון נבואה:

(פסקא שם)

דבור [הקל] ddd. **ודברתם אל הסלע** (במדבר כ.ח):

----

ccc בערי הנוסח ״וטוב״ (בטעות, שהוא מלשון בבלי ברכות כח ע׳ א בדרשה על
תהילים קכח.ב) במקום ״ייטב״ (לשון הפסוק של כבוד אב ואם דברים ה.טז)
״והארכת ימים״ (בטעות, שהוא מן הפסוק של שלוח הקן, דברים כב.ז) במקום
״יאריכון ימיך״ (דברים ה.טז) ותקנתי לפי הבבלי קרושין מ ע׳ א:

ddd יש עוד נוסח בכ״י -- רבר [הקל]:

General Index

Abbahu, 29
Abraham, 12, 42
Academy, 17, 29, 37
Afterlife, 54
Akiba, 27, 28, 29, 33, 37, 50, 52
Albeck, Ch., 41
Alexandrian, 46
Alter, R., 5
Alter, R., 5
Amoraic, 38, 55, 59, 60, 63
Amos, 51
Angels, 4, 5, 6, 10, 46, 68, 69, 70
Angels, 5, 10, 68
Antiquities (Josephus), 43
Apocrypha, 2
Augustine, 21
Avodah Zarah, 53- 55, 57-62
Azulai, H., 77

Babylonia, 4, 16, 17, 33, 35
Babylonian Talmud (tractates) 6, 12-
18, 20, 23, 25, 26, 32-37, 47, 48, 52-62,
70
Bacher, W., 53
Balaam, 25-30
Banquet, 50, 51
Baptism, 30
Basser, H., 17, 52, 53
Belial, 22
Ben Azzai, 47
Berachot, 59b, 21; 27b, 48
Bickerman, E., 24
Bietenhard, H., 1, 78
Brit Avraham, 27, 77, 79

Candelabra, 50
Cane, 7
Cassuto, U., 52
Censors, 27
Classification, 35
Cleanliness, 3

Commentary, 1, 2, 3, 18, 31, 44, 50, 64,
69, 77, 78, 79
Converts, 41
Corinthians, 46
Covenant, 4
Creation, 9

Deborah, 4
Decalogue, 75
Divine, 3, 4, 5, 6, 7, 8, 21, 30, 43-52, 57,
70-72

Ecclesiastes, 8
Editor, 28, 51, 63, 64
Egypt, 19, 72
Egyptians, 20
Elazar ben Azariah, 47, 48
Elazar HaQappar, 26ff
Elders, 22, 45, 46
Eliezer, 26-29
Enoch, 24
Ephraim, 29
Esau, 12
Esther, 5, 15, 55
Exodus, 9, 20, 45, 70, 72, 75
Ezekiel, 4, 5, 6, 10, 70
Ezra, 76, 77

Father, 22, 40, 55, 57, 58
Finkelstein, L., 40, 56-65,
First Born, 8
Folklore, 23
Folktales, 53
Fox, H., 17
Fraade, S., 78
Fraenkel, J., 54, 56

Gabriel, 5
Galatians, 44
Gamliel, 48
Geiger, A., 33
Genesis, 10, 43, 70
Ginzberg, L., 37
Gnosticism, 5
Greek, 7, 20, 24

Habakkuk, 8, 11
Hadrianic, 47, 48, 50, 68
Haftarah, 60
Hagiga, 48
Halakhah, 4, 7, 19, 30-41,
Halivni, D., 35
Halpern, B., 3
Hammer, R., 1, 37, 78
Hanina ben T'radyon, 49-63
Hartman, L., 22
Heavens, 5, 9, 10, 21, 22, 24, 30, 68, 69, 70, 72
Heavens, 9, 10, 71, 72
Heinemann, J., 14, 16
Hermeneutic, 30, 34, 35
History, 3, 4, 7, 17, 22, 23, 24, 25, 28, 36, 44, 50, 51, 52, 54, 57, 60, 66, 68, 72, 76
Hoffman, D., 37
Horowitz-Rabin (Mechilta, 72, 75

Idolatrous, 27, 31
Instruction, 9, 10
Instruction, 9, 22, 24
Intercessor, 42
Isaiah, 52, 53, 60, 63, 65, 67, 69, 70, 71
Israel, 1-20

Jannes and Jambres, 21
Jeremiah, 15, 70
Jerome, 21
Jerusalem, 2, 8, 14, 20, 23, 24, 36, 38, 39, 49, 52, 54,56, 57, 58, 77, 78
Jesus, 19, 26, 27, 30, 44, 45, 46
Jew, 8
Jordan, 10
Josephus, 2, 20, 21, 40-47
Joshua, 10, 25, 26, 28, 29, 48, 75

Kahana, M., 63- 66, 77, 78
Kiddushin, 38
Klausner, J., 24
Kritot, 35
Kugel, J., 25

Lactantius, 28
Law, 8, 18, 21, 25, 31, 33, 41, 45-61
Lichtstein, A., (Zera Abraham), 78
Lieberman, 49, 53, 56-63
Literature, 1, 3, 18, 35-40, 45, 50, 59
Literature, 14, 16, 38

Marqah, 67
Martyrdom, 47-60
Matthew (gospel of), 19, 42
Megilla, 6, 17,
Meir, 50, 69, 74
Mekhilta, 19, 38, 39, 40, 47, 48, 63-77
Menahot, 12
Menasseh, 28
Messiah, 12, 51
Midrash, 1, 2, 4, 6, 7, 19, 26, 27, 30, 31, 33, 34, 35, 37, 41, 46, 66, 71, 78
Midrashic, 24, 52
Moed Katan, 53, 59
Moses, 14, 15, 16, 20, 22, 23, 27, 28, 39, 44, 45, 46, 47, 67, 68, 69, 70, 72, 74, 75

Naphtali, Testament of, 27
Neusner, J., 1, 35, 37, 38, 78

Ohana, Soliman , 77, 78

Paul, 43-47
Pesher, 18, 38
Petichta, 16, 17
Philo, 2, 8, 18, 21, 40, 46, 47, 67, 68
Philosophus, 55, 56
Piska, 27, 67, 68
Praepositor, 56
Praise, 10, 15, 66
Preachers, 17, 52, 53, 59, 60
Prooftext, 14, 16, 17, 46, 66, 68, 76
Proverbs, 9, 11, 12, 14, 15, 16, 17, 25, 26, 27, 41, 43
Psalms, 9, 10, 11, 12, 14, 17, 53, 69
Pseudepigrapha, 2, 24
Purim, 53, 59
Purity, 2, 3

Yishmael, 5, 40-42
Yohanan, 6, 26-7, 30

Zevahim, 36, 47-49
Zion, 12
Zuckermandel, (Tosefta), 55

Rapoport, S.J., 17
Revelation, 3, 4, 5, 44
Righteous, 27, 28, 48, 49, 60, 67, 68

Sadducees, 18
Sanhedrin, 8, 39, 47, 53, 59
Segal, E., 17
Septuagint, 40, 65, 70
Shimon bar Yochai, 33, 34
Sifra, 33, 35, 38
Simaye, 9, 10
Sin, 3, 9, 42, 45, 72
Sinai, 6, 11, 13, 74, 75
Sota, 53
Soul, 5, 9, 10, 18, 30, 49, 54, 56, 57, 59, 61

Ta'anit, 32, 61
Talio, 40
Talmud, 5, 7, 13, 17, 21, 34, 35, 36, 37, 39, 54, 56, 58, 60, 67
Tamid, 47
Tanak, 17
Tanhuma, 21, 31
Tanna, 28, 32
Tannaitic, 1, 28, 29, 30, 34-41, 53, 56, 59, 60, 71, 76
Targum, 74, 45
Theodor -Albeck, (Bereschit Rabba) 29
Theophany, 76, 77
Tigris, 21
Torah, 4-20, 35, 37, 40, 41, 42,-60, 63, 69-78
Torture, 50, 59
Tosefta, 36, 37, 55

Ugolino, B., 1, 79
Urbach, E.E., 8, 24, 27, 52, 57

Yalkut Shimoni, 12, 24, 25-31, 71, 79
Yefeh Eynaim, 59
Yerushalmi Talmud (tractates), 8, 9, 36, 39, 41, 46, 61, 64, 70, 75, 76, 83

Index of Passages to Rabbinic Literature

Mishnah Tamid 5:1, 47
Mishnah Yadaim 4:2, 47
Mishnah Yadaim 4:5, 19
Mishnah Zevahim 1:3., 49

Tosefta Megilla 1, 48
Tosefta Sotah 7, 48
Avot de R. Natan A 18, 48

Jerusalem Talmud

y Megilla 1:1, 7
y Megilla 1:4, 55
y Megilla 1:9, 7
y Moed Katan 3:7, 53, 59
y Sanhedrin 3:9, 71
y Sanhedrin 1:1, 8
y Shabbat 16:1, 33
y Ta'anit end 2:1, 30
y Ta'anit 4:5, 61

Babylonian Talmud

b Avodah Zarah 17b-18a, 53-61
b Baba Kama 25b, 35
b Baba Metzia
    33a-b, 34
    78b, 55
b Berachot
    12a, 47
    27b, 45
    59b, 20
    61b, 52
b Gittin 58a, 61
b Hagiga
    3a, 48
    15a, 24
b Kiddushin 49b, 38
b Kritot 13b, 35
b Megilla

7a, 5
32a, 6
b Menahot
    99b, 64
    53a, 12
b Sanhedrin
    29a, 71
    86a, 38
    101a, 59
b Shevuot 41b, 38
b Sota 49b, 44

Minor Tractates

Kallah, end, 55
Semachot 8, 49ff

Mekhilta
    to Exodus 12:1, 72
    to Exodus 13:14, 20
    Exodus 20:18, 75ff

Sifra
    3:5-6, 31
    2:3, 40

Sifre Numbers 305-6, 28

Sifre Deuteronomy
    306, 9, 23, 68, 70, 72ff
    307, 52ff, 70
    310, 23
    311, 8
    313, 75
    329, 63
    333, 68, 74
    338, 29

Midrash Rabba

Genesis Rabba 1:1, 43
    61:3, 30
    33:11, 24

Shmot Rabba 15:2, 13

Leviticus Rabba 1:6, 15, 17

Numbers Rabba 12:3, 7

Ecclesiastes Rabba to Eccl. 12:12, 8

Other Midrashim

Midrash Proverbs 27, 27

Pesikta Rabbati 21, 6

Tanhuma Ki Tisa 19, 21

Yalkut Balak 766, 25ff

Index to Passages in Hebrew Scriptures
(Alphabetical order)

Amos 9:11, 50

Canticles 2:8, 11

Daniel
   8:17-19, 4
   10:11, 4

Deuteronomy
   5:23, 42
   6:4, 10, 67
   17:8, 11
   26:7, 14
   32:1, 9,10,24,67,71,72,
   32:2, 10,72,73,74,
   32:3, 10,67,74
   32:4, 54
   32:6, 11
   32:7, 24
   32:8, 8
   32:10, 75,76
   32:11, 11,12
   32:13, 11,12
   32:15, 12,52
   32:24, 70
   32:39, 64ff
   32:43, 68
   33:2, 11

Ecclesiates 12:12, 8

Exodus
   1:22, 14
   12:18, 19
   12:38, 18
   13:8, 19
   20:18, 75
   20:19, 9
   21:29,30, 41
   34:25, 45

35:27, 17

Ezekiel
   1:28-2:2, 4
   47:9-10, 10

Genesis
   2:14, 21
   22:17, 10

Habakkuk 3:3, 11

Hosiah 6:5, 50-62

Isaiah
   5:2 54
   5:30, 55
   44:6, 64

Job
   1:6, 10
   38:7, 10

Leviticus
   1:1, 15
   1:3, 32
   19:17, 19

Numbers
   13:30, 11
   23:19, 28ff

Proverbs
   8:22, 12
   8:30, 43
   27:14, 25
   20:15, 16
   23:23, 7

Psalms
   78:54, 11
   80:4, 12

Index of New Testament Passages

2Cor. 3:12-4:6, 44

Galatians 3., 44

Luke 20:27, 42

Mark 12:18, 42

Matthew 5:43-4, 19
         22:31-33, 42
         15:5 42

Index of authors and books cited

Alter, R., *The Art of Biblical Narrative*, Basic Books, 1981, 5

Basser, H.,*Midrashic Interpretations of the Song of Moses*, Berne, Peter Lang 1984, 1

Bietenhard, H., *Sifre Deuteronomium*, Berne, Peter Lang 1984., 1

Clifton, C. Black II, "The Rhetorical Form of the Hellenistic Jewish and Early
    Christian Sermon," *HTR* 81:1 (1988), 25

Finkelstein, L., *Midrash, Halakhot and Aggadot*, Yitzhak F. Baer Jubilee Volume,
    Jerusalem, 1960, 41

Finkelstein, L., "Prolegomena to the Sifre," *PAAJR*, 1931-32, 37

Fox, H., " The Circular Proem," *PAAJR*, 49 (1982), 17

Halpern, Baruch, *The First Historians*, San Francisco: Harper and Row, 1988, 3

Hammer, R., *Sifre: A Tannaitic Commentary on the Book of Deuteronomy*, New
    Haven and London, Yale University Press, 1986, 1

Heinemann, J., "The Proem in the Aggadic Midrashim," *Studies in Aggadah and
    Folk Literature, Scripta Hierosolymita* xxii: Jerusalem, 1971, 14

Herr, M.D., "Persecution and Martyrdom in Hadrian's Days, *Scripta Hierosolymitana*
    23, 1972, 54

Kahana, M., Commentaries to Sifre buried in manuscripts," *Rabbi Isaac Nissim
    Memorial Volume*, Jerusalem, 77

Kahana, M., "Pages from the Mekhilta to Deuteronomy Ha'azinu and Vezot
    Haberakhah," *Tarbits*, 57 (1988), 63

Lieberman, S., *Hellenism in Jewish Palestine* New York, 1962, 58

Lieberman, S., *Tosefta Kifshutah* VIII, Sota, New York, 1973, 53

Lieberman, S., in *Jubilee Volume in honor of Salo Baron on the occasion of his
    eightieth birthday*, Jerusalem, 1975, 57

Marmorstein, A., *Studies in Jewish Theology*, Oxford, 1950, 49

Melamed, E.Z., *Benjamin DeVries Memorial Volume*, Jerusalem, 1968, 58

Neusner, J., *Sifre to Deuteronomy: An Analytical Translation*, Atlanta, Scholars's
    Press, 1987, 1

Neusner, J., *Sifre to Deuteronomy: An Introduction to the Rhetorical, Logical and
    Topical Program*, Atlanta, Scholar's Press, 1987, 37

Neusner, J.,"Sifra's Critique of Mishnaic Logic,"Hebrew Studies, 1988, 35.

Neusner, J.,*Paradigms in Passage*, Lanham, NewYork, London, University Press of
    America, 1988, 38

Noy, D., *Scripta Hierosolymitana: Studies in Aggadah and Folk-literature* vol. 22,
    Jerusalem, 1971, 45

Philo, ed. Colson, "On Virtues", ch., 11-12, 53

Scholem, G., *Jewish Gnosticism, Merkabah Mysticism and Talmudic Tradition*, New
    York, 1965, 5

Ugolino, B., *Thesaurus Antiquatum Sacrarum Comlectens*, Venice 1753, vol 15, 1

Urbach, E., *The Sages*, Jerusalem 1975, 8

Urbach, E., "Ascesis and Suffering in Talmudic and Midrashic Sources," *Baer Jubilee
    Volume*, Jerusalem, 1960, 52